AF835175

Property and Trust Law in Portugal

Property and Trust Law in Portugal

Second Edition

Sandra Passinhas

This book was originally published as a monograph in the International Encyclopaedia of Laws/Property and Trust Law.

Founding Editor: Roger Blanpain
General Editor: Frank Hendrickx
Volume Editors: Alain Verbeke & Vincent Sagaert

Wolters Kluwer

Published by:
Kluwer Law International B.V.
PO Box 316
2400 AH Alphen aan den Rijn
The Netherlands
E-mail: international-sales@wolterskluwer.com
Website: lrus.wolterskluwer.com

Sold and distributed in North, Central and South America by:
Wolters Kluwer Legal & Regulatory U.S.
7201 McKinney Circle
Frederick, MD 21704
United States of America
Email: customer.service@wolterskluwer.com

Sold and distributed in all other countries by:
Air Business Subscriptions
Rockwood House
Haywards Heath
West Sussex
RH16 3DH
United Kingdom
Email: international-customerservice@wolterskluwer.com

ISBN 978-94-035-1743-8

e-Book: ISBN 978-94-035-1791-9
web-PDF: ISBN 978-94-035-1835-0

This title is available on www.kluwerlawonline.com

The Author

Sandra Passinhas (27 August 1971) is Professor at Coimbra Law School. She teaches Property Law, Contracts, Family Law, Successions and several seminar courses on Consumer Law. In 2010, she received her PhD in Law from the European University Institute, Florence, with a thesis entitled *Dimensions of Property under European Law: Fundamental Rights, Consumer Protection and Intellectual Property Rights – Bridging Concepts*? In 2016, she received a PhD in Law from Coimbra Law School, with a thesis entitled *Property and Personhood on Portuguese Civil Law*. She is also the author of a book on condominiums, corresponding to her master thesis, with the title *A Assembleia de Condóminos e o Administrador na Propriedade Horizontal* (Coimbra, Almedina, 2002), and of several articles in the subject. She also develops her research on European Private Law and is a regular member of the Group on Property Law in the Common Core Project.

The Author

Table of Contents

Table of Contents

List of Abbreviations

Although I have translated into English the names which the abbreviations refer to, I have maintained the abbreviations that are normally used by Portuguese scholars and courts:

BFD	Coimbra Faculty of Law Journal [*Boletim da Faculdade de Direito da Universidade de Coimbra*]
CC	Civil Code [*Código Civil Português*]
CDADC	Copyright and Related Rights Code [*Código dos Direitos de Autor e dos Direitos Conexos*]
CE	Expropriations Code [*Código das Expropriações*]
CIRE	Insolvency and Corporate Recovery Code [*Código da Insolvência e da Recuperação de Empresas*]
CMVM	Securities Market Commission [*Comissão do Mercado de Valores Mobiliários*]
CN	Notary Code [*Código do Notariado*]
CPC	Civil Procedure Code [*Código do Processo Civil*]
CPI	Industrial Property Code [*Código de Propriedade Industrial*]
CRegP	Land Registry Code [*Código do Registo Predial*]
CRP	Constitution of the Portuguese Republic [*Constituição da República Portuguesa*]
DL	Decree-Law [Decreto-Lei]
DR	Official Journal [*Diário da República*]
NRAU	New Tenancy Law [*Novo Regime do Arrendamento Urbano*]
RARF	Legal Regime for Rural and Forrest Land Tenancies [*Regime do Arrendamento Rural e Florestal*]
RJUE	Legal Regime on Urban Occupation [*Regime Jurídico da Urbanização e da Edificação*]
ROA	Professional Order of Attorneys Journal [*Revista da Ordem dos Advogados*]
STJ	Supreme Court of Justice [*Supremo Tribunal de Justiça*]

List of Abbreviations

General Introduction

§1. General Background of the Country

I. Geography, Climate and History

1. Portugal is a coastal nation in south-western Europe. Its mainland is located on the Iberian Peninsula and borders only Spain, to the east and north, with a total border length of 1,214 km. On the west and south, Portugal is bound by the Atlantic Ocean, with a coastline that is 837 km in length. The country's shape is roughly rectangular, with its shorter sides on the north and south and its longer sides on the east and west.

Portugal is crossed by three large rivers that rise in Spain, flow into the Atlantic, and divide the country into three markedly different geographic areas. The Minho River, part of the northern boundary, cuts through a mountainous area that extends south to the vicinity of the Douro River. South of the Douro, the mountains slope to the plains around the Tejo River. The remaining division is the southern one comprised of Alentejo and Algarve.

In addition to continental Europe, Portugal consists of two autonomous regions in the Atlantic Ocean, which are the archipelagos of Madeira and Azores. Madeira is located on the African Tectonic Plate, and comprises the main island of Madeira, Porto Santo, and the smaller Savage Islands. It lies in the Atlantic about 861 km southwest of Lisbon. The Azores stretch over 547 km in the Atlantic and consist of nine islands with a total area of 2,335 sq. km, located between the junction of the African, the European and the North American Plates, straddling the Mid-Atlantic Ridge. The nine islands in this archipelago are usually divided into three groups (Western, Central, and Eastern) and the several smaller Formigas (rock outcroppings) located between the São Miguel and the Santa Maria Islands. Both island groups are volcanic in nature, with historic volcanology and seismic activity persisting to the present day.

2. In sum, Portugal has an area of 92,391 sq. km of which 91,951 sq. km is land and 440 sq. km is water. Portugal has the third largest Exclusive Economic Zone (EEZ) in the European Union (EU) and the eleventh in the world. The sea zone over which Portugal has special rights over the exploration and use of marine resources covers an area of 1,727,408 sq. km (Continental Portugal 327,667 sq. km, Azores Islands 953,633 sq. km, and Madeira Islands 446,108 sq. km).

3. Portugal has a Mediterranean climate, Csa in the south and Csb in the north, according to the Köppen climate classification. Both the Azores and the Madeira Islands have a subtropical climate with mild, rainy winters and mainly dry, warm summers. The sea surface temperatures in these archipelagos vary from 16ºC to 18ºC in winter to 23ºC–24ºC in the summer, occasionally reaching 26ºC.

4. Portugal was one of the first European kingdoms to establish stable borders and has a long and rich history. The history of Portugal dates back to the Early Middle Ages. At the end of the eleventh century, the Burgundian knight Henry became Count of Portugal and defended his independence, merging the County of Porto (at the time, Portucale) and the County of Coimbra. Although Henry had claimed independence for Portugal – while a civil war raged between León and Castile – he died in April 1112 without achieving his aim. After his son Afonso Henriques had taken control of the county, the lords of the cities of Coimbra and Porto, together with the Braga's clergy,[1] demanded again the independence of the county. Portugal traces its national origin to 24 June 1128, with the Battle of São Mamede. Portuguese forces led by Afonso Henriques defeated the forces led by his mother Teresa of León and her lover Fernão Peres de Trava. Afonso proclaimed himself first Prince of Portugal and in 1139, as the first King of Portugal. By 1143, at the Conference of Zamora, with the assistance of a representative of the Holy See, Cardinal Guido de Vico, Portugal was formally recognized as independent, and Afonso Henriques was addressed as *Dux Portucalensis*. In 1179, Afonso I was finally declared by the Pope as the first King of Portugal, through the papal *bull manifestis probatum*. Since the Battle of São Mamede, the first capital of Portugal had been Guimarães. From 1129, the King shifted his court to Coimbra. This was a strategically important move, since Coimbra was a better base from which to prosecute the Reconquest.[2] In fact, the Kingdom of Portugal emerged in the twelfth century linked to the process of the Christian Reconquest of the Iberian Peninsula. In the eyes of the Christian world, that signified the birth of a new kingdom, which would reinforce the fight against the infidels. In fact, that would prove to be true. From 1249 to 1250, the Algarve, the southernmost region, would finally be re-conquered by Portugal from the Moors, and in 1255, the Portuguese capital shifted to Lisbon. Portugal's land-based boundaries have been notably stable in history. The border with Spain has remained almost unchanged since the thirteenth century.

5. In the fifteenth and sixteenth centuries, Portugal ascended to the status of a world power during Europe's 'Age of Discovery' as it built a vast empire including possessions in South America, Africa, Asia and Australasia. Portuguese navigators mapped the coasts of West Africa between 1430 and 1490 and discovered a sea route around the Cape of Good Hope. Between 1490 and 1520, they sailed from

1. Braga was, at the time, the unofficial Catholic centre of the Iberian Peninsula.
2. A. Ross Disney, *A History of Portugal and the Portuguese Empire*, I (Cambridge: CUP, 2009), 75.

Europe to India, Indonesia and China, and discovered and charted the coasts of Brazil. In 1520, during his global circumnavigation voyage, Fernão de Magalhães was the first European to navigate the Magellan Strait and made the first crossing of the pacific.[3]

During the Golden Age, the kingdom attained considerable prosperity as a consequence of overseas trade and expansion. But gradually, the kingdom was overtaken by an array of economic and political problems, culminating in the defeat of Al-Ksar al-Kabir and the ensuing loss of independence in 1580. The country was under the rule of the Spanish monarchy from 1580 to 1640, and Portuguese colonies were attacked by Spain's opponents, especially the Dutch and the English who aspired to dominate both the Atlantic slave trade and the spice trade with the Far East. During the fifteenth and sixteenth centuries, Portugal would gradually lose much of its wealth and status as the Dutch, the English, and the French would take an increasing share of the spice and the slave trades (the economic basis of the empire) by surrounding or conquering the widely scattered Portuguese trading posts and territories, leaving it with ever fewer resources to defend its overseas interests.

6. By 1750, Sebastião José de Melo (later the first Marquis of Pombal) was appointed as Prime Minister. He abolished slavery in Portugal and in the Portuguese colonies in India, reorganized the army and the navy, and restructured the University of Coimbra. He also implemented strong economic and financial reforms, through the creation of several companies and guilds to regulate commercial activities. He has also demarcated the region for production of wine in Oporto, to ensure the wine's quality.

7. On 1 November 1755, Lisbon was struck by a violent earthquake with an estimated magnitude of nine on the Richter scale. The city was razed to the ground by the earthquake and the subsequent tsunami and ensuing fires. Sebastião de Melo immediately embarked on the rebuilding of the city, with his famous quote, as follows: *'What now? We bury the dead and feed the living.'* The Portuguese capital was designed and planned in accordance with rational eighteenth century principles. The buildings and big squares of the Pombaline Downtown of Lisbon still remain an important tourist attraction.

8. The ideals of the French revolution were violently imposed in Portugal during the *'French Invasions'*, which took place in 1807, 1808, and 1810. On 27 November 1807, the royal family fled to Brazil, retaining Portugal's independence and its government, even ruling from overseas. Meanwhile the British, taking advantage of several popular uprisings all over the Peninsula against the French dominion, sent troops to Portugal. At the end of the Napoleonic Wars, England would enjoy a privileged governmental position controlling all commercial relationships with the colonies and with the rest of the world. The moving of the Portuguese capital to Rio de Janeiro had accentuated the economic, institutional, and social crises in mainland Portugal, which was administered by English commercial and military interests under William Beresford's rule in the absence of the monarch.

3. Malyn Newitt, *Portugal in European and World History* (London: Reaktion Books, 2009), 49.

9. The aftermath of the war, influences from both the American and the French Revolution, a discontent for absolutism, and a general indifference shown by the Portuguese Regency towards the plight of its people, have strengthened liberal ideals. So, in 1820, a group of liberals organized an uprising in Oporto that spread throughout the country and arranged the expulsion of the British. The liberal revolution had begun. The government was in the hands of a temporary committee whose task was to organize the first elections and write a constitution, which would be published in 1822.[4] This is how a constitutional monarchy was born in Portugal.

10. Lisbon regained its status as the capital of Portugal when Brazil declared its independence from Portugal in 1822. The loss of Brazil in 1822, however, would bring a period of troubled times to the liberals. The remaining supporters of the absolutist system initiated a civil war that lasted until 1834, when the liberals led by D. Pedro won the war against the absolutist wing led by his brother D. Miguel.

11. Although Portugal still maintained its colonies, the monarchical government had to face two problems: on one hand, the people's dissatisfaction, and on the other hand, the growing group of republican supporters. On 1 February 1908, in an attack against the royal family, D. Carlos and the heir prince D. Luís Filipe were killed. D. Manuel II (the second son of D. Carlos) was recognized as the King of Portugal by the end of that same year. He was the last King of Portugal. During the last two years of his reign, the revolutionary movements kept growing. On 5 October 1910 the Republic was proclaimed in Lisbon, and the royal family was expelled from the country. A republican constitution was approved in 1911, inaugurating a parliamentary regime with reduced presidential powers and two chambers of parliament.[5]

12. The Republic provoked important fractures within the Portuguese society, notably in the essentially monarchist rural population, in the trade unions, and in the Church. Political chaos, several strikes, harsh relations with the Church, and considerable economic problems aggravated by a disastrous military intervention in the First World War led to the military *coup d'état* on 28 May 1926, installing the '*Second Republic*' that would later become the *Estado Novo* in 1933, led by António de Oliveira Salazar, which transformed Portugal into a proto-Fascist Axis-leaning state, which later evolved into some mixture of single party corporative regime.

13. In 1961, the Portuguese army was involved in armed action in its colony in Goa against an Indian invasion (Operation Vijay). The operations resulted in a humiliating Portuguese defeat and the loss of the colonies in India. Independence movements also became active in Portuguese Angola, Portuguese Mozambique, and Portuguese Guinea, and the Portuguese Colonial War began. Portugal, during this period, however, was never an outcast, and was a founding member of the North

4. M. J. Almeida Costa (with collaboration of Rui de Figueiredo Marcos), *História do Direito Português*, 5th edn (Coimbra: Almedina, 2012), 446; J.J. Gomes Canotilho, *Direito Constitucional e Teoria da Constituição*, 7th ed (Coimbra: Almedina, 2003), 129 et seq.
5. Cf. Articles 7 et seq. of the Portuguese Constitution 1911.

Atlantic Treaty Organization (NATO), the Organisation for Economic Co-operation and Development (OECD), and the European Free Trade Association (EFTA).

Salazar suffered a stroke in 1968 and died the following year. He was replaced by Marcello Caetano, an academic lawyer and historian.

14. The downfall of the Portuguese corporate state happened on 25 April 1974, when the Armed Forces Movement seized power in a nearly bloodless coup and established a provisional military government (Carnation Revolution).[6] Democracy was back again after forty-eight years of dictatorship. In May 1974 was gathered the first temporary cabinet with members of all the political parties, which followed the programme written by the army group, as follows: the constitution of political parties and unions, the organization of free elections, the extinction of the political police, and the abolishment of censorship. All political prisoners were set free and the exiled were authorized to return to their motherland.

In 1975, the government nationalized banking, transportation, heavy industries, and the media. On 25 April 1975, the first free election took place for a representative convention, which later would write a new constitution (the Constitution of 1976, published on 2 April 1976).

Yet in 1975, Portugal granted independence to its Overseas Provinces in Africa (Mozambique, Angola, Guinea-Bissau, Cape Verde, and São Tomé and Príncipe). Nearly one million Portuguese, or persons of Portuguese descent, left these former colonies as refugees. In that same year, Indonesia invaded and annexed the Portuguese province of Portuguese Timor (East Timor) in Asia before independence could be granted. The Asian dependency of Macau, after an agreement in 1986, was returned to Chinese sovereignty in 1999. Portugal applied international pressure to secure East Timor's independence from Indonesia, as East Timor was still legally a Portuguese dependency, and recognized as such by the United Nations. After a referendum in 1999, East Timor voted for independence and Portugal recognized its independence in 2002. The Portuguese empire ended de facto in 1999 when Macau was returned to China, and de jure in 2002 when East Timor was declared independent.

15. In 1986, Portugal entered the European Economic Community (EEC) and left the European Free Trade Association (EFTA) which was founded by Portugal and its partners in 1960. In 1999, Portugal became a founding member of the European Economic and Monetary Union (EMU). Portugal's economy, in fact, is based on traditional industries such as textiles, clothing, footwear, cork and wood products, beverages (wine), porcelain and earthenware, and glass and glassware. In addition, the country has increased its role in Europe's automotive sector and has a world-class mould-making industry. Services, particularly tourism, are playing an increasingly important role. EU expansion into Eastern Europe has erased Portugal's historic competitive advantage and relatively low labour costs. The government is now working to change Portugal's economic development model from one

---

6. Malyn Newitt, *Portugal in European and World History* (London: Reaktion Books, 2009), 209 et seq.

based on public consumption and public investment to one focused on exports, private investment, and development of the high-tech sector.

II. Cultural Situation

16. Portuguese colonial history has long since been a cornerstone of its identity, as its geographic position at the south-western corner of Europe, pointing out towards the Atlantic Ocean. Portugal is also culturally influenced by the traditions of western European countries especially Spain, France, and Italy. The existence of a single religion, Catholicism, and a single language have contributed to Portuguese ethnic and national unity after the expulsion of the Moors and the Sephardi Jews (in the late fifteenth century). Freedom of religion and of conscience, nonetheless, is constitutionally granted in Portugal.[7]

17. Portugal has a relatively homogeneous population. The Portuguese official bureau of statistics estimated that in 2013, the population was 10,457.30 of which 52.4% was female and 47.6% was male. Portugal has 398,268 inhabitants who are legal immigrants. Portugal, long a country of emigration (the vast majority of Brazilians have some Portuguese ancestry), has now become a country of net immigration, and not only from the last Indian (Portuguese until 1961), African (Portuguese until 1975), and Far East Asian (Portuguese until 1999) overseas territories. Since the 1990s, along with a boom in construction, several new waves of Ukrainians, Brazilians, people from the former Portuguese colonies in Africa and other Africans have settled in the country. Those communities currently comprise the largest groups of immigrants in Portugal. The Romanians, the Moldovans, and the Chinese have also chosen Portugal as their destination. A number of EU citizens mostly from the United Kingdom, but also from the Nordic countries, are permanent residents of the country, with the British community being mostly composed of retired pensioners choosing to live in Algarve and Madeira.[8] Portugal's Romani population, estimated at approximately 40,000, offers another element of ethnic diversity. Most Romani live apart, and primarily in the south. They can often be found at rural markets selling clothing and handicrafts.

18. Portuguese is a Romance language that grew from the Latin-descended Galician-Portuguese language that was spoken in the medieval Kingdom of Galicia. It also absorbed influences from the Romance and the Arabic languages spoken in the areas that were conquered by the Portuguese Christian Reconquest. With over 260 million speakers, Portuguese is the sixth most spoken language in the world, the most widely spoken in the southern hemisphere, and the third most spoken in the Western world. It is the fifth language most used on Internet and the third on Facebook and Twitter. In addition to Brazil and Portugal, it is used in Angola, Cape Verde, Guinea-Bissau, Macau, Mozambique, São Tomé and Príncipe, and East

7. Article 41 of the Portuguese Constitution 1976, and Law 16/2001, of 22 June (Law on Freedom of Religion).
8. Further information in <www.pordata.pt>.

Timor, as well as in the former territories of Portuguese India (Goa, Daman, Isle of Angediva, Simbor, Gogol, Diu, and Dadra and Nagar Haveli) and in small communities that were part of the Portuguese Empire in Asia as Malacca, Malaysia, and East Africa as Zanzibar, Tanzania. Contemporary Portuguese comprises of two internationally recognized standards (*European Portuguese* and *Brazilian Portuguese*).

19. An Orthographic Agreement was signed in Lisbon, on 12 October 1990, by the Lisbon Academy of Sciences, the Brazilian Academy of Letters and delegations from Angola, Cape Verde, Guinea-Bissau, Mozambique and S. Tome & Príncipe, in order to strengthen the role of the Portuguese language internationally and to guarantee linguistic uniformity among those eight member states of the Community of Portuguese Language Countries (CPLP). The Portuguese language spelling reform came to effect on the 1 of January 2012 for all state organisms and entities in Portugal.

20. During the Reconquest, Portuguese art was limited to a few paintings in churches, convents, and palaces. During the Golden Age of Portugal, in the late fifteenth and early sixteenth centuries, Portuguese artists were influenced by Flemish art, and were in turn influential on Flemish artists of the same period. In the nineteenth century, naturalist and realist painters such as Columbano, Henrique Pousão and Silva Porto revitalized painting against a decadent academic article. The twentieth century saw the arrival of Modernism, and the most prominent Portuguese painter Amadeo de Souza-Cardoso, who was heavily influenced by French painters. Another great modernist painter/writer was Almada Negreiros. He was deeply influenced by both Cubist and Futurist trends. Prominent international figures in visual articles in the late twentieth century included painters Vieira da Silva, Júlio Pomar, and Paula Rego. Joana Vasconcelos, born in 1971, is nowadays considered the most pre-eminent artist of her generation.

21. Adventurer and poet Luís de Camões (around 1524–1580) wrote the epic poem *The Lusíadas,* with Virgil's Aeneid as his main influence. Modern Portuguese poetry is rooted in neoclassical and contemporary styles, as exemplified by Fernando Pessoa (1888–1935). Modern Portuguese literature is represented by authors such as Almeida Garrett, Camilo Castelo Branco, Eça de Queirós, Sophia de Mello Breyner Andresen, and António Lobo Antunes. Particularly popular and distinguished is José Saramago, winner of the 1998 Nobel Prize for literature.

22. Portuguese music encompasses a wide variety of genres. The most renowned genre of Portuguese music is *fado – since* 2011, it is considered Intangible Heritage of Humanity – a melancholy urban music, usually associated with the Portuguese guitar and *saudade,* or longing. Coimbra *fado,* a unique type of *fado,* is also noteworthy.

Portugal has a rich traditional folklore *(Ranchos Folclóricos)* with great regional variety. The traditional Cante Alentejano (Alentejano Song), a polyphonic singing from Alentejo, southern Portugal, was also listed by UNESCO as Intangible Cultural Heritage of Humanity, in November 2014.

Amália Rodrigues, Carlos do Carmo, Mariza, Mísia, Madredeus, and the pop singerTony Carreira are internationally known performers.

23. As regards theatre, Gil Vicente, known as the father of Portuguese theatre, was the leading Portuguese playwright in the sixteenth century, satirically portraying the society of the time. António Ferreira (1528–1569) is considered the father of Renaissance culture in Portugal. António José da Silva (1705–1739), commonly known as '*O Judeu*' because of his Judaic origins, wrote several noteworthy works. Luís Miguel Cintra (actor and director), Eunice Munoz, Ruy de Carvalho, and Diogo Infante developed a noteworthy body of work. In the twentieth century, theatre in Portugal became more popular with the '*Revista*'– a form of humorous and cartoonish theatre designed to expose and criticize social (and political) issues. The most important actors in this genre were Vasco Santana, Beatriz Costa, and Ivone Silva. Filipe la Féria is an acclaimed Portuguese theatre director of several masterpieces.

24. Portuguese cinema has a long tradition, reaching back to the birth of the medium in the late nineteenth century. Directors Manoel de Oliveira (1908-2015) and João César Monteiro (1939-2003) receive international attention.

In Portugal, a mixed television system is maintained, as apart from public-owned channels there are privately owned ones. Both radio and press have a strong tradition in Portugal.

25. As regards architecture, although Portugal has been the location of important construction since the second millennium BC, it developed significantly in the second century BC with the arrival of the Romans. They built aqueducts, bridges and roads, along with theatres, temples, circuses, and other public buildings. Romanesque and Gothic influences have given Portugal some of its greatest cathedrals, and in the sixteenth century a national style *(Arte Manuelina)* was synthesized. There are numerous examples of Restoration architecture (1640–1717), the Baroque style (1717–1755), the Pombaline style (1755–1780), which is a secular, utilitarian architecture used after the 1755 Lisbon earthquake. Modern Portugal has given the world renowned architects such as Eduardo Souto de Moura, Álvaro Siza Vieira and Gonçalo Byrne. Paulo Moreira, Jorge Moura, and the young David Mares are also noteworthy. One of the top architecture schools in the world, known as 'Oporto School', is located in Portugal. *Azulejos,* which are glazed ceramic tiles, were introduced by the Moors, and use both geometric and representational patterns. They normally cover the facades and interiors of churches, government buildings, and private homes.

26. In the field of sport, football (soccer) is the most known, loved, and practiced sport. The legendary Eusébio is still a symbol of Portuguese football history, and Luís Figo and Cristiano Ronaldo are among the numerous examples of other world-class footballers born in Portugal and noted worldwide. José Mourinho, nicknamed 'the Special One', is widely regarded as one of the best coaches in the game and led numerous top European teams to national and European honours.

Portugal has a successful rink hockey team, with fifteen world titles and twenty European titles, making it the country with the most wins in both competitions. The most successful Portuguese rink hockey clubs in the history of the European championships are F.C. Porto S.L. Benfica . Portugal won the CERH European Roller Hockey Championship more than 20 times, and often gets a place in the top three (fourteen silver medals and 9 bronze medals).

The national rugby union team ('os lobos') made a dramatic qualification into the 2007 Rugby World Cup and became the first all-amateur team to qualify for the World Cup since the dawn of the professional era. It is now the 28th on the world rugby ranking. The Portuguese national team of rugby sevens has performed well, becoming one of the strongest teams in Europe, and has proved its status as the European champion in several occasions.

Francis Obikwelu is a sprint athlete, who has won several gold, silver, and bronze medals in the European, World, and Olympic Games competitions in the 100 meter and the 200 meter categories. Naide Gomes in pentathlon and long jump, is another Portuguese elite athlete. In the triathlon, Vanessa Fernandes has won a large number of medals and major competitions across the world and in 2007, became the world champion both in the Triathlon and the Duathlon. Nelson Évora is a former triple jump Olympic and world champion. Cycling, with *Volta a Portugal* being the most important race, is also a popular sporting event. Noted Portuguese cyclists include, among others, Joaquim Agostinho, Marco Chagas, José Azevedo, Sérgio Paulinho, Ricardo Mestre and Rui Costa.

The country has also achieved notable performances in sports such as fencing, surfing, windsurfing, kitesurfing, kayaking, sailing, and shooting, among others. The Paralympic athletes have also acquired many medals in sports such as swimming, boccia, and wrestling. Portugal has its own original martial art, *jogo do pau*, in which the fighters use staffs to confront one or several opponents.

27. Portuguese cuisine is characterized by rich, satiating and full-flavoured dishes and is a prime example of a Mediterranean diet. The influence of Portugal's former colonial possessions is evident in the wide variety of spices used. Olive oil is one of the bases of Portuguese cuisine, both for cooking and for flavouring meals. Portuguese wines have earned international recognition since the times of the Roman Empire, which associated Portugal with their God 'Bacchus'. In 2013, the Mediterranean Diet was listed by UNESCO as Intangible Cultural Heritage of Humanity.

28. Science and technology in Portugal is mainly conducted within a network of research and development units belonging to public universities and state-managed autonomous research institutions. According to the Innovation Union Scoreboard 2014, Portugal is one of the moderate innovators with a below average performance. Relative strengths are in open, excellent, and attractive research systems, finance, support, and innovators. Relative weaknesses are in firm investments, intellectual assets, and outputs.

The sole Portuguese science-related Laureate, who was awarded the Nobel Prize in Medicine in 1949, was Egas Moniz.

III. Political System

29. Portugal moved from authoritarian rule to a parliamentary democracy following the 1974 military coup against the dictator Marcello Caetano, himself a continuation of the long-running dictatorship of Antonio Salazar. After a period of instability and communist agitation, Portugal ratified a new constitution in 1976,[9] which is still in force. Under the constitution of 1976, Portugal is a democratic parliamentary republic.

According to Article 3 of the Portuguese Republic Constitution 1976 (hereinafter 'CRP'), sovereignty shall be single, indivisible, and shall lie with the people, who shall exercise it in the forms provided for in the Constitution. The state shall be subject to the Constitution and shall be based on the democratic rule of law. In a similar vein, the validity of laws and other acts of the state, the autonomous regions, local government, and any other public bodies shall be dependent on their conformity with the CRP.

Article 10 provides that the people shall exercise political power by means of universal, equal, direct, secret, and periodic suffrage, referendum, and the other forms provided for in the CRP. Political parties shall contribute to the organization and the expression of the will of the people, with respect for the principles of national independence, the unity of the state, and political democracy.

30. Article 110 of the CRP lists the bodies that exercise sovereign power: the President of the Republic, the Assembly of the Republic, the Government, and the Courts. These bodies shall be separate and interdependent. No body that exercises sovereign power shall delegate its powers to other bodies, except in such cases and under such terms as are expressly laid down by the Constitution and the law.

31. The President, elected to a five-year term by direct, universal suffrage is also commander-in-chief of the armed forces. Presidential powers include confirming the appointment of the Prime Minister and the Council of Ministers, dismissing the Prime Minister, dissolving the Assembly to call for early elections, vetoing legislation (which may be overridden by the assembly), and declaring a state of war or siege.[10] The President has an advisory body, known as the Council of State, which is composed of six senior civilian officers, former Presidents elected under the 1976 constitution, five members chosen by the Assembly, and five members selected by the President.

32. The Government is headed by the Prime Minister, who is nominated by the Assembly for confirmation by the President. The Prime Minister then appoints the Council of Ministers. A new Government is required to present its governing platform to the Assembly for approval.[11]

---

9. As amended by the Constitutional Laws 1/82, of 30 September; 1/89, of 8 July; 1/92, of 25 November; 1/97, of 20 September; 1/2001, of 12 December; 1/2004, of 24 July; and 1/2005, of 12 August.
10. *See* <www.presidencia.pt/>.
11. <www.portugal.gov.pt/PT/GC18/Pages/Inicio.aspx>.

33. The Assembly of the Republic is a unicameral body composed of up to 230 deputies. Elected by universal suffrage according to a system of proportional representation, deputies serve four-year terms of office, unless the president dissolves the Assembly and calls for new elections.[12]

34. Courts also exercise sovereign powers. The national Supreme Court is the court of last appeal. Military, administrative, and fiscal courts are designated as separate categories of courts. A thirteen-member Constitutional Court reviews the constitutionality of legislation.

35. Article 6 of the CRP provides that the state shall be unitary and organized and shall function in such a way that it respects the autonomous island system of self-government and the principles of subsidiarity, the autonomy of local authorities, and the democratic decentralization of the Public Administration. The Azores and Madeira archipelagos are autonomous regions with their own political and administrative statutes and self-government institutions. A regional autonomy statute promulgated in 1980 established the Government of the Autonomous Region of the Azores; the Government of the Autonomous Region of Madeira operates under a provisional autonomy statute in effect since 1976.

Article 227 of the CRP sets forth an extensive list of the powers of the autonomous regions. The autonomous regions have legislative autonomy with respect to matters set out in the respective political and administrative statutes as are not the exclusive responsibility of bodies that exercise sovereign power. In the absence of specific regional legislation on a matter that is not the exclusive responsibility of bodies that exercise sovereign power, the current provisions of the law shall apply to the autonomous regions.[13]

36. Continental Portugal is divided into eighteen districts [*distritos*]. Portugal has an administrative structure of 308 municipalities [*concelhos*], which are, after 2013, subdivided into more than 3,000 parishes [*freguesias*]. Their legal status is set in the Constitution.

37. The creation of administrative regions is foreseen in Article 255 of the CRP. Their de facto institution is still dependent on the approval of individual laws instituting each one, and on an affirmative vote by the majority of the registered electors who cast their votes in a direct national ballot covering each of the regional areas.

§2. Legal Background of the Country

I. Legal Family or Tradition

38. The Portuguese legal system is part of the civil law legal system, also called the family of continental legal systems. Laws are written into a collection, codified,

12. <www.en.parlamento.pt/>.
13. Article 228 CRP.

and not (as in common law) primarily determined by judges. Statutory law is unequivocally the most important source of law in Portugal. It is as follows:

> invariably sought to solve any concrete problem, based on the assumption that the adequate resolution of all problems will be found in it. At this level, we can therefore speak of seeking plenitude or comprehensiveness in legal regulations, based on a set of accepted methodological principles both for the drafting of laws (based on the great abstraction of legally enshrined rules) and for their subsequent interpretation and integration … .[14]

39. Codes exist for the main branches of law: the Civil Code (1966, as amended) and the Penal Code (1982, as amended). Other relevant laws are the Commercial Code (1888, as amended), the Civil Procedure Code (2013, as amended), the Commercial Companies Code (1986, as amended), the Criminal Procedure Code (1987, as amended), and the Labour Law Code (2009, as amended).

40. The custom, which is the repeated and habitual adoption of a particular line of conduct that is generally believed to be mandatory, assumes scarce practical relevance in Portugal. It can be regarded as a source of law, for instance, in the field of public international law. Usage – repeated social practices that are not considered to be mandatory – may be taken into account by the courts where provided for by law and where it is not 'contrary to the principles of good faith' (Article 3 of the CC). Legal rules cannot, therefore, be created independently through usage, and usage cannot be considered a genuine source of law.[15]

41. Case law and doctrine also play a secondary role as sources of law. As Pereira Nunes and Ferreira de Almeida wrote, they lack innovative capability, and are used exclusively as a means of disclosing (or identifying and clarifying) pre-existing legal standards or solutions, generally from a legal source.[16] The doctrine plays an important role in the scientific and technical development of legal knowledge. Seldom have they promoted the true *praeter legem* development of the legal system by upholding and divulging specific solutions.

42. Case law, that is, the set of principles emerging from judgments and decisions handed down by the courts, is significant merely in revealing the meaning of legal provisions. The Portuguese legal system[17] is unbound by precedent and is composed of specially trained judicial officers with a limited ability to interpret law. The structure of Portuguese courts' decisions encompasses the object of the case in question, the relevant facts to render the judgment upon it, the issues on which the correct decision depends, and last, the resolution of the case. Courts mandatorily

---

14. V. Pereira Nunes & C. Ferreira de Almeida, 'Portuguese Law System as Civil Law', in *Portuguese Law – an Overview*, ed. C. Ferreira de Almeida, Assunção Cristas & Nuno Piçarra (Coimbra: Almedina, 2007), 31.
15. *Ibid.*
16. *Ibid.*, 32.
17. *Ibid.*, 33.

decide with express reference to the legal rules on which the decision is based. Although court decisions normally contain several references to previous decisions and doctrinal works – where the same legal issues had been addressed – those references usually seek to identify previous references presenting the same interpretation of the same legal rules and not references establishing *ex novo* solutions for the same problems.

Article 9 of the CC provides that when a lacuna does exist and there is no rule applicable by analogy to fill it, it is necessary to resort to the so-called *analogia juris* or the rule which the legislator would have created within the spirit of the system, had the omitted issue or lacuna been provided for.[18]

Finally, courts are empowered to formulate, with regard to certain specific cases submitted for their assessment, legal rules appropriate to the specific features of those cases, relying on general principles of justice and the ethical awareness of the judge. Article 4 of the CC reads as follows:

> The courts may decide on the basis of equity only where: (a) there is a legal provision allowing it; (b) there is agreement between the parties and appeal to a higher court is possible; or (c) the parties have previously agreed to rely on equity.

43. The rules and principles of general or common international law shall form an integral part of Portuguese law. The rules set out in duly ratified or passed international agreements shall come into force in Portuguese internal law once they have been officially published, and shall remain so for as long as they are internationally binding on the Portuguese state. Further, rules issued by the competent bodies of international organizations to which Portugal belongs shall come directly into force in Portuguese internal law, subject to the precondition that this is laid down in the respective constituent treaties.[19] Citizens enjoy a wide range of protections of fundamental civil and political rights which are outlined in the Constitution with specific reference to the Universal Declaration of Human Rights (UDHR). Portugal also accepts the compulsory jurisdiction of the International Court of Justice (ICJ) with reservations.[20]

44. The provisions of the treaties that govern the EU and the rules issued by its institutions in the exercise of their respective responsibilities shall apply in Portuguese internal law in accordance with EU law and with respect for the fundamental principles of a democratic state based on the rule of law.[21] The principle that 'rules issued by the competent bodies of international organizations to which Portugal belongs shall come directly into force in Portuguese internal law, on condition that this is laid down in the respective constituent treaties' covers the direct effect of

18. *Ibid.*, 33.
19. Article 8 of the CRP. *See* Gomes Canotilho, *Direito Constitucional e Teoria da Constituição*, 7th ed (Coimbra: Almedina, 2003), 822–828.
20. Notice 251/2005, of 27 May 2005.
21. Article 8 of the CRP.

European regulations and of directives and decisions addressed to the Member States. The transposition of EU legislation and other legal acts into the internal legal system shall take the form of a law, an executive law, or a regional legislative decree.[22] Doctrine and the Portuguese courts commonly agreed that the hierarchical position of the EU law in the Portuguese legal order was superior to that of ordinary national law. According to Miguel Maduro and Francisco Coutinho:

> [A]t the same time that is accepts the supremacy of EU law limits it in two ways: first, the supremacy of EU law, contrary to the conception of the European Court of Justice does not derive from its own independent claim of authority but from the authority given to it by the national constitution; and second, this reasoning also assumes that such supremacy only extends insofar as it is determined by national constitutional law and, therefore, it does not extend to national constitutional norms themselves.[23]

Portuguese law was applied in the former colonies and territories and continues to be the major influence for those countries. The Portuguese variant of civil law legal systems is used in various countries and territories around the world, including the following: Portugal (Portuguese Republic), Macau (Macao Special Administrative Region the People's Republic of China), Goa – now part of India, Cape Verde (Republic of Cape Verde), Mozambique (Republic of Mozambique), and, to a lesser extent, Brazil (Federative Republic of Brazil).

II. Relation and Hierarchy Between the Sources of Law

45. The authorities empowered to adopt rules of law are Parliament, the Government, the Regional Governments and Legislative Assemblies of the Azores and the Madeira, local authorities, and certain administrative authorities. In accordance with the previous section, the sources of law in Portugal are as follows: constitutional laws (comprising the Portuguese Constitution and other constitutional laws); the rules and principles of general or common international law; rules set out in duly ratified or approved international agreements; rules issued by the competent bodies of international organizations to which Portugal belongs, on the conditions laid down in the respective constituent treaties, the 'the provisions of the treaties that govern the European Union and the rules issued by its institutions in the exercise of their respective responsibilities';[24] ordinary laws, which comprise laws enacted by the Assembly of the Republic, decree-laws issued by the Government and regional legislative decrees adopted by the Legislative Assemblies of the Autonomous

22. Article 112(8) CRP. *See* Jónatas Machado, *Direito da União* Europeia, 2nd ed (Coimbra: Coimbra Editora, 2012) 213 et ff, and Miguel Gorjão Henriques, *Direito da União*, 7th edn (Coimbra: Almedina, 2014) 283 et seq.
23. M. Poiares Maduro/F. Pereira Coutinho, 'EU Law and Portuguese Law', in *Portuguese Law – an Overview*, ed. C. Ferreira de Almeida, Assunção Cristas & Nuno Piçarra (Coimbra: Almedina, 2007), 53.
24. Article 8 CRP.

Regions of the Azores and the Madeira;[25] instruments with effect equivalent to that of laws, such as acts approving international conventions, treaties or agreements, generally binding decisions of the Constitutional Court declaring measures to be unconstitutional or illegal, collective labour agreements and other collective instruments regulating labour relations; regulations aiming at supplementing laws and stating the details so that they can be applied or implemented, such as regulatory decrees, regulations, decrees, regional regulatory decrees, decisions, rules, ministerial orders, executive rulings, municipal orders, and regulations.

46. The hierarchical order of the different sources according to their method of creation is as follows: the Constitution and constitutional laws; the rules and principles of general or common international law and international agreements; laws and decree-laws; regional legislative decrees; instruments having an effect equivalent to that of laws; and regulations. Without prejudice to the subordination to the corresponding laws of executive laws that are enacted under legislative authorization and of those that develop the basic general elements of the legal systems, laws and executive laws shall possess equal force. Organizational laws, laws that must be passed by a two-thirds majority, and laws which under this Constitution are compulsory legal pre-requisites for other laws or which must be obeyed by other laws, shall possess superior force. No law shall create other categories of legislation, or grant other types of act the power to interpret, integrate, modify, suspend or revoke any of its provisions in such a way as to produce effects in relation to third parties.[26]

47. Article 62 of the CRP, on the right to private property, provides as follows:

1. Everyone is guaranteed the right to private property and to the transmission thereof in life or upon death, in accordance with the Constitution.
2. Requisitions and expropriations in the public interest may only be undertaken on a legal basis and upon payment of just compensation.

Article 65(1) of the CRP, on housing and urbanism, sets forth as follows:

> Everyone has the right for himself and his family to have an adequately sized dwelling that provides hygienic and comfortable conditions and preserves personal and family privacy.[27]

---

25. Article 112 CRP.
26. Article 112(4) CRP.
27. Fundamental rights are set forth in Part I of the Portuguese Constitution from Articles 12 to 79. Fundamental rights are divided into two separate groups: rights, freedoms and guarantees and economic, social and cultural rights and duties. The former belong to the category of provisions with direct and immediate effect, whilst economic, social, and cultural rights have a merely programmatic nature.

    The legal protection to housing rights is not immediately enforceable and their fulfilment depends on the availability of favourable social and economic conditions. Moreover, housing rights are not generically enforceable, as they are essentially addressed to public authorities, binding them to the realization of the existing constitutional programme on economic and social matters. I am referring

A. Constitutional Framework

48. The most important role in the settlement of conflicts arising between different legal rules is played by the Constitutional Court, which must declare as unconstitutional any rule that conflicts with the Portuguese Constitution or the principles enshrined therein. Further, when considering specific cases presented before them, the courts cannot apply provisions that infringe the Constitution or the principles deriving from it.

49. The courts must settle the conflicts arising between different legal rules, always having regard to the above-mentioned hierarchy of sources. In doing so, they must consider the Portuguese legal system as a unified whole, weighing the circumstances underlying the adoption of the rules and the specific conditions prevailing at the time when the proceedings take place, always requiring a minimum verbal correspondence, even if imperfectly expressed, with the approach taken and assuming that the legislature opted for the *'most judicious'* solutions and was able to 'express its intentions in appropriate terms'.[28] A special administrative action may be instigated for the main purpose of requesting a declaration of illegality of a measure adopted under the provisions of administrative law.[29]

B. Parliament and Legislative Process

50. Article 164 of the CRP lists matters regarding which the Assembly of the Republic possesses exclusive responsibility to legislate. Article 165 of the CRP sets forth the matters regarding which the Assembly of the Republic shall possess exclusive responsibility to legislate, unless it authorizes the Government to do so. As regards property law, I would emphasize the following matters: the general rules governing requisitions and expropriations in the public interest; the basic elements of the rules for protecting nature, the ecological balance and the cultural heritage; the general rules governing rural and urban rentals; the creation of taxes and the fiscal system, and the general rules governing duties and other financial payments to public bodies; the definition of sectors of ownership of the means of production, including that of basic sectors in which private businesses and other bodies of a similar nature shall be forbidden to act; the means and forms of intervention, expropriation, nationalization, and privatization of and in relation to means of production and soils in the public interest, together with criteria for determining compensation in such cases; the rules governing economic and social development plans and the composition of the Economic and Social Council; the basic elements of the agricultural policy, including the determining of the maximum and minimum limits for

---

to J. Bacelar Gouveia, 'Fundamental Rights', in *Portuguese Law – an Overview*, ed. C. Ferreira de Almeida, Assunção Cristas & Nuno Piçarra (Coimbra: Almedina, 2007), 96–97.

28. Article 9 CC.
29. Article 2(2)(a) of the Code of Procedure of the Administrative Courts [*Código de Processo nos Tribunais Administrativos*], approved by Law 15/2002, of 22 February, as amended (last amendment by DL 214-G/2015, of 2 October). *See* Vieira de Andrade, A justiça administrativa 16th ed. (Coimbra: Almedina, 2017), pp. 183 et seq.

farming units; the definition of, and the rules governing, property in the public domain; the rules governing means of production that are integrated into the cooperative and social sector of ownership; the basic elements of town, country, and urban planning. Laws that grant authorization to legislate shall define the object, purpose, extent, and duration of such authorization, which may be extended. Without prejudice to their use in partial stages, authorizations to legislate shall not be used more than once. Authorizations shall lapse upon the resignation or removal of the Government to which they were granted, at the end of the legislature, or upon the dissolution of the Assembly of the Republic.

51. The way in which rules are adopted varies according to the specific procedures to be followed by each body responsible for adopting the rules.[30] The most complex procedure, involving the Parliament, comprises steps that can be summarized as follows:

Initiation of legislation: the power to initiate legislation lies with Members of the Assembly, parliamentary groups and the Government, and also, subject to the terms and conditions laid down by law, with groups of registered electors. The power to initiate legislation in relation to the autonomous regions lies with the respective Legislative Assembly (Article 167(1) of the CRP).

Initial admission, publication, registration, numbering, and assessment: this phase involves consideration of the admissibility of the bill, publication of the text in the Parliament's Official Gazette, administrative processing and, finally, evaluation of its content.

Discussion and approval: this involves a debate on general issues, another debate on specific points, a vote on the bill as a whole, a vote on specific points, and a final overall vote. For a bill to be passed, a simple majority, an absolute majority, or a qualified majority may be required.

Scrutiny by the President of the Republic within the period laid down by law, following which he/she either promulgates the proposed text or exercises his right of veto. In the latter event, the measure is re-discussed by the Parliament. If the veto is confirmed or amendments are made, the text is again forwarded to the President for promulgation, which must also take place within a pre-established period of time. The President of the Republic is responsible for promulgating laws and signing resolutions of the Assembly of the Republic that approve international agreements.[31]

Publication: once it has been promulgated, the President must order the text of the new legislation to be published in the Official Journal of the Portuguese Republic.[32]

52. The procedure whereby the Government adopts legislation comprises of the following main steps: the draft legislation is put forward by the ministerial departments (initiation); during this stage, the minister proposing the draft must canvass

30. Cf. Articles 167–170 CRP.
31. Article 134(b) CRP.
32. Laws shall be binding only after publication in the Official Journal, according to Article 5 CC, and Law 74/98 of 11 November, as amended (last amendment by Law 43/2014, of 11 July).

opinions, and the bodies specified by the Constitution and by law must also be consulted (enquiry); proposals are examined and evaluated once they have been initially endorsed (preliminary and detailed assessment); approval of the draft; within forty days of the receipt of any government decree for promulgation, the President of the Republic shall either promulgate the decree or exercise his right of veto. In the latter case, he/she shall inform the Government, in writing, of the reasons for so doing (Article 136(4) of the CRP); publication of the definitive text in the Official Journal.

C. Common Law and Judicial Process

53. Courts are sovereign bodies *'which possess the responsibility to administer justice in the name of the people'*.[33] In administering justice, the courts shall ensure the defence of those citizens' rights and interests as are protected by law, repress breaches of the democratic rule of law, and rule on conflicts between public and private interests. Their function is to ensure the defence of the legally protected rights and interests of the citizenry, to redress the violation of democratic legal rights, and to settle disputes of public and private interests. They shall be independent and subject only to the law.[34] Court hearings are public, except when the court itself, in a well-founded decision, decides otherwise for the purpose of guaranteeing and safeguarding the dignity of persons and public morals or ensuring their normal operation. The decisions of the Courts are binding on all public and private entities, and prevail over the decisions of any other authorities.

54. Article 20 of the CRP guarantees everyone access to the law and the courts in the defence of their legally protected rights and interests, and justice cannot be denied to anyone due to lack of financial means: everyone has guaranteed access to the Courts for the defence of their legally protected rights and interests; and everyone is entitled to legal information and advice, to the protection of the Courts, and to be represented by a lawyer before any authority.

55. The Constitutional Court shall be the court with specific responsibility for administering justice in matters of a legal and constitutional nature, as defined in Article 221 of the CRP. In addition to the Constitutional Court, the following categories of courts exist: the Supreme Court of Justice and the judicial courts of first and second instance; the Supreme Administrative Court and the other administrative and fiscal courts; and the Court of Auditors. Maritime, Arbitration, and Magistrates Courts may also exist.

56. Portuguese judicial organization is ruled by Law 62/2013, of 26 August (as amended).[35] According to Article 29, a distinction shall be made between ordinary

33. Article 202 CRP. *See* A. Vieira Cura, *Organização Judiciária Portuguesa* (Coimbra: Gestlegal, 2018), 11–15.
34. Article 203 CRP.
35. Last amendment by Law 27/2019, of 28 March.

jurisdiction (courts of law) and administrative jurisdiction. Administrative jurisdiction is composed of the administrative and tax courts, and is restricted to disputes arising from legal relationships classified as being of an administrative or tax nature. The administrative and tax courts shall try contested suits and appeals, the purpose of which is to settle disputes arising from administrative and fiscal legal relations. Article 212 of the CRP, referring to Administrative and tax courts, provides that without prejudice to the specific responsibilities of the Constitutional Court, the Supreme Administrative Court shall be the senior body in the hierarchy of administrative and tax courts.

57. Article 211 of the CRP lays down that the courts of law shall be the general courts in civil and criminal matters and shall have jurisdiction over every area that is not allocated to other judicial bodies.[36] The courts of law collectively forming the ordinary jurisdiction are divided into three levels or instances as follows: (i) the Courts of First Instance, (ii) the Courts of Appeal, and (iii) the Supreme Court of Justice.

58. The Courts of First Instance *(tribunais de comarca)* have specialized and specific competence. Courts with specialized competence deal with specific matters, irrespective of the applicable form of proceeding. The Courts of Appeal are, as a rule, Courts of Second Instance. At present, the Courts of Appeal are in Lisbon, Oporto, Coimbra, Évora, and Guimarães. The Courts of Appeal also include civil, criminal, and social divisions with objective competence on a par with that which is indicated in relation to the Supreme Court of Justice. They may also include sections on Family and Children, Commerce, Intellectual Property and Competition, and Regulation (Article 67 LOSJ). The Supreme Court of Justice is the superior hierarchical body of the judicial courts. Its headquarters are in Lisbon. It consists of civil, criminal, and social divisions (Article 47 LOSJ). It functions under the direction of a President (Presiding Judge) as a full bench of the Court, in specialized divisions and sections. The civil sections are competent to cases that are not allocated to other divisions; the criminal sections judge cases of a criminal nature; the social sections are for cases for which the Labour Courts have competence. The Supreme Court of Justice, save in the case of legally enshrined exceptions, only deals with matters of law. The Supreme Court has no power to choose the cases that it will decide, but it has the possibility to harmonize jurisprudence in matters wherein there is no consensus within the superior courts.

59. In Portugal, jurisdiction is divided among the different courts according to the matter in question (i.e., the nature of the dispute), hierarchy (i.e., the levels of jurisdiction of the courts – First Instance, Second Instance and the Supreme Court

36. V. Pereira Nunes/C. Ferreira de Almeida, 'Portuguese Law System as Civil Law', in *Portuguese Law – an Overview*, ed. C. Ferreira de Almeida, Assunção Cristas & Nuno Piçarra (Coimbra: Almedina, 2007), 33.

of Justice), the amount in question (i.e., the monetary value of the economic benefit being sought), and the territory (i.e., the geographical area to which the facts to be considered should be connected).[37]

60. Cases involving property rights such as the division of jointly owned property, eviction, separation of inherited property from the existing estate of the heir, and foreclosure, as well as those cases involving reinforcement, substitution, reduction, or releasing of mortgages should be brought to the court having jurisdiction over the area where the property in question is located. Cases for the reinforcement, substitution, reduction or releasing of mortgages on ships or aircrafts will, however, be brought in the court having jurisdiction over the area in which the item in question is registered. If the mortgage covers movable assets registered in several districts, the plaintiff can opt for any of these. When the object of the case is a group of movable items belonging to the same person and intended for a single use, or movable and immovable assets, or real estate assets situated in different districts, the case in question will be brought in the court in the district where the most valuable immovable assets are located. For this purpose, the Land Registry values will be used. If the immovable asset which is the object of the case is located in more than one district, the case can be brought in any of those districts. Cases for demanding the fulfilment of obligations, compensation for non-fulfilment or incomplete fulfilment of obligations and the termination of a contract due to non-fulfilment will be brought, at the choice of the creditor, in either the court of the place where the obligation should have been fulfilled or in the court of the place where the defendant lives.

For civil liability cases based on illegal acts or hazards, the court with jurisdiction is that of the area in which the act occurred. The court with jurisdiction over divorce cases or cases for legal separation and division of property is that of the area of domicile or residence of the plaintiff. For probate (to end community of property after a person's death), the court with jurisdiction is that of the area of the final place of domicile of the deceased.

61. With regard to protective measures (set in motion by procedural steps aimed at safeguarding the effectiveness of a decision to be taken in a particular case), and steps taken before a case is brought, the following points should be noted: the seizure (legal apprehension of goods) and impounding of goods (consisting of listing, valuing, and delivering the goods to a depository) can either be requested at the court in which the main proceedings are to be brought or in the court of the district in which the goods are located, or if the goods are located in several districts, in any of the respective courts; for the embargoing of new work (an urgent measure aimed at suspending new work), the court with jurisdiction is that of the district in which the work is being carried out; for other restraining measures, the court with jurisdiction is that in which the respective case is to be brought. The preliminary measures taken before a case for producing proof are requested in the court of the district in which measures are to be made.

---

37. Article 37 of LOSJ. *See* A. Vieira Cura, *Organização Judiciária Portuguesa* (Coimbra: Gestlegal, 2018), 132-228.

62. Arising from these two jurisdictions, the Constitutional Court, the Audit Court,[38] the Jurisdiction Disputes Court (which settles disputes between civil and administrative jurisdictions – as conflict-resolution tribunals), Maritime Courts, Justices of the Peace, and the Arbitration Courts complete the scheme of the Portuguese courts.

63. All disputes resulting from a legal relationship which the parties can terminate through negotiation, even renouncing the rights arising from their agreement, and which are not reserved by law solely to the judicial courts, can be settled by Alternative Dispute Resolution (ADR) mechanisms. Portuguese law has institutionalized non-judicial instruments and means of alternative dispute resolutions. Alternative means available for resolving disputes are conciliation, mediation, and arbitration. These are all directed towards the resolution of disputes through non-judicial routes. Resorting to such routes enables the quick and effective delivery of justice. The involvement of the parties favours the creation of conditions which enable them to maintain relationships after the disagreement has been resolved.

64. Although of a judiciary nature, conciliation is an alternative to Court adjudication. Under this process, the judge invites parties to discuss the matter on which they disagree and helps them to reach a voluntary agreement.[39] The conciliator draws attention to the objective aspects of the dispute, presses for a rapid, non-exhaustive solution to the matter and helps the parties in dispute to reach an agreement under their own responsibility. In comparison with a mediator, the conciliator takes a more active stance. He/she may even propose a solution to the dispute, and, because the conciliator has the ultimate power to adjudicate the dispute, the dynamic of conciliation is quite different from the one of mediation, under Portuguese law.

65. Mediation is an alternative means of resolving disputes which is confidential and voluntary in nature. The responsibility for coming up with the decisions to be taken resides with the parties involved. In general, mediation is informal in nature. In this type of resolution process, the parties in dispute, helped by an impartial and neutral third party, try to reach an agreement settling their dispute – the empowerment of the parties is what distinguishes mediation.

Unlike a judge or an arbitrator, the mediator does not make any decision regarding the result of the argument. Instead, the mediator guides the parties, promoting

---

38. The Audit Court, according to Article 214 CRP, shall be the senior body with authority to scrutinize the legality of public expenditure and judge such accounts as the law may require to be submitted to it. It shall particularly be responsible for the following: (a) issuing an opinion on the General State Accounts, including the social security accounts; (b) issuing an opinion on the accounts of the Azores and the Madeira Autonomous Regions; (c) enforcing liability for financial infractions, as laid down by law; and (d) fulfilling such other responsibilities as the law may confer upon it. Without prejudice to the provisions of Article 133(m), the term of office of the President of the Audit Court shall be four years. The Audit Court may operate in a decentralized manner, in regional sections, as laid down by law. In the Azores and the Madeira Autonomous Regions there shall be sections of the Audit Court with full responsibility for the matter in question in the respective region, as laid down by law.
39. Articles 591, 594 and 604 CPC.

the dialogue between them and enabling the exchange of points of view, in such a way that the parties themselves can come up with the basis for an agreement ending the dispute. As this process always involves a third party, we can consider this to be an intermediate process between conciliation and arbitration. As mediation allows the relationship between the parties in dispute to be maintained, it is particularly suitable for settling disputes inside family and between neighbours. Mediation is regulated in general by Law 29/2013, of 19 April. It is also specifically envisaged in the legislation which created the Justices of the Peace [*Julgados de Paz*] (bodies similar to courts which have the task of settling civil cases involving amounts not more than Euros (EUR) 15,000.00)[40] and in the Civil Procedure concerning custody arrangements.[41] Specific regulation concerning mediation in Family Law, Criminal Law and Labour Law, also exist in Portugal.

66. The 'Justices of the Peace', as a dispute settlement tool,[42] requires the promotion of mediation prior to the settlement of a dispute submitted to any Peace Court. The act regulating the competence, organization, and functioning of the Justice of the Peace expressly provides for the mediation services created within each Court. In these courts, it is possible for disputes to be settled on the basis of *aequitas*, in those cases wherein the disputes involve values lesser than 7.500,00 Euro and the parties to the dispute accept that the decision should be issued in accordance with such a criterion. Peace Courts are entitled to adjudicate disputes until 15.000,00 Euro, as mentioned, their jurisdiction being restricted to judging issues deriving from the law of obligations and rights in rem. The jurisdiction of a Peace Court is only of a declaratory nature and, therefore, in order to enforce decisions issued by the Peace Courts, the parties have to resort to an executive procedure in the Courts of the civil jurisdiction.[43]

67. The 'Justices of the Peace' courts have jurisdiction in the civil area over the following matters related to property law: actions aimed at ensuring that obligations are fulfilled, except for those involving pecuniary benefits and for which the original creditor is or was a legal person; cases involving the transfer of movable assets; cases involving the rights and duties of joint property owners, whenever the respective assembly of joint owners has not made it mandatory for there to be an arbitration to settle disputes between joint owners, or between the joint owners and the administrator; actions to settle disputes between property owners related to temporary forced passage, natural drainage of waters, works to protect against flooding, sharing of drains, channels, ditches, hedges, opening of windows, doors, balconies and similar works; eavesdropping, planting of trees and bushes, erection of walls and partitions; actions for taking possession, adverse possession and accession; cases regarding the right to use and administer jointly owned property, superficies rights, usufruct, use and habitation and the real right of periodical habitation; cases

40. According to Article 8 of Law 78/2001, of July 13th, as amended by Law 54/2013, of 31 July.
41. Cf. Article 24 of Law 141/2015, 8 September.
42. *See* A. Vieira Cura, *Organização Judiciária Portuguesa* (Coimbra: Gestlegal, 2018), 285-301.
43. V. Pereira Nunes & C. Ferreira de Almeida, 'Portuguese Law System as Civil Law', in *Portuguese Law – an Overview*, ed. C. Ferreira de Almeida, Assunção Cristas & Nuno Piçarra (Coimbra: Almedina, 2007), 36.

involving urban leases, except actions for eviction; cases involving contractual and extra-contractual civil liability; cases involving contractual default, except for employment contracts and rural leases; cases involving the general guaranteeing of obligations.

68. It is not necessary for parties to appoint lawyers when attempting to settle a dispute through mediation. In mediation, the parties are called upon to become actively involved in seeking a solution. However, the role of lawyers in providing assistance to the parties should not be underestimated. The lawyer can ensure that the process unfolds in such a way that the interests and objectives of the client are respected; he/she can identify points of law, assess the desirability or the value of a settlement to the opposing party, and can prepare or check the text of the agreement. The agreement reached by mediation is made in writing and may, upon request, be ratified by the judge.[44] The enforcement of a mediation agreement is a matter for the Court of First Instance, under the conditions laid down in the Civil Procedure Code.[45]

69. Arbitration is also a regular means of settling disputes and is regulated, in Portugal, by Law 63/2011, of 14 December. Voluntary arbitration is a private method of settling disputes in which the parties, on their own initiative, choose people known to be arbitrators, who come up with a decision which is binding on the parties in settling their differences. In this process, the impartial third party makes a decision regarding the dispute dividing the parties. It is equivalent to litigation, since the decision is not taken by the parties in dispute. For enforcement purposes, arbitration decisions are considered to be equal to those taken by normal courts and are enforceable by them. Only if parties have agreed on their right of appeal and did not have authorized the arbitrator to reach an judgment grounded on equity, can an appeal be made against arbitration decisions to the Court of Appeal.[46] Arbitration in consumer disputes is regulated by Law 144/2015, of 8 September (as amended), implementing Directive 2013/11/EU of the European Parliament and of the Council of 21 May 2013 on alternative dispute resolution for consumer disputes.[47]

'Institutionalized arbitration' is the term given to voluntary arbitration carried out by entities authorized by the Ministry of Justice to engage in such an activity.[48] These entities are called 'Arbitration Centres' [*Centros de Arbitragem*]. The main characteristic of voluntary institutional arbitration is the fact that the said Centres which carry out such work are located in several cities throughout Portugal. The Centres are permanent and predate the disputes which they may settle. These Centres can have general competence or might be specialized in certain areas. There are

44. Article 14 of Law 29/2013. The same applies, mutatis mutandis, when the agreement is reached in the context of a judicial procedure (cf. Article 273 CPC).
45. Article 9 of Law 29/2013.
46. Article 39, 4, of Law 63/2011, of 14 December.
47. Sandra Passinhas, Alterações recentes no âmbito da resolução alternativa de litígios de consumo", Instituto Jurídico da Faculdade de Direito de Coimbra (ed.), *O contrato: na gestão do risco e na garantia da equidade* (Coimbra: 2015), pp. 357-388.
48. *See* A. Vieira Cura, O*rganização Judiciária Portuguesa* (Coimbra: Gestlegal, 2018), 293-295.

some Centres which have regional jurisdiction and are only involved in disputes occurring in a certain geographical area. There are others which cover the entire country and can deal with disputes from all over Portugal. In addition to the Arbitration Centres which have general jurisdiction, there are several Arbitration Centres which deal with specific sectors. These include consumer disputes arising from public and private works, disputes on automobile accidents and insurance.

70. In accordance with the Voluntary Arbitration Law, any dispute which does not have to be settled in court or by compulsory arbitration and which does not concern inalienable rights can be submitted by the parties to arbitration. In Portuguese law, inalienable rights include those considered to be related to matters of individual freedom and personal status, rights regarding labour relations in the context of employment contracts, and rights recognized by social security law. They also include those rights connected with legal relationships which the parties cannot alienate of their own will and which they cannot, therefore, waive by means of a legal transaction. Should such rights be invoked, arbitration or other alternative means of settling disputes cannot be deployed. An arbitration clause (*'cláusula compromissória'*) must specify the legal relationship of the disputing parties and must be binding on the parties. Likewise, there is nothing to prevent the contracting parties from agreeing to resort to other types of ADR, in particular mediation, to settle any disputes arising from the contractual relationship.

It is not necessary for a lawyer to be appointed when settling disputes by arbitration. The parties can designate anyone to represent them or to be present at the arbitration court. However, a legal representative must be appointed in an arbitration case when an appeal is lodged.

In voluntary arbitration, the process ends with an arbitration decision which may consist in the ratification of the agreement reached during a conciliation phase. This decision carries the weight of a court judgment and is enforceable in the same way as a decision by a Court of First Instance. The enforcement of the arbitration decision is a matter for the Court of First Instance, under the conditions laid down in the Civil Procedure Code.

D. Executive Powers and Administrative Law

71. The Portuguese Public Administration encompasses the following types of public bodies: the State; Public Agencies [*Institutos Públicos*]; Public Associations [*Associações Públicas*]; Autonomous Regions; Local Authorities [*Autarquias Locais*]; State-owned companies [*Empresas Públicas*]; some private companies and charities which are submitted to an administrative legal regime or subjected to Government supervision [*Entidades Particularesde Interesse Público*].[49] Administrative regulations [*regulamentos administrativos*] are legal rules issued by an administrative body or agency empowered by law and enforced within the limits of its powers. Administrative decisions [*actos administrativos*] are unilateral decisions taken

49. D. Freitas do Amaral & João Caupers, 'Administrative Law', in *Portuguese Law – an Overview*, ed. C. Ferreira de Almeida, Assunção Cristas & Nuno Piçarra (Coimbra: Almedina, 2007), 102.

by public bodies or agencies, under a specific provision of law, which allows a decision to be taken that is binding upon the individual concerned. Administrative contracts [*contratos administrativos*] are contracts between an administrative body or agency and an individual or company not ruled by civil, but instead by administrative law.

72. Administrative Procedure is ruled by the Administrative Procedure Code of 2015.[50] The major principles of law which govern Portuguese administrative procedure are as follows: the rule of law, cooperation with individuals and their right to be heard, accountability, and the power of coercive enforcement. In 2002, Portugal enacted a new Administrative Courts Statute [*Estatuto dos Tribunais Administrativos e Fiscais*][51] and, for the very first time, a detailed Administrative Courts Procedure Code [*Código de Processo nos Tribunais Administrativos*],[52] which approaches the German model of full jurisdictional control of administrative activities. In the words of Freitas do Amaral and João Caupers:

> Significantly enough, administrative tribunals, which during almost two centuries (1832-2002) could not punish or issue injunctions against public bodies, received full powers of punishment and injunction, with the sole limitation that tribunals cannot invade the area of administrative discretion, so that the separation of powers can be preserved and fully respected. In other words, administrative tribunals can now command the Administration to perform a legal duty, but they are not allowed to give instructions on how the Administration shall use a legal power or exercise a legal right.[53]

§3. Introduction to the Law of Property and Trust

73. In Portugal, the trust is a not general institution or object of legal treatment. The expression 'Law of Property' relates to patrimonial Civil Law, encompassing both Contracts and Obligations.

I. Historical Origins and Evolution

A. *Legal History*

74. Portugal has an ancient legal system based on Roman law. Roman law[54] was applied throughout the Roman province of Hispania, which largely corresponds to

50. DL 4/2015, of 7 January.
51. Law 13/2002, of 19 February, as amended (last amendment by DL 2214-G/2015, of 2 October).
52. Law 15/2002, of 22 February, as amended (last amendment by DL 2214-G/2015, of 2 October).
53. D. Freitas do Amaral/João Caupers, 'Administrative Law', in *Portuguese Law – an Overview*, ed. C. Ferreira de Almeida, Assunção Cristas & Nuno Piçarra (Coimbra: Almedina, 2007), 101.
54. I am referring to vulgar Roman law, as coined by H. Brunner, *Zur Rechtsgeschichte der römischen und germanischen Urkunde* (Berlin: weidmann 1880).

the Iberian Peninsula. It was, however, strongly influenced by the customs of the indigenous people as well as various pre-legal traditions. Nonetheless, Roman law would survive in the law of the Visigoths, the Germanic people who replaced the Roman authorities in the Iberian Peninsula in 446 AD. Despite the codification work developed by them (Code of Eric, *Lex Romana Visigothorum, and Codex of Reccesvindus*), day-to-day life continued to be ruled by unwritten legal principles and communitarian norms of behaviour accepted by peninsular Gothic-Roman communities.[55]

From the thirteenth century onwards, Roman Law became the European common law, through the influence of the interpretative work carried on by the Italian Glossators and Commentators. These Italian lawyers, using the scholastic method, integrated Roman law, canon law and local law, such as the law of the kingdoms, within a homogeneous body. The *Glossa Ordinaria* of Accursius (1220–1234), the work of Commentators (especially Bartolus' opinions, 1313–1354) and later, the *communis opinion doctorum*, became texts of authority for Portuguese lawyers, as well as the subsidiary law in Portugal.[56]

75. Although no distinction can be found in Roman texts between property rights and obligatory rights, this distinction was, however, subjacent to the dichotomy between *actiones* in rem and *actiones* in personam (real or proprietary actions and personal actions).[57] In the *actio* in rem, the plaintiff claims a right (*ius mihi esse*), whereas in the *actio* in personam the plaintiff claims a duty in charge of the defendant.[58] The *actio* in rem was a claim for a physical thing, rather than the assertion of a right available against everyone, and an *actio* in personam, in its origin, was thought of rather as a claim to a person. But, for classical law and later, the two types may be regarded as means for the enforcement of, respectively, rights in rem and rights in personam.[59]

The absolute separation between property rights and personal rights was also evident in the organization of legal institutions. Contracts and property rights were absolutely separate categories. That is the reason why the transfer of ownership was not the direct effect of a contract, but demanded a transfer of the thing although the

55. C. Nogueira da Silva, 'Legal History', in *Portuguese Law – an Overview*, ed. C. Ferreira de Almeida, Assunção Cristas & Nuno Piçarra (Coimbra: Almedina, 2007), 16; M. J. Almeida Costa (with collaboration of Rui Figueiredo Marcos), *História do Direito Português*, 5th ed (Coimbra: Almedina, 2012), 201 et seq.
56. *Ibid.*, 17. Ruy de Albuquerque & Martim de Albuquerque, *História do Direito Português*, vol I, 10th edn (Lisboa: Paulo Ferreira, 1999), 321 et seq.
57. In classical times, the distinction between *actio* in rem and *actio* in personam is crossed by the distinction between actions *civiles* and actions *honorariae*. Both actions *civiles* and *honorariae* may be either in rem or in personam. Fritz Schulz, *Classical Roman Law* (Oxford: Clarendon Press, 195), 33.
58. Biondo Biondi, *Corso di istituzioni di diritto romano* I (Catania: Ed. Siciliana Tipografica, 1929), 97; Rudolph Sohm, *The Institutes, A Textbook of the History and System of Roman Private Law*, trans. James Crawford Ledlie, 3rd edn (Oxford: Clarendon Press, 1907), 263 et seq.
59. W.W. Buckland, *A Text-Book of Roman Law from Augustus to Justinian* (Cambridge: CUP, 1932), 675.

delivery was more symbolic than real.[60] The civil law methods of acquiring ownership were *mancipatio, in iure cessio,* and *traditio.*

76. No Roman definition of ownership exists in the available sources, and it may be safely assumed that the classical lawyers never attempted to provide such a definition. In republican times, when *dominium* and *proprietas* had not yet become technical legal terms, ownership was designated by describing its principal content. *Dominium* would include the *jus utendi*, or the right of appropriating its use; the *jus fruendi*, or the right of appropriating its fruits whether natural or civil; the *jus abutendi*, which involved the right of destruction, consumption, and free disposition.

Although not unlimited, the *dominium* would involve the highest and most absolute control which a person was permitted, under the law, to exercise with reference to an object. It was, in general, indefinite as to its extent, unlimited as to its duration, and unrestricted as to its disposition. The owner, or *dominus*, could hold the object to the exclusion of all other persons; he/she could use it according to its own free will; he/she could reap all the benefits capable of being legitimately derived therefrom; and he/she could freely dispose thereof during his lifetime or at his death.[61] It can be assumed that this conception of property was prominent in Portugal until the fourteenth century.

With the revival of Roman Law in the twelfth century in Italy, by way of the work of the Glossators and Commentators, a new conceptualization arose. The Glossa maintained that '*dominus dicitur qui rei vindicationem habet*'. The shift, however, was to come later on, due to Bartulus: '*[d]ominium est ius de re corporali perfecte disponendi nisi si quis lege prohibeatur*',[62] and Baldus: '*[d]ominium absolute* dictum *est plena proprietas cum alienandi potestate*'.[63] These definitions were adopted, with slight variations, by Alciatus (*[d]ominium est ius perfecte disponendi*), Duareno (*[d]ominium sic definimus: ius de re aliqua corporali plene ac libere disponendi extra quam si quid lege prohibeatur*); Cuiacio (*[v]ulgo dominium definitur hoc modo: ius re corporali perfecte disponendi aut vindicanti nisi quod lex aut conventio prohibetur*); and Noodt (*[e]st dominium ius pro arbitrata de re disponendi praeter quam si quid vi aut iure prohibeatur*).[64]

60. Reinhard Zimmermann, *The Law of Obligations, Roman Foundations of the Civilian Tradition* (Munich: Juta and Beck, 1990), 230 et seq. *See* also A. Vieira Cura, 'O Fundamento Romanístico da Eficácia Obrigacional e da Eficácia Real da Compra e Venda nos Códigos Civis Espanhol e Português', in *Jornadas Romanísticas* (Coimbra Editora: 2003), 73 et seq, and 'Compra e Venda e Transferência da Propriedade no Direito Romano Clássico e Justinianeu (a Raiz do "Sistema do Título e do Modo")', *BFD* Volume Comemorativo do 75.º tomo (2003), 69 et seq.

61. Although classical ownership did not imply an unlimited right over a thing, the right of *dominium* is the most extensive real right which a person can legally exercise over a thing. The powers of a slave-owner were restricted by imperial constitutions. Ownership of land was limited not only with regard to the interest of neighbours but also by public law. But it is evident that under classical law the bounds of ownership were very wide, according to the liberal principle which demanded that ownership should be as unrestricted as possible and that the greatest possible latitude should be given to individual action and initiative.

62. *See* Vittorio Scialoja, *Teoria della proprietà nel diritto romano*, vol. I (Roma: Attilio Sampaolesi Editore, 1928), 264 et seq.

63. *Ibid.*

64. *Ibid.*,265.

77. In Portugal, from the fifteenth century onwards, royal legislation acquired a growing importance. The first codifications of Portuguese law were published as follows: *Ordenações Afonsinas* (1446); *Ordenações Manuelinas* (1514–1521) and *Ordenações Filipinas* (1603) present the first example of European Early Modern codifications. The latter remained in force until 1867 (in Portugal) and 1917 (in Brazil). The *Ordenações Afonsinas* stated that the kingdom's law (statute law, case law, and customs) should prevail as the main source of law. Canon law ruled on spiritual matters and certain temporal matters according to a criterion defined by Bartolus. Roman law was valid as subsidiary law in temporal matters. Last, the King was vested with the authority to fill any lacunae. In the subsequent *Ordenações Manuelinas*, the common law doctrine gave way to the common opinion, bestowing upon the courts the last word in the determination of the relevant law. Guided by the common opinion, judges were liberated from blind obedience to the Italian jurists and began to devise new solutions, which were more capable of meeting the social requirements.[65]

The decisions (*Assentos*) of palatine courts (*Casa da Suplicação and Relação do Porto*), as well as the overseas High Courts (Goa, Baía, and Rio de Janeiro), were registered and had a binding effect.

Outside the palatine courts, local customs still prevailed amidst the 'rustic judges', who were not familiar with the national law. These customs were recognized by the official legal system as a valid source of law, provided they met some basic pre-requisites.[66]

78. During the closing years of the eighteenth century, the rationalism and voluntarism of European modern natural law changed the underlying assumptions of pre-modern law. Natural law, rooted in reason, became the basis of every legal norm. The enlightened will of the monarch, bestowed with the mission of rendering positive the law of nature, became the pre-eminent source of positive law. Within this framework, a statute of 1769 (*Lei da Boa Razão*) reformed the hierarchy of sources of Portuguese law, reasserting the primacy of royal statute law, as well as the merely subsidiary value of Roman law, filtered by the criterion of rationality. Common law doctrine ceased to be applicable. Canon law was abolished as a source of law in civil cases. The value of jurisprudence was restricted and, finally, custom was practically excluded from the set of valid legal sources. To a significant extent, political, economic, commercial and maritime matters came under the influence of the law of the *'Christian, enlightened and civilized nations.'* This provision would serve as a basis for new doctrinal suggestions and an innovative case law, both inspired by the French Civil Code of 1804.[67]

---

65. C. Nogueira da Silva, 'Legal History', in *Portuguese Law – an Overview*, ed. C. Ferreira de Almeida, Assunção Cristas & Nuno Piçarra (Coimbra: Almedina, 2007), 18; Mário Júlio Almeida Costa, *História do Direito Português*, 5th ed (Coimbra: Almedina, 20012), 313 et seq.
66. C. Nogueira da Silva, *supra,* 18.
67. M.J. Almeida Costa, *História do Direito Português*, 5th ed (Coimbra: Almedina, 2012), 402 et seq; Rui Marcos, *A Legislação Pombalina: Alguns Aspectos Fundamentais* (Coimbra: Almedina, 2006), 156 et seq.

79. Following the Portuguese Liberal Revolution of 1820, constitutional movements ensued. Portuguese Constitutions from the period of liberal monarchy (1820–1910) were marked by their individualism, recognition of civil rights, national sovereignty, a representative system, the division of powers as a way of limiting powers, monarchical government, and the institution of a census to the exercise of electoral rights.

80. The first Portuguese Civil Code appeared in 1867. It was characterized by an underlying liberal and individualistic philosophy, yet tempered by notions of solidarity, as well as social unity and integration. Some of the innovations brought by the code included the demolition of communitarian rights as well as the religious and moral restrictions that had previously imposed heavy limitations in property law and contractual law. In spite of all the social, economic, and cultural changes of the late nineteenth and twentieth centuries, the Civil Code of 1867, in combination with foreign influence on national jurisprudence and doctrine, remained in force until 1966.[68]

81. In 1910, the Portuguese monarchy was overthrown by a Republican revolution, and a new Constitution was approved (1911). This Constitution, in accordance with the new democratic model, organized a lay and democratic republican regime. It preserved, however, some elements of the previous constitutional tradition, as follows: national sovereignty (Article 5), separation of powers through a bicameral system (Article 7), as well as a liberal vision of society, marked by an absence of social rights and by indifference regarding political parties, which would only be formally acknowledged in 1919 in a constitutional revision.[69] Legislation on tenancy matters [*Leis do Inquilinato*] which helped poor industrial workers, who lived in extremely overcrowded conditions, to rent houses, was one of the most significant social measures of the Republican regime.

82. An authoritarian project of the Constitution, prepared by Salazar, was later approved in a plebiscite in 1933. This Constitution imposed a Presidential model[70] and installed a Corporatist Regime, which attributed representative powers to so-called intermediate bodies, such as the family, professional corporations, the church and municipalities, through a corporative chamber (Articles 102–106).[71]

83. After the April 1974 Revolution, a Constituent Assembly was elected, which voted upon the central principles of the new political regime. The nationalization of banks and other basic economic sectors (transport, energy, assurance companies, communications, and others), as well as a general programme of agrarian reform that included the collectivization of land property, were some of the means chosen to realize a socialist society. Nonetheless, this 'socialist way', which was adopted in the new Constitution of 1976, would be gradually replaced by another social and

68. C. Nogueira da Silva, *supra*, 22. M. J. Almeida Costa, *supra*.
69. C. Nogueira da Silva, *supra*, 23.
70. Cf. Article 81.
71. C. Nogueira da Silva, *supra*,24.

economic development model, which was similar to that followed by member countries of the European Community, to which Portugal has accessed in 1986.[72]

84. The actual Portuguese Civil Code (hereinafter 'CC)' was approved by Decree 47344 of 25 November 1966 and entered into force on 1 June 1967. However, after the approval of the Portuguese Constitution of 1976, some of the rules of the Civil Code – such as those which benefited children born within wedlock and which disadvantaged the married woman in relation to her husband – became unconstitutional. These rules were against the new constitutional principles such as the non-discrimination between offsprings born in and out of wedlock, or the equality between spouses.

In 1977, an important reform, introduced by Decree Law 496/77 of 25 November, would reconcile the Civil Code with the new constitutional framework. The marital power had disappeared, as well as the prohibition on a wife from trading without her husband's consent. The 1977 Reform also brought two important alterations in the field of succession law, as regards the position of the surviving spouse.[73] In the 1867 Code and in the first version of the 1966 Civil Code, nephews and siblings were placed before the surviving spouse. Today, in both mandatory and supplementary succession, the spouse is first in line for inheritance along with descendants, and in second place, when there are no descendants but only surviving ascendants. In addition, the spouse is treated more favourably, since under certain circumstances, he/she is entitled to a larger share than the other necessary or legal heirs, and he/she has the right to the allocation of the family house.[74] Recently, Law 48/2018, of 14 August, has allowed spouses to be married under the matrimonial regime of separate assets, to renounce to the quality of mandatory heir (although they remain legal heirs, they can be overturned by an opposite testamentary disposition).

B. The University

85. The year 1290 was the year of the creation of the Portuguese General Study [*Estudo Geral*] by means of the document '*Scientiae thesaurus mirabilis*', signed by King Dinis on the 1 March 1290, and confirmed by the bull '*De statu regni Portugaliae*', issued by Pope Nicholas IV, on the 9 August 1290.[75] The Faculties of Arts, Law, Canon Law, and Medicine were the first to be created. Only around 1380 did theology, formerly reserved to Dominican and Franciscan convents, become part of university education in Portugal. In 1308, the General Study was transferred from Lisbon to Coimbra and, in 1309, it received its first Statutes with the name of

72. C. Nogueira da Silva, *supra*, 28.
73. The 1977 Reform has reduced the family nucleus, for the effects of succession, to the fourth degree in the collateral line. In the absence of these, rights of succession are attributed to the State.
74. *See* Guilherme de Oliveira, 'Family Law in Portugal', in *International Encyclopedia of Laws: Family and Succession Law*, ed. Robert Blanpain (The Hague: Kluwer Law International, 2012), 28.
75. For a general overview, *see* João Caupers & Tiago Duarte, 'Legal Studies', in *Portuguese Law – an Overview*, ed. C. Ferreira de Almeida, Assunção Cristas & Nuno Piçarra (Coimbra: Almedina, 2007), 43 et seq.

'*Charta magna privilegiorum.*' The University moved back to Lisbon in 1338 and back again to Coimbra in 1354; it returned to Lisbon in 1377 and was definitively established in Coimbra in 1537.[76] During the Moyen Age and the Early Modern Period, Roman Law was the main subject to be learnt at the Faculty of Law.

86. In the eighteenth century, the Marquis of Pombal, Minister of the kingdom, made radical reforms in the University, especially regarding the teaching of sciences, in accordance with Enlightenment trends and his anticlerical creed. In 1770, he established a special board for educational affairs (*Junta de Providência Literária*) to conduct a thorough review of the University. This board handed down its report to King José in August 1971, and, in 1772, the University received the 'Pombaline Statutes.'[77] It was a comprehensive new set of statutes which, among other aspects, created the new disciplines, namely *Institutions of Portuguese Law*. Property law was, by that time, taught along with other matters of Civil Law.[78] Mello Freire, Professor of Coimbra (in 1794, he became the Professor of *Institutions of Portuguese Law*), wrote the *Institutiones Juris Civilis Lusitanos cum Publici tum Privati*. Book Three was dedicated to property law. *Institutions* was the first manual written by a Portuguese author to be used in the Faculty of Law. They have remained the basis of the Civil Law from 1779 to mid-nineteenth century.[79] Coelho da Rocha wrote the *Instituições de Direito Civil Portuguez* by 1857, and Guilherme Moreira wrote *Instituições do Direito Civil Português* in 1907. Civil Law was then a unitary matter, taught during a period of three years.

87. In 1923, the Faculty of Law of Lisbon (created in 1911)[80] and the Faculty of Coimbra adopted a new programme of studies (Decree 8578 of 12 January). It was the basis for the autonomy of property law. António José Teixeira de Abreu, Manuel Rodrigues, José Tavares, and Pinto Coelho were important authors by that time.[81] From Coimbra, Pires de Lima, Antunes Varela, Orlando de Carvalho, Carlos Mota Pinto, Henrique Mesquita, Santos Justo, Paulo Mota Pinto, and Mónica Jardim; from Lisbon, Jaime de Gouveia, Oliveira Ascensão, Menezes Cordeiro, Carvalho Fernandes, Pedro de Albuquerque, Rui Pinto Duarte, Henrique Sousa Antunes and José Alberto Vieira are well-known authors.

---

76. As pointed out by Ross Disney, *A History of Portugal and the Portuguese Empire*, I (Cambridge: CUP, 2009) 96, though the University was, for a long time, modest in size and reputation, it provided – along with various monastic and cathedral schools – an opportunity for the Portuguese to acquire learning without ever leaving the kingdom.
77. The objective was to modernize Portugal's only university, since Évora had been closed when the Jesuits were expelled in 1759 and rid of its alleged moribund Scholasticism. *See* Ross Disney, *supra*, 309.
78. For a general overview, Rui Marcos, *A História do Direito e o Seu Ensino na Escola de Coimbra* (Coimbra: Almedina, 2008), 44 et seq.
79. *See* José Alberto Vieira, *Direitos Reais, Perspectiva Histórica do Seu Ensino em Portugal* (Lisboa: Coimbra Editora, 2008); and Pedro de Albuquerque, *Direitos Reais – Relatório sobre o Programa, Conteúdo e Métodos de Ensino* (Coimbra: Almedina, 2009).
80. M. J. Almeida Costa, *História do Direito Português*, 5th edn (Coimbra: Almedina, 2012), 507.
81. M. J. Almeida Costa, *supra*, 516 et seq.

88. Initial steps towards some convergence of European higher education systems were taken with the signature of the Sorbonne Declaration in 1998 by the Ministers in charge of higher education in France, Italy, the United Kingdom, and Germany, and later in 1999, with the signature of the Bologna Declaration. The Bologna process aimed at creating a European Higher Education Area by implementing a comparable degree structure, common quality assurance standards, and by promoting mobility of students and faculties. This was one major revolution in Europe's higher education. In Portugal, after the adoption of the new Bologna Process model, property law remains an autonomous matter in all graduation courses.

II. Concept of Ownership

A. General Introduction

89. Ownership is the highest real right in Portugal. It is the widest power that may impinge upon a thing, as follows: it comprises the possible uses and exploitations that the goods which form the object of ownership may be subject to. Ownership can be defined as an individual right endowed with real efficacy and characterized as a result of its all-embracing content, which Article 1305 of the CC describes by using the terms 'enjoying' and 'disposing of' an object.

By 'enjoying', it shall be understood as the right of use and the right of appropriating its fruits, whether natural or civil. The term 'disposing of' means the owner's power to alienate and encumber the object of ownership (*ius disponendi*). As for alienation, it must be understood as any kind of contract by means of which property can be transferred from one person to another (e.g., sale, exchange, donation, contribution of goods to a company), while encumbrance means the constitution of any limited real right in specific goods, whether it is a right of enjoyment (e.g., usufruct, easement), a right of guarantee (e.g., mortgage, pledge), or a right of acquisition (a pre-emption right). The owner may also transfer the goods by means of inheritance, which distinguishes ownership from other limited real rights, which end as a result of the owner's death.[82]

The owner may also voluntarily renounce his/her right, either in favour of a specific person, in which case renunciation will normally be done onerously, or without the aim to favour any specific person, as occurs when the owner of movable goods abandons them, enabling such goods to become a *res nullius*.

90. It is possible to identify four basic features concerning the right of ownership: abstraction, elasticity, perpetuity, and exclusivity.

91. Abstraction means that ownership comprises an indeterminate number of powers.[83] The content of property rights will differ according to different social

82. *See* the specific legal regime of the right of superficies.

83. Sandra Passinhas, *Dimensions of Property under European Law: Fundamental Rights, Consumer Protection and Intellectual Property – Bridging Concepts* (Florence: EUI, 2010), 73 et seq, available at <http://cadmus.eui.eu/bitstream/handle/1814/13759/2010_Passinhas.pdf?sequence=2>.

resources, as some rights may exist with regard to specific resources but not with regard to others. Certain objects of property determine the contours of the property relationship, conditioning its rights and duties (such as duties of stewardship or obligations to use in a certain manner). As a general idea, the powers of the owner of immovable property are not the same as those of the owner of movable property, and even here the power of the owner of a car is not the same as the power of the owner of an animal.

In contrast to ownership, the powers that limited real rights comprise can be defined accurately. To a certain extent, it can be said that the powers which ownership includes become actualized only when they are separated from the nucleus of the owner's right, forming part of the content of a limited real right.

92. Ownership is an elastic power that returns to its original shape after the restriction or change, which deformed or distorted it, is removed. Limited rights act as a strain. For example, when the usufruct ends, in the event of its holder's death, the power to use and enjoy return to the bosom of the right of ownership. Elasticity means that ownership always remains a sort of residual power, capable of resuming its original shape after being stretched or compressed.

93. Perpetuity means that the property tends to last as much as its object does, and not as long as its owner lives, that is to say, the length of a property right is defined by the physical or economic permanence of the object it falls upon, which allows to distinguish property from certain limited rights that have a life span. For this reason, legal protection for property is closely connected with the legal protection for the right of inheritance.

94. Finally, exclusivity means also that two rights of ownership protected fully and simultaneously in favour of two different owners cannot exist at the same time. Limited real rights are not exclusive, in the sense that they always depend on the existence of a previous right of ownership that they will compress (e.g., a mortgage is a restriction on ownership).[84]

95. Although ownership is composed of an indeterminate number of powers, and despite the existence of limited real rights, it would be wrong to define ownership as an unlimited right.

The law lays down structural conditions that modulate the exercise of the right by its holder. Those limits have the aim of favouring interests for other individuals (personality rights protection), favouring the exercise of other property rights by their holders (neighbourhood law), or favouring general social interests (justified by the requirement that property fulfils a social function).[85]

---

84. Co-ownership is characterized by a single property right held in common by several holders. *See* Ch. 5.
85. *See* para. 151.

B. *The Object of Ownership: Immovable Property, Movable Property and Animals*

96. Article 1302 of the CC states that property rights can only relate to tangible things. The following Articles provide that copyright and industrial property are governed by special laws and that the rules of the Civil Code are applied to these rights on a subsidiary basis. Some authors construe the category of property rights as embracing only tangible things and others extend it to intangible things. It should be emphasized that the Civil Code permits both the usufruct and the pledge of credits and other rights.[86]

97. Under the category of tangible goods, immovable property might be distinguished from movable property. That distinction is very important. It can be explained in general terms as follows: contracts over immovable property must be written in a public deed;[87] a contract qualifies as a lease or a tenancy depending on the object; powers of disposal are different regarding movable and immovable property;[88] and the competence of companies might differ towards different categories of goods. Law 8/2017, of 3 March, established a new legal status for animals. Considered as things until then, animals were through this new regime expressly recognized as sensitive beings. Consequently, ownership of animals must now vest new rights and duties. Specially, it should take into consideration the welfare of the animal according to its species (Article 1305-A CC), that is, its maintenance and health. It is now expressly stated that ownership over an animal does not include the power to abuse it, by infringing unjustified pain. What is unjustified pain remains, however, unclear, since, in Portugal, bullfights are considered a cultural tradition, as well as pigeon shooting. In what is not expressly ruled, the general rules on ownership still apply (Article 1302, 2).

98. In the field of property law, several rights might impinge only upon immovable property, as follows: apartment ownership, right of use; superficies; easements; and time-sharing; several rights might impinge upon immovable and movable property subject to registration, as rent assignment; mortgage; preliminary contract; contractual pre-emption rights; the pledge can only impinge upon movable things. As regards the acquisition of real rights: occupation is suitable only for movable things (Articles 1318 and 1345 of the CC); accession by nature is only for movable property (Article 1327 of the CC). The time required for *usucapio* is longer for immovables than for movables. Industrial accession has a different regime, depending on the immovable or movable nature of the things at stake. *Ius retentionis* also varies according to the nature of the good.

99. Finally, real rights over immovables are subject to registration, whereas those over movables are not. A public registry has been created, similar to the Land Registry, with the aim of giving legal publicity to property and some other real

86. R. Pinto Duarte, *Curso de Direitos Reais*, 3rd ed. (Lisboa: Principia, 2013), 194 et seq.
87. According to Articles 875 and 947, and Article 22 of DL 116/2008, 4 July.
88. Cf. Articles 1678(1)(e); 1682 and 1682-A; and 94(3) CC.

rights in certain chattels (e.g., ships, airships, train wagons, motor vehicles, and commercial establishments). Publicity is mainly given trough registration and not through possession.[89]

1. Immovable and Real Property

100. According to Article 204 of the CC, there are different kinds of immovable property: land (Article 204(1)(a) of the CC); waters (Article 204(1)(b) of the CC); trees, bushes, and fruits (Article 204(1)(c) of the CC), while connected to the soil; and the rights pertinent to the above-mentioned things (Article 204(1)(d) of the CC). Article 204(1)(e) of the CC categorizes as immovables the fixtures [*partes integrantes*], that is, things that are attached to a principal thing. Attachment causes them to lose their character as individual things, and become part of the principal thing.

101. It remains controversial whether Article 204 of the CC is a taxative enumeration of things to be considered as immovable property, as defended by Castro Mendes,[90] Carvalho Fernandes,[91] and Menezes Leitão.[92] Oliveira Ascensão,[93] Menezes Cordeiro,[94] and José Alberto Vieira,[95] claim that provision is merely exemplificative and, therefore, things not listen in Article 204 cc can also be considered as immovable property.

102. Portuguese law does not accept the medieval idea that *qui dominus est soli sominus est usque ad coelos usque ad inferos* (whoever owns the soil, it is theirs all the way up to heaven and down to hell). Article 1344 foresees several restrictions according to the practical interest of the owner and several parts of the subsoil in the public domain. Therefore, the owner cannot prevent aeroplanes from flying over his land, but he/she has the right to exploit minerals in the subsoil. He/she can use stones, sand, and common minerals in construction.[96]

103. The Portuguese legal order distinguishes between public and private waters. The Civil Code regulates private waters. Public waters are regulated by

89. Article 205(2) CC.
90. João Castro Mendes, *Teoria Geral do Direito Civil I* (Lisboa: Universidade Católica, 1978), 395.
91. Carvalho Fernandes, *Teoria Geral do Direito Civil I*, 6th ed (Lisboa: Universidade Católica Editora, 2012), 689.
92. Menezes Leitão, *Direitos Reais* (Coimbra: Almedina, 2019), 645.
93. Oliveira Ascensão, *Teoria Geral I* (Coimbra: Coimbra Editora, 2000), 359–360.
94. Menezes Cordeiro, *Tratado De Direito Civil Português I*- Parte Geral, II- Coisas, 3rd ed (Coimbra: Almedina, 2005), 120.
95. José Alberto Vieira, *Direitos Reais* (Lisboa: Coimbra Editora, 2008), 145.
96. Menezes Leitão, *supra*, 69.

Laws 54/2005, of 15 November[97] and Law 58/2005, of 29 December.[98] Decree-Laws 226-A/2007, 31 May (as amended); 97/2008, of 11 June; and 100/2008, of 16 June complete that regulation.[99]

104. Trees, bushes, and fruits (Article 204(1)(c) of the CC), while connected to the soil are considered immovable. When that connection ceases, they are considered movable property.

105. Rights pertinent to the above-mentioned things are also immovable property. A right of usufruct over a house is immovable property and can be, for example, subject to a mortgage or a pre-emption right.

106. The fixtures [*partes integrantes*] are permanently attached to the land, and they cannot be removed without, substantial or slight, damage to the land. If the fixture is removed, it will become an autonomous thing. Fixtures shall be distinguished from component parts [*partes constituintes*], that is, things that are incorporated into a principal thing. Incorporation causes them to lose their character as individual things, and become part of the principal thing. They are immovable goods 'by means of incorporation'.

107. In a sale of land, fixtures are treated as part of the land, and may not be removed or altered by the seller prior to the transfer of the land. Accessory things are chattel not attached to land though maintained permanently for the service of that immovable. Indeed, they can be physically detached without causing damage to the immovable they belong to, which means that in this case the link is mainly economic in nature. The chattel, such as ornamental objects, industrial machinery, agricultural fertilizers, or breeding places, is used in order to enhance the use of property. In a sale of land, accessory things may be legally removed by the seller prior to the transfer of the land, unless parties agree otherwise.[100]

97. As amended (last amendment by Law 31/2016, of 23 August).
98. As amended (last amendment by Law 44/2017, of 18 June).
99. *See* Decisions STJ, of 28 October 2014 [Process: 750/03], available at http://www.dgsi.pt/jstj.nsf/954f0ce6ad9dd8b980256b5f003fa814/83367b9d6b7dc14780257d8000382a95?OpenDocument; of 9 February 2012 [Process: 161/06], available at http://www.dgsi.pt/jstj.nsf/954f0ce6ad9dd8b980256b5f003fa814/a9c0f46f8420098a8025799f0043dc5c?OpenDocument; of 20 January 2010 [Process: 678/1999], available at http://www.dgsi.pt/jstj.nsf/954f0ce6ad9dd8b980256b5f003fa814/031ea094ad1cf432802576b100573df0?OpenDocument; and of 9 December 2008 [Process: 08A3107], available at http://www.dgsi.pt/jstj.nsf/954f0ce6ad9dd8b980256b5f003fa814/021dbcf452b58f7b80257524003cda01?OpenDocument.
100. Article 210 CC.

2. Movable and Personal Property

108. The category of movable goods is defined in Article 205(1) of the CC by means of a simple contrast with regard to the catalogue of immovable things contained in Article 204(1) of the CC, in such a way that all the rest of the goods considered to be the object of property must be considered chattels, are not included in the said catalogue.[101]

109. Movable things have traditionally been considered those endowed with lesser value within the individuals' personal patrimony. This tendency has started to change in the last decades, since it has been shown that some chattels have an equal or superior value than many immovable goods, which has currently allowed several loans to be granted on the basis of movable guarantees.

110. The legal status of the most expensive movable goods (e.g., artworks, ships, airships, motor vehicles) is the status of movable things, unless otherwise regulated. This holds true even for movable goods subject to registration.[102]

3. Who May Own Property

111. Legally speaking, a person is either a human being or a corporation while holding rights and being responsible regarding obligations. The legal personality consists, therefore, in the possibility to actually have rights and obligations.

a. Physical Persons

112. Human beings are deemed to have legal personality the moment they are completely born and alive. Thereafter, they shall be designated as physical persons. The law entitles rights to *nascituri* (*lato* and *stricto sensu*), but the actual acquisition of such rights depends on their being born alive.[103] Either *nasciturus stricto sensu* (already conceived) or *nodum* (not yet conceived) may acquire rights by donation or by succession (voluntary succession), as far as they are children of a specific person who is alive at the time the donor made his/her statement or at the time succession is open.[104] Under legal provisions, the *nasciturus* who had already been conceived at the time the succession opening has 'successor capacity'– understood as the expectation to be called upon legal succession when attaining his/her legal personality.[105]

---

101. Energy is also to be considered a movable thing. Cf. Menezes Cordeiro, *Tratado De Direito Civil Português I*- Parte Geral, II- Coisas, 3rd ed (Coimbra: Almedina, 2005), 146 et seq; José Alberto Vieira, *Direitos Reais* (Lisboa: Coimbra Editora: 2008), 158; Menezes Leitão, *Direitos Reais* (Coimbra: Almedina, 2019), 73.
102. Article 205(2) CC.
103. Article 66(2) CC.
104. Articles 952 and 2033(2)(a) CC.
105. Article 2033(1) CC.

113. As a rule, all physical persons can have any rights and obligations. Therefore, they may, in principle, be a part of any legal relation; exceptions are to result from the law.[106] The capacity of physical persons consists in their ability of exercising, either personally and freely, or through a representative appointed by them, their rights and obligations.

Minors not emancipated are, as a rule, considered not to have legal capacity. Their incapacity shall be overcome by parental authority, and subsidiarily, by the guardianship.[107]

Persons subject to guardianship are those who, due to health issues, disability, behaviour, are unable to take care of themselves and to manage their property.[108] They are assisted by a curator [*o acompanhante*] whose authorization is required for the disposal of assets *inter vivos* and for any other acts that, in view of the circumstances of the case, shall be specified in the Court's decision.[109] The recent Law 49/2018, of 14 August, adapted the Portuguese Civil Code to the Convention on the Rights of Persons with Disabilities, adopted on 13 December 2006 at the United Nations. The most innovative feature of this new regime relates to the measures to be adopted. They are proportional and tailored to the person's circumstances, apply for the shortest time possible and are subject to regular review by a competent, independent judicial body.

b. Corporations

114. Corporations also have legal personality, once they are legally constituted and in certain cases registered, or upon their administrative assessment.[110] They are organizations aimed to the fulfilment of collective purposes. Private corporations fall under one of the following categories: associations [*associações*], foundations [*fundações*], trading companies [*sociedades comerciais*], and civil companies under commercial statutes [*sociedades civis sob forma comercial*].[111] Associations and foundations are governed by the Civil Code; trading companies and civil companies under commercial statutes are governed by the Commercial Company Act.[112]

115. Corporations are entitled to the rights and subject to the duties suited to their legal nature.[113] Their capacity covers only the rights and obligations necessary or adequate to the achievement of their purposes (principle of the specialty) and they cannot have, as is obvious, rights and obligations prohibited by law or adjacent

106. Article 67 CC.
107. Articles 123–124 CC.
108. Article 138(1) CC.
109. Article 153 CC. For a general overview, *see* Guilherme de Oliveira, 'Family and Succession Law in Portugal', in *International Encyclopedia of Laws: Family and Succession Law*, ed. Robert Blanpain (The Hague: Kluwer Law international, 2012), 525.
110. Article 158 CC.
111. Civil companies do not have, as such, legal personality. Professional companies may adopt a commercial form and in doing so, they become subject to the rules regarding commercial companies (Article 27, 2, of Law 2/2013, 10 January).
112. DL 262/86, of 2 September, as amended (last amendment by Law 49/2018, of 14 August).
113. Article 160 CC.

only to the legal personality of a physical person. Corporations are to be represented by those designated by the law or by its statutes.

116. Article 6 of the Commercial Company Act provides that the capacity of a company shall include the rights and obligations necessary or adequate to the pursuit of its corporate purpose, with the exception of those which are prohibited by law or inseparable from the legal form of a sole trader. Liberalities which can be considered usual, according to the circumstances of the time and the conditions of the company itself, shall not be considered to be contrary to its purpose. The provision of real or personal guarantees for any debts of other entities shall be considered contrary to the purpose of the company, except where the company has a justified interest or it is in a group or controlling relationship.

c. Property among Spouses

117. In Portugal, spouses are free to choose their matrimonial property system, either by choosing one of the systems laid down in the Civil Code or by stipulating their own rules.[114]

The default property regime among spouses, in the absence of ante-nuptial accord, is that of community of acquired assets. Under the system of community of acquired assets, there is or there may be joint property and personal property of each spouse. Whatsoever someone brings into the marriage or receives individually through gifts or inheritances remains his/hers, but whatsoever someone earns or acquires during the marriage is co-owned by both spouses, regardless of who earned it or whose name is on the title. Property that is brought to the couple or acquired individually is not communicated; only property acquired after marriage onerously is joint property. This is the core of the system and basically corresponds to the idea that only that which expresses the collaboration of both spouses in the patrimonial effort of marriage will become joint property.[115]

118. The Portuguese Civil Code also typifies a system of general community of assets or a system of separate assets. The system of general community of assets is characterized by the fact that the joint property is constituted by all present and future property of the spouses that is not exempted by law. Under the system of separate assets,[116] there is complete and absolute separation between the properties of the spouses. Under Article 1735 of the CC, each owner retains ownership and enjoyment of all their present and future property, which they can freely dispose of as they wish. The system of community of assets and the system of separate assets

114. On the limits of the freedom of the spouses, *see* Guilherme de Oliveira, 'Family and Succession Law in Portugal', in *International Encyclopedia of Laws: Family and Succession Law*, ed. Robert Blanpain (The Hague: Kluwer Law international, 2012), 202 ff.

115. Francisco Pereira Coelho & Guilherme de Oliveira, *Curso de Direito da Família*, 5th ed (Coimbra: Imprensa da Universidade, 2016), 506.

116. There are two cases in which the law imposes the system of separate assets: marriages celebrated without being preceded by the process of publication of bans, and marriages involving anyone who is already sixty years of age.

is in force if it is stipulated by the intended spouses in the ante-nuptial deed or in the document drawn up before the registrar of the civil registry office.

§4. Trust and Fiduciary Mechanisms

I. The Numerus Clausus Principle

119. Real rights or property rights are rights over things,[117] which can be characterized in two ways. First, they entitle their holder to a direct and immediate power over the goods, and second, the holder's power is endowed with an *erga omnes* efficacy. As regards enforceability against third parties, real rights are exclusive. In this context, exclusivity means that every property right holder has the right to exclude any non-authorized action from another person that affects the goods which are the object of his/her property (*iura excludendi omnes alios*).[118] The duty to respect property by non-interference does not involve the person who owes the duty in any personal dealing with the owner in order to respect his ownership. The relation is mediated via the thing the owner own and not on the basis of his personal interactions. The practice of property protects the ownership relation by instituting a blanket prohibition on the interference with things that others own. This duty illustrates the way in which property rights are rights in rem. The scope of the right is not to be visualized as an owner's possession of billions of personal rights against others, each of which has individuated personal duties towards every owner of property. Rather, people simply have a duty not to interfere with the property of others; in general, if it is not ours and we have no permission from the owner, we are not entitled to interfere with it. The right to exclude others entails a duty, enforceable by state coercion, to defer to the owner's will. In this sense, the state confers a property right by granting a specific person or group of persons the right to call on the aid of the state to prevent others from using particular resources without the owner's consent.[119]

120. Ownership and limited real rights, rights in rem, are the opposite category to claims or rights of credit, which are rights in personam. The main differences between them arise both from their content and from the effects that they produce with regard to third parties (people who have not taken part in its constitution). Rights of credit are characterized by their relative efficacy, since they may only be asserted against a specific subject – the debtor, who is held to carry out a specific performance in favour of the creditor (related to a thing or not), and to whom the hypothetical action will be brought against in case of violation of the creditor's

117. Sandra Passinhas, *Dimensions of Property under European Law: Fundamental Rights, Consumer Protection and Intellectual Property – Bridging Concepts* (Florence: EUI, 2010), 70 et seq, available at <http://cadmus.eui.eu/bitstream/handle/1814/13759/2010_Passinhas.pdf?sequence=2>.

118. *Ibid.*, 71–72.

119. *Ibid.*, 74–75.

interest (*inter partes* efficacy). Real rights, however, give the holder a power of exploitation over a definite thing, which can be asserted against any third party (*erga omnes* efficacy).

121. The Portuguese Civil Code of 1967 imposes a strict standardization of property rights. Property law is considered to be a closed system, including a restricted list of entitlements which allows us to rely on a number of property interests or real rights. Article 1306 of the CC provides that save as otherwise stated in the law, restrictions cannot be created with real nature on the right of property or on rights that correspond to parts of the same.[120] The *numerus clausus* principle is a mandatory principle governing Portuguese property law. The standardization of property provides individuals with a limitative typology of real rights. In a taxative typology, there is no possibility to model new forms, different from those specified by law. The principle of the closed number of property rights implies that it is not possible for private individuals to create or to transfer any property rights other than those expressly recognized as such by the law. A private norm can be modelled only according to those types which have been previously shaped by law. The *numerus clausus* principle states that divided interests in property must be strictly confined to a small number of well-defined, controlled, and limited types.[121] The assumption that underlies such a principle is that as property law settles the general ordination of goods, it needs to be easily perceptible by individuals. Quoting Mattei:[122]

> We do not need to enter into subtleties of comparative discussion to say that property rights do affect the allocation of scarce resources in a much deeper way than contractual rights. This is one of the reasons behind the civilian theory of the numerus clausus of real rights that precludes the parties from creating limited property rights outside of the typical scheme provided by the code.

122. Article 1306 of the CC reads as follows: 'The constitution neither of real restrictions to ownership neither of fragmentation interests is allowed except in cases legally previewed; every restriction agreed upon out of, these conditions has contractual nature.' The Portuguese property rights system is characterized by a limited number of forms which are not subject to contractual modification. Legal scholarship in Portugal has tried, however, to minimize the effects of such a restrictive disposition. For instance, it has outlined that consuetude can create property rights, and it supports the idea that the interpreter can also qualify a figure as real, despite the fact that the legislator had not considered it that way.

---

120. J. Oliveira Ascensão, *A Tipicidade dos Direitos Reais* (Lisboa: Petrony, 1968); R. Pinto Duarte, *Tipicidade e Atipicidade dos Contratos* (Coimbra: Almedina, 2000).
121. Ugo Mattei, *Basic Principles of Property Law: a Comparative Legal and Economic Introduction* (London: Greenwood Press, 2000), 14.
122. Ugo Mattei, *supra*, 39.

123. Even where the limitative standardization of property rights is accepted without reservation, the *numerus clausus* principle is usually attenuated. First, in order to achieve this, an open structure of the type is usually adopted. The type description does not have to contain every relevant element of the aimed normative effects, but only those necessary for the practical effect. 'Type' represents a fundamental cadre or a description, but does not exclude relevant elements that arise a posteriori. A fact or situation can have extra-type content. In *numerus clausus* systems, we generally find open types. Second, the effective rigidity of a closed system strictly depends on the flexibility of the real rights admitted; they can be extended in such a way that supplies all imaginable needs. As a general characteristic, the strictness of the *numerus clausus* is balanced by the extension of the definition of servitude.

124. Limited real rights can be classified into three groups: rights of use)*direitos reais de gozo*), rights of guarantee (*direitos reais de garantia*), and rights of acquisition (*direitos reais de aquisição*). Rights of use, such as the usufruct or the servitude, give the holder some power to use/enjoy someone else's goods. Guaranteed real rights are constituted to ensure the fulfilment of an obligation. This second group of real rights gives the holder the power to demand the compulsory sale of another person's goods (the goods given as guarantee), as well as to apply the price so obtained in order to satisfy its right of credit. Finally, rights of acquisition are real rights (when they are effective against third parties) that entitle their holder to acquire a thing, under certain circumstances. They can be foreseen specifically by law or agreed upon in a contract. For example, the tenant,[123] the joint owner,[124] and the owner of the land,[125] have pre-emption rights in case of sale or *datio in solvendo* of property. In order to create a real right of acquisition through contract, parties shall declare their intention and have it registered. Therefore, contractual rights of acquisition must impinge upon immovable property or movable property subject to registration.[126] There is no specific chapter in the Portuguese Civil Code on real rights of acquisition.

II. Unity and Fragmentation

125. Unity is a main characteristic of ownership in Portugal and constitutes a general principle of property law. Fragmentation of ownership is not lawful in Portugal: upon one thing, only one ownership right must impinge (although this right might be hold in common by several holders). *Emphyteusis* was considered a partitioning of ownership, rather than a *ius in rem*. As such, it was an undesirable vestige of feudal law. In accordance with this idea, this right was extinguished after the Revolution of 1974. *Emphytheusis* [*enfiteuse*] on rural land was extinguished by

123. Article 1091 CC.
124. Article 1409 CC.
125. According to Article 1535, the owner of the land has a pre-emption right in case of the sale of the *right of superficies*.
126. Cf. Article 421 CC.

Decree-Law (hereinafter 'DL') 195-A/75,[127] of 16 March and *emphiteusis* on urban land was abolished by DL 233/76, of 2 April.[128]

126. The right of ownership over a good might be compressed by a limited real right. Contrary to ownership, the other real rights are known as limited real rights, since their content consists of only a part of the utilities that goods are able to provide. As they are always constituted in favour of someone distinct from the holder, they are called *iura in re aliena* (rights in rem over a thing owned by another). Similar to estates in land, limited real rights are rights in land for a particular duration of time. It should also be emphasized that several limited real rights can co-exist in the same piece of land (e.g., a mortgage and a servitude). Finally, limited rights accompany the things encumbered.

III. Fiduciary Mechanisms in Portugal

127. In Portuguese law, although not sealed in the legislation, some fiduciary mechanisms with exceptional character are admitted. In Part IV, the fiduciary mechanisms with a goal of management (*fiducia cum amico*) and the fiduciary mechanisms with a goal of guarantee (*fiducia cum creditore*) will be analysed in detail. Also, a distinction between *inter vivos* and *mortis causa* fiduciary mechanisms will be made.

§5. Possession and Title

128. In Portugal, transfer of property requires the existence of a legal title over it. The title may also refer to a formal document that serves as evidence of ownership. Conveyance of the document may be required in order to transfer ownership in the property to another person. Title is distinct from possession, a power that often accompanies ownership but that is not necessarily sufficient to prove it. In many cases, both possession and title may be transferred independently of each other.

129. Given the *erga omnes* efficacy of real rights, it is necessary that their holder can be known by anyone, and not only by the contracting parties that have respectively conveyed and acquired the right at issue. In this sense, the transfer of a real right by means of a contract (e.g., sale or donation), even when put in writing, does

---

127. Amended by DL 546/76, of 10 July.

128. Amended by DLs 82/78, of 2 May; 73-A/79, of 3 April; and 226/80, of 15 July. *See* Gomes Canotilho and Vassalo Abreu, 'Enfiteuse sem extinção. A propósito da dilatação legal do âmbito normativo do instituto enfitêutico' *RLJ* 3967 (2011), 206 et seq; Rui de Figueiredo Marcos, 'O regresso da enfiteuse', in FDUL, *O sistema contratual romano: de Roma ao direito actual* (Coimbra: Coimbra Editora, 2010) 980 and ff; M. J. Almeida Costa, *Origem da enfiteuse no direito português* (Coimbra: 1957). *See* also the Decision of the Supreme Court of Justice [hereinafter STJ], of 30 October 2014 [Process: 5658/07], available at http://www.dgsi.pt/jstj.nsf/954f0ce6ad9dd8b98025 6b5f003fa814/aaa9c7b2035ba47280257d8200372fde?OpenDocument.

not give enough legal publicity to the purchaser's right. The publicity of property and real rights is based on another kind of act, which permits one to state that not only did someone acquire from another one specific right on one specific date, but also that the right at issue currently belongs to a specific individual. Possession is a method of legal publicity for real rights admitted by law. The most sophisticated system of legal publicity for property and other real rights is the recording of the same in a public Registry.

130. Possession [*posse*] is the de facto control over an object that is manifested by an activity corresponding to the exercise of ownership or another real right of use over the property.[129] The factual control exercised by the possessor must be an expression of a real right over the thing or a claim of right.[130]

131. The main effect of possession is the legitimization of the possessor, who will be able to act as the holder of the item possessed.[131] According to Article 1268(1) of the CC, the possessor is presumed to be the holder of the corresponding real right over the property. The law presumes that the person who possesses a thing is the real holder of it. By means of possession, it is possible to make a provisional or presumable assignment of property and other rights in goods. If *A* acts over a rural property as the owner, the appearance of an authentic right arises. Therefore, if *C* is the legal owner of that property, there is the consequent reversal of the burden of proof, and *C* has to prove his/her right in order to succeed in his/her claim.

132. A possessor enjoys certain judicial protection against third parties even if he/she is not the owner. Every possessor, due to the simple fact of possessing, has the power to demand a judicial protection against anyone who disturbs his/her possession. This protection is not subject to proof of an acquisition title, but to proof of the simple fact that the plaintiff had previous possession of the goods or right at issue.

133. Possession is also shaped as a means to become the authentic owner of an object, in the event that the possessor was not already the owner because of a failure in his/her acquisition title. This significant effect, known as adverse possession [*usucapio*], can take place in the course of time. On the adverse possession as a way of acquisition of property and other real rights, *see infra*, Part III.

Portugal does not accept the principle *en fait de meubles possession vaut titre* (as far as immovables are concerned, possession equals title). The person who, in good faith, acquires movable goods from the hands of a trader, will not be maintained in his/her acquisitions if it is subsequently proved that the transferor was not the authentic owner of the transferred goods.[132] Possession does not amount to title. The

129. Article 1252 CC.
130. A claim of right exists if the person believes he/she has rightful claim to the property, even if that belief is mistaken. A negative example would be a timber thief who sneaks onto a property, cuts timber not visible from the road, and hauls the logs away at night. His/her actions, though they demonstrate actual possession, also demonstrate knowledge of guilt, as opposed to claim of right.
131. This presumption declines before presumption resulting from prior registration.
132. Article 1301 CC.

owner has vindicatory power upon payment of the price previously paid for the good. He/she remains, therefore, entitled to restitution.

The owner may demand judicial protection for his/her right, supposing that interference on it exists. The action that the owner may bring to demand the retrieval of goods which are the object of property in question from the person who possesses it unlawfully is known as *vindicatio*, and is foreseen in Articles 1311 to 1315 of the CC.

134. The Portuguese legal order foresees several mechanisms for the protection of property. Vindication is a real action brought by the owner (not the possessor) against the person in possession (but not the owner). *Vindicatio* aims at having the real right recognized by the Court and retrieving that same object of property from the person who unlawfully possesses it. The plaintiff must prove: (a) his/her own title over the object to which the action refers; (b) the possession of the object by the defendant. Under Portuguese law, the holder of a real right has a power to pursuit the property against any person (*C* or *D*) in unlawful possession of the property. If *A* can prove that he/she has a real right over the property and that *C* is in possession of the property, *A* can petition the court for a declaration of his/her rights and a mandatory order against *C* for return of the property (Article 1311 of the CC read with Article 1315 of the CC).[133] The exercise of this remedy is not subject to a time limit.[134]

135. *Actio negatoria* and action *confessoria* are modalities of *actio vindicatoria*. A *actio negatoria* is designed to ensure that property is left free from the interference of third parties. The denial action is one exercised by the owner with the twofold purpose of asking the judge both to declare that the ownership is free from any kind of charge, and to bring it back to him/her into the full enjoyment of his/her right. For example, if *B* claims that he/she has a servitude right over a property belonging to *A*, *A* might ask the Court to deny the existence of that right.

An *actio confessoria* is designed to ensure that the holder of a limited real right might enforce his/her right against the owner of the property who contests that right. If *B* has a servitude in a property belonging to *A*, but *A* contests his/her right or prevents the free enjoyment of the servitude, *B* might ask the Court to declare the existence of the servitude and to condemn *A* to respect it.

133. *See* Decisions STJ, of 4 October 1984 [Process: 071598], available at http://www.dgsi.pt/jstj.nsf/954f0ce6ad9dd8b980256b5f003fa814/bbe279b72b343aff802568fc003a49ea?OpenDocument; of 26 May 2009 [Process: 09AO531], available at http://www.dgsi.pt/jstj.nsf/954f0ce6ad9dd8b980256b5f003fa814/e743fb0c118e4135802575da004826c8?OpenDocument; of 4 February 2012 [Process: 314/2000], available at http://www.dgsi.pt/jstj.nsf/954f0ce6ad9dd8b980256b5f003fa814/9ae80583c8a2a66f80257c7b005ecfad?OpenDocument; of 19 November 2015 [Process: 779/14], available at http://www.dgsi.pt/jstj.nsf/954f0ce6ad9dd8b980256b5f003fa814/756ba2bc8055560680257f0200564e6e?OpenDocument.

134. Article 1313 CC.

136. Article 1346 of the CC, dealing with nuisance, provides that the holder of a real right[135] may approach the court for an interdict against unpleasant smells or noises that substantially interfere with the use or enjoyment of the property and do not result from the normal use of the property.[136]

Since the holder of a limited real right has the same protection under Portuguese law as an owner to protect his/her right (Article 1315 of the CC), a usufructuary can act directly against a dispossessor to stop the disturbance of his/her limited interest, by using a negatory action to ensure cessation of the disturbance.[137] If the disturbance affects the rights of both the holder and the owner, the usufructuary and the usuary are placed under an obligation to warn the owner. Failure to notify the owner in such circumstances may result in an action for damages against the holder of the personal servitude.[138] Whereas, the nude owner can obtain a preliminary and urgent order from the court to prevent the usufructuary from committing acts which diminish the value of the property. However, the usufructuary who does not comply with his duties cannot be placed under the management of the court or a professional manager. The most effective way to defend the property would thus be to terminate the usufruct. The above-mentioned applies to a use and habitation right[139] and to superficies.[140]

137. It is possible, under Portuguese procedural law, to bring a summary action in order to retrieve the lost possession of an object, provided the plaintiff is able to prove that he/she has been in the possession of that object before. The general principle is that a person in possession of land or goods, even as a wrongdoer, is entitled to take action against anyone interfering with the possession unless the person interfering is able to demonstrate a superior right to do so.[141]

These summary proceedings on possession are only aimed at restoring the factual situation in which the possessor found himself/herself, thus forbidding acts of dispossession, even if the same arise from the actual owner. They do not serve to solve other legal issues, which must be clarified in the suitable vindicatory judgment. Likewise, the summary proceedings on possession serve to protect everyone who possesses goods, whether his/her possession is based on a right that enables him/her to possess them or not.

The protection extends to the forbidding of unlawful acts of dispossession by judicial procedures [*embargos de terceiro*].[142] I will now describe the claim for the recovery of lost possession and the action for maintenance of possession.

---

135. Since a remedy based on nuisance is not considered a possessory remedy, its availability is restricted to the holder of a real right.
136. In this sense, the term 'nuisance' signifies the resulting condition rather than the action causing the interference. The nuisance must be continuous. It need not be constant or unceasing but it must occur often enough to be almost continuous.
137. Henrique Mesquita, *Direitos Reais* (Coimbra, 1967), 178.
138. Articles 1475 and 1490 CC.
139. Article 1490 CC.
140. Article 1536(1)(a) and (2) CC.
141. *See* Decision of the Supreme Court of 16 November 1988 [Process: 076888], available at http://www.dgsi.pt/jstj.nsf/954f0ce6ad9dd8b980256b5f003fa814/198eb691ea9c7e19802568fc003a7b07?OpenDocument.
142. Articles 342-350 of the CPC.

138. The possessor is entitled to institute a claim for the recovery of lost possession [*acção para a restituição da posse*] (corresponding to the Roman *interdictum recuperandae possessionis*), on account of wrongful deprivation of the factual control over the property.[143] Restitution will be ordered without a consideration of the merits of the case, for example, an investigation concerning the right of ownership.[144] The deprivation does not need to be by force or fraud; any unlawful deprivation would suffice. Nevertheless, if the dispossession was effected by the use of violence against the property or the person[145] of the former possessor, the court might order summary restitution without giving the dispossessor an opportunity to defend himself/herself.[146] In the most urgent cases, the holder of a real right who is deprived of his possession can use self-help to recover possession over the thing.[147]

The claim for restitution can be pursued not only against the dispossessor and his/her heirs, but also against any third person who has acquired possession of the property with the knowledge of the unlawful dispossession.[148] He/she can sue the dispossessor within a year of the deprivation or in the case of clandestine deprivation, within a year after it came to his/her knowledge. In appropriate circumstances, the possessor is also entitled to institute a claim for damages.[149]

Possessors are also entitled to an action for the maintenance of possession [*acção para a manutenção da posse*], corresponding to the Roman *interdictum retinendae possessionis*. According to Article 1277 of the CC, the possessor who is unlawfully disturbed in the exercise of his/her possession can request that the court uphold his/her possession until the merits of the case are decided.[150] Portuguese law does not require the disturbance to be effected by force or fraud.

139. The procedure for maintenance of possession can only be pursued against the person who disturbed the possession.[151] The possessor can sue the disturber within a year after overt disturbance or, within a year after clandestine disturbance has come to his/her knowledge.[152] The use of self-help and a claim for damages against the holder will lie in the same circumstances as in the case discussed above for deprivation of possession.

---

143. Article 1277 CC.
144. Article 1278 CC.
145. *See* Decision STJ, of 25 November 1998 (Process: 98B410), available at http://www.dgsi.pt/jstj.nsf/954f0ce6ad9dd8b980256b5f003fa814/caa65c43ace202a7802568fc003b9554?OpenDocument. The Decision STJ, of 25 June 1998 [Process: 97B846], at http://www.dgsi.pt/jstj.nsf/954f0ce6ad9dd8b980256b5f003fa814/a2fa02a2cbc0ae50802568fc003b72ab?OpenDocument concluded that the breaking of a door in order to gain possession of a building amounts to violence against property.
146. Article 1279 CC and Articles 377 ff CPC.
147. Article 316 CC read with Articles 1314 and 1315 CC.
148. Article 1281(2) CC.
149. Article 1284 CC. *See* Decision STJ, of 3 October 2013 [Process: 9074/09], available at http://www.dgsi.pt/jstj.nsf/954f0ce6ad9dd8b980256b5f003fa814/3c72ad6bd9befdfa80257c0c0031dfc6?OpenDocument.
150. Article 1278 CC.
151. Article 1281(2) CC.
152. Article 1282 CC. *See* Decision of the Supreme Court of 22 July 1982 [Process: 070217], available at http://www.dgsi.pt/jstj.nsf/954f0ce6ad9dd8b980256b5f003fa814/2fb7b74c1b3e98fd802568fc0039cf17?OpenDocument.

140. Portuguese law extends possessory protection to certain holders [*detentores*], for example, lessees and borrowers for use, in case of disturbance or deprivation of their withholding [*detenção*] of the property. Quasi-vindicatory remedies and remedies based on nuisance are not, however, available to the lessee and the borrower for use if their right is disturbed. Under Portuguese law, the kind of control that a lessee or borrower for use acquires over the property under a contract of lease or loan for use amounts to mere withholding and not to possession of the property. Article 1037 provides expressly that the lessee has the same protection as the possessor when he/she is deprived of or disturbed in the exercise of his/her rights. This remedy may be sought even against the lessor, if the latter disturbs the control of the lessee or prevents him/her from exercising his/her right.

141. In a similar vein, the borrower is entitled to use the possessory remedies to have his/her possession restored.[153] Those remedies can even be used against the lender who obstructs or restricts the use of the property. It should be emphasized, however, that as a general principle, the lender does not have a duty to protect the borrower against attacks from third parties.[154]

142. Protective measures [*procedimentos cautelares*] are procedural measures necessary to secure the effectiveness of the legal action.[155] They are measures taken before and by a court to ensure that the decision in the case will be effective and thus will entirely fulfil the practical purpose sought by the party who brought the action and has won the case.[156] Interim protective measures of this kind are taken if there is merely a likelihood that the right asserted or to be asserted in court is real and if there is a risk of infringement of that right. The measures are granted on the basis of a summary demonstration and on an assessment of probability or plausibility. They are intended to prevent irreparable loss by eliminating the risk associated with the length of proceedings, that is, the risk of a change in basic circumstances which may potentially be caused by the time lag.

143. Protective measures may be precautionary measures [*conservatória*] or interim measures [*antecipatória*], meaning that they are intended to maintain the status quo, so that the decision in the main proceedings does not become divorced from reality and impossible to enforce (e.g., measures to prevent the dissipation or loss of assets which may be the subject of an execution order in the future), or to anticipate the court's decision prior to the final judgment (e.g., a measure awarding a provisional monetary payment for the subsistence, accommodation, and clothing of a claimant for maintenance).

144. Some protective measures are typified in the Civil Procedure Code. They follow a pattern laid down in procedural law and are subject to a set of specific requirements and assumptions, and specific decision content. The following are the

153. Article 1133(2) CC.
154. Article 1133(1) CC.
155. Article 2(2) CPC.
156. Article 362 CPC.

statutory protective measures laid down in the Portuguese system of civil law: (a) provisional restitution of possession (Articles 377-379 of the CPC); (b) suspension of corporate decisions; (c) provisional maintenance; (d) provisional compensation; (e) seizure (Articles 391-396 of the CPC); (f) embargo on new work (Articles 397-402 of the CPC); (g) impounding of goods (Articles 403-409 of the CPC).

145. The provisional restitution of possession [*restituição provisória da posse*] is used when the holder has been deprived of his/her property against his/her will by physical or psychological coercion, and wishes to have his/her property provisionally returned to him. The seizure [*arresto*] allows a creditor who is justifiably afraid of losing the assets guaranteeing his/her claim to obtain judicial seizure of goods. The embargo on new work [*embargo de obra nova*] is available to anyone who considers that his/her right to sole or joint-ownership or any other right in rem or in personam of use or ownership is infringed as a result of new work or a new service which causes or is likely to cause him loss. In such a situation, the immediate suspension of the work or service may be request.[157] The embargo can also be imposed out of court, provided that it is subsequently confirmed by a court. The request for confirmation must be made within five days. Finally, the procedure for impounding goods [*arrolamento*] must be launched where there is a reasonable fear of the loss, concealment or dissipation of movable or immovable property or documents, to obtain a description of the goods in the court record (with an indication of the value assigned them by an expert) and have them handed over to a depositary pursuant to Articles 403 and 406 of the CPC.

Non typified protective measures are not subject to any pre-defined procedure and it is for the court to adopt the appropriate measure to secure the effectiveness of the right at risk.[158] They are not used if the risk of loss is covered by a specific measure and are based on procedural rules that apply by default to statutory measures.

146. Except for the embargo on new work, for which it is possible to take initial out-of-court action followed by an application for confirmation by a court, all the other protective measures are based on an initial application to a court. The court with jurisdiction to order such measures is determined on the basis of the following criteria laid down in Article 78 of the CPC. Applications for seizure and impounding of goods may be made to the court where the related proceedings are to be brought (i.e., the proceedings which will decide on the right to be secured by the protective measure) or in the place where the assets are located or, if there are assets in a number of districts, in one of them. For an embargo on new work, the court where the work is to be done has jurisdiction. For the other protective measures, the court with jurisdiction is the court before which the related action is to be brought.

147. When assessing the criteria for ordering a protective measure, the court must always examine whether the fear invoked is grounded and how serious and how difficult it will be to repair the potential infringement of the right at issue. It will also assess whether the precautionary or interim measure is appropriate in the

157. Article 397(1) CPC.
158. Article 362(1) CPC.

specific case at issue with a view to safeguarding the right alleged to be at risk. It must establish that there is a risk associated with any delay. It will also examine whether the proceedings are actually or potentially dependent on an action brought or to be brought that is based on the right safeguarded. In this type of proceeding, it is for the court to obtain a summary (i.e., less rigorous than in the main proceedings) demonstration that there is a real likelihood that the right to be safeguarded exists and that the fear of its being infringed is sufficiently justified. Under Article 368(2) of the CPC, protective measures may be refused by the court if the resulting damage to the defendant would be significantly greater than the loss which the claimant wishes to avoid. The right which is to be safeguarded by the protective measure may already exist or may arise from the decision pending.

148. All protective measures are regarded as urgent. Article 363 of the CPC provides that they are always urgent and have priority over any other non-urgent judicial acts and that actions brought before the relevant court must be decided at first instance within two months at the most or, if the defendant does not have to be summoned, within fifteen days.

149. Since they are ordered by the courts, protective measures are binding on all public and private entities and take precedence over measures adopted by any other authority pursuant to Article 205(2) CRP. In procedures pertaining to the seizure and impounding of goods, if the debtor is made the depositary of the goods and disposes of them, this constitutes a public order offence. The legal transaction to this effect will be null and void if the aim to circumvent the measure ordered is shared by the parties to the transaction, pursuant to Article 281 of the CC. In other situations, although the act is valid, it is ineffective as far as the claimant for seizure is concerned.[159]

150. The measures are valid until the decision in the related main proceedings can take effect. For example, in provisional maintenance and provisional compensation proceedings, it is the point at which the first payment is made, while in seizure proceedings, it is the point at which seizure is done. If the defendant has not been heard before the protective measure is ordered, he/she is merely notified of the decision ordering it. If he/she wishes to contest it in order to submit facts or evidence not taken into account by the court and which may remove the basis for the protective measure or cause it to be reduced,[160] he/she must do so within ten days of being notified. After this deadline, if necessary, the evidence required or determined by the court is produced pursuant to Article 367(1) of the CPC. An appeal brought against an order which rejects outright the initial application for a protective measure or which does not order it, suspends the effect of the decision against which the appeal is brought. An appeal against a decision ordering the protective measure does not have suspensive effect.

159. Article 622(1) CC.
160. Article 372(1)(b) CPC.

Part I. Immovable Property and Real Property

Chapter 1. General Classification

§1. Social Function of Property

151. Objects of property determine the contours of the property relationship, conditioning its duties (such as duties of stewardship or obligations to use in a certain manner) and rights. In understanding property, neither rights nor duties are prior to each other, as some rights or obligations may exist towards specific resources but not with others. For most kinds of resources, owners will mainly have rights and non-owners will mainly have duties, but recognizing the possibility of duties in rem for some resources is an important addition to a fuller understanding of this institution. The particular social goals pertaining to a specific resource are a necessary part of understanding private property.[161]

Contrary to other legal systems, the social function of property is not expressly imposed as a limit to property in the Portuguese Constitution of 1976. Nonetheless, regulations and restrictions on property rights must be made, considering the social aims enshrined in the fundamental law (e.g., environmental issues) and reconciled with other fundamental rights (e.g., the regulation that imposes accessibility for disabled people in private buildings).[162]

Although it is not expressly stated, the social function of property is considered a general principle of property law as regards the exercise of the private right to property, namely, the use of property. The idea that property fulfils a social function is, hence, consolidated in the prohibition of abuse of rights. Article 334 CC states that the exercise of a right is to be considered unlawful wherein it goes against good faith, morality, or the economic or social function of that right.[163]

---

161. Cf. Sandra Passinhas, *Dimensions of Property under European Law: Fundamental Rights, Consumer Protection and Intellectual Property – Bridging Concepts* (Florence: EUI, 2010), 74, available at <http://cadmus.eui.eu/bitstream/handle/1814/13759/2010_Passinhas.pdf?sequence=2>.
162. *See* DL 163/06, of 8 August.
163. Pires de Lima & Antunes Varela, *Código Civil Anotado*, 2nd ed, III (Coimbra: Coimbra Editora, 1987), 92–93.

§2. URBAN PROPERTY

152. As regards urban land, Article 65(4) of the CRP states the following:

> [T]he state, the autonomous regions and local authorities shall lay down the rules governing the occupancy, use and transformation of urban land, particularly by means of planning instruments and within the overall framework of the laws concerning town and country planning and urban planning, and shall expropriate such land as may be necessary to the fulfillment of the purposes of public-use urban planning.

The participation of the interested parties in the drawing up of urban planning instruments and any other physical town and country planning instruments is guaranteed.[164]

153. An important shortage of decent and affordable housing in urban areas has characterized the Portuguese housing situation for decades.[165] Since the 1970s, the private rental sector has undergone a significant decline; it represented no more than 21% of the stock occupied as usual residence (including 3.9% of dwellings owned by close relatives of the occupant). Supply constrains in this sector were at the origin of its decline. They were due to several reasons, as follows: the protracted rent controls, the strict legal regulation protecting tenants, and also the new financial and savings context which tended to divert savings from legal estate.

The relative liberalization of the rental market after 1990[166] has produced a dual rental sector with an old, large, and low-rent sub-sector, where market mechanisms were completely absent, and a new but small market characterized by high and uncompetitive rents (as compared to home ownership).

154. Without an active, dynamic rental market (private or social), a significant supply failure of low-cost affordable housing arose. Portuguese home-seekers, independently of their preferences for home ownership, have been compelled to buy or build their own homes. In Portugal, for the majority of home-seekers, the housing issue has meant the need to choose the timing of access to owner-occupation and find the best way to finance access to home ownership, rather than decisions associated with a tenure choice between ownership and rental housing.

155. In 1991, the owner-occupied sector represented 65% of the total stock occupied as usual residence; in 2001, the share of the owner-occupied sector grew to 76%. Home-ownership became almost the only available alternative to those seeking a home. Unable to produce effective changes in the private rental housing

---

164. Article 65(5) CRP.

165. *See* V. M. Leite Neves, *The Demand for Residential Mortgage Finance in Portugal: Theory, Methodology and Empirical Analysis* (Coimbra: FEUC, 2002).

166. I am referring to the Tenancy Law Regime [*Regime do Arrendamento Urbano*- RAU] implemented by Decree Law 321-B/90, of 15 October, amended by the Decrees-Law 278/93, of 10 August, 257/95 of 30 September, 64-A/2000 of 22 April, and 329-B/2000 of 22 December.

market (and without any commitment to develop a stronger rental sector), the Portuguese governments used to base their housing policy almost exclusively on a subsidized mortgage credit system designed to help households purchasing or building owner-occupied housing. This system was launched in Portugal for the first time in 1976 and, with several changes since then, constituted the main instrument of Portuguese housing policy until 2002.

156. Since 2001, there was a significant reduction of new mortgages contracted, mainly linked to the behaviour of interest rates (and its consequent impact on the accessibility indicator) as well as to a huge drop of consumer confidence. In 2013, only 31.216 contracts were celebrated.[167] *157.* A major legal reform in tenancy law, in 2006,[168] has tried to launch a more dynamic tenancy market and overlap the difficulties of the old low-rent sub-sector. In 2011, 27.90% of the dwellings were rented.[169]

167. https://www.ine.pt/xportal/xmain?xpid=INE&xpgid=ine_indicadores&indOcorrCod=0001080&contexto=pi&selTab=tab0 [last visited: 30 April 2019].

168. The New Tenancy Law [*Novo Regime do Arrendamento Urbano*- NRAU] was introduced by Law 6/2006, of 27 February.

169. https://www.ine.pt/xportal/xmain?xpid=INE&xpgid=ine_indicadores&indOcorrCod=0007889&contexto=bd&selTab=tab2 and https://www.ine.pt/xportal/xmain?xpid=INE&xpgid=ine_indicadores&indOcorrCod=0007890&contexto=bd&selTab=tab2 [last visited 30 April 2019].

Chapter 2. Legal Interests

157. In Portugal, the distinction between legal interests and equitable interests is not known. Under the Portuguese legal system all property rights are legal interests, in the double sense that they have a statutory origin, and that they have a general efficacy by which they become enforceable against third parties. Real rights entitle their holders a direct and immediate power over a thing, and the holders' power is endowed with an *erga omnes* efficacy, the power to exclude others from the use or other benefits of the thing. Portugal borrowed the Roman category of real rights, in the sense of rights upon things, which includes both ownership and limited rights (*iura in re aliena*).

Ownership entitles the owner the widest powers to use, enjoyment, modification and disposition over the object (object of the right), normally identifying the right with its object (often the term property or properties is associated with the object or objects themselves on which somebody's right of property falls). The so-called limited real rights, which are always compatible with the owners' right, do not give so wide powers for action. On the contrary, they entitle the holder with only concrete and specific powers. The law sets forth the exact way that limited real rights compress ownership. Further, whilst ownership has a perpetual character (it is transferred to owner's heirs upon death), duration of *iura in re aliena* is generally submitted to a limitation imposed by law, normally coincident with the holder's life term.

158. Depending on the powers that can be exercised over goods, the *iura in re aliena* are classified as rights of enjoyment, rights of guarantee, and rights of acquisition.

Rights of enjoyment entitle the holder to use another's goods, and in certain cases to take the fruits that the goods produce. Within this category are included, among others, the rights of use and habitation, the right of usufruct and the easements.

Guarantee rights allow the holder, creditor of a pecuniary amount, to urge the mandatory sale of the goods in which the guarantee lies, as well as to be paid with preference before other creditors with regard to the value obtained by this sale. The real guarantee rights may be claimed against anyone who happens to be the owner of the goods to which they pertain.

Acquisition rights entitle their holder with the power to acquire a good in the future, either through a pre-emption right or through a preliminary contract of transfer of property.

Chapter 3. Equitable Interests

159. Equitable interests are not recognized under Portuguese Property Law. The Portuguese legal system is very formal and title-based.

160. The Portuguese statutory basis for land registration is the Land Registration Code approved by DL 224/84, of 6 July (hereinafter 'CRegP').[170] In Portugal, legal registration of land and property is in charge of the Land Registry, where rights acquired and transferred concerning distinct real estate are inscribed.[171] Registrars are legally certified government officials that work on a functional autonomy basis: they depend on the Ministry of Justice, through the Institute of Registries and Notaries [*Instituto dos Registos e do Notariado*]. Land registration aims at giving publicity to the legal rights pertaining to each property, in order to improve security on real estate transmissions.[172] Each property is described in a separate file, filled with the physical description of the land, the name of the owner, and other eventual real rights (such as usufruct, superficies, mortgages) to which the property is subject. Therefore, Articles 2 and 3 of the CRegP enunciate the facts (e.g., constitution, recognition, acquisition or modification of *rights* in rem) and the judicial proceedings (cases brought before a court aiming at the recognition, constitution, or modification of facts subject to registration; cases aiming at the reformulation, declaration of nullity, avoidance of a registration, or its cancellation; and the final decisions of these proceedings) subject to registration.

161. Data inserted in the Land Registry can be freely accessed by everyone, according to Article 104 of the CRegP.[173] An abstract of the title [*certidão do registo predial*] certifies who owns the property, and the inscriptions of proprietary right in force. Since the Land Registry is held in electronic form, and DL 116/2008, of 4 July, abolished the territorial jurisdiction of Land Registry offices, with effect from 1 January 2009, an abstract of the title can be asked in any Land Registry office, regardless of where the property is located. It shall be required in an official sample, and might be handed over in the Land Registry Office, sent by post or fax, or through the use of an internet-based inquiry service.[174] The requisition of a certificate must contain the identification of the submitter, the number of the description of the building in the Land Registry, the parish, and the city where the building is located.

---

170. As amended (Last amendment by Law 89/2017, of 21 August).
171. There is no general cadaster in Portugal. There is a descriptive database of the physical configuration of properties; its goal is mainly fiscal, in order to set real estate evaluations and calculate the adequate taxes.
172. Article 1 CRegP.
173. Only the staff has direct access to the books, folders, and documents; only in special circumstances are judicial authorities and other entities also granted with direct access.
174. Article 41-B *ex vi* Article 111(3) CRegP.

162. No one can acquire registrable property from someone else unless it is registered as the latter's property. The notary or the public official in charge of conveyance of the transfer must ask for a certification of the Land Registry (or check for it on the internet) that the transferor is the registered owner of the immovable.[175]

If someone acquires property for someone else, and registers his/her acquisition, his/her right becomes enforceable against third parties.[176] The question of whether good faith is required remains controversial in the doctrine. The debate is set among those who consider good faith as a general principle in Portuguese legal system,[177] and those who consider that good faith is not relevant as regards protection from registration.[178] Further, if someone acquires in good faith, for consideration, an immovable from a registered owner, and registers his/her acquisition, he/she will be protected against any invalidity of the registration within one year, according to Article 17 of the CRegP.

163. The fact that someone is registered as the owner of the immovable does not mean that he/she is in fact the owner. However, registration produces important effects, such as the following: it offers a rebuttable presumption (*juris tantum*) that the registered owner is entitled to property, that is to say, that the registered proprietary right exists and is vested in the person inscribed in the register.[179] Conversely, it also allows the assumption that a right which has been cancelled (e.g., an easement or a usufruct) no longer exists. In accordance with this, if someone is registered as the owner of the property, he/she is presumably the owner of the said property, and the burden of proof to the contrary is reversed.

164. Under the Portuguese legal system, registration is not necessary for the creation or transfer of a real right, except as for mortgages.[180] Ownership and real rights over property are validly acquired without the necessity of registering them. Facts subject to registration are still effective *inter partes* and may be invoked by their heirs.[181] Since the function of Land Registry in Portugal is to provide publicity to the legal status of the property, registration of the legal act that impinges upon property is necessary for its enforceability [*oponobilidade*] against third parties.[182]

175. Article 9 CRegP.
176. Article 5(1) CRegP.
177. Menezes Cordeiro, *Tratado De Direito Civil Português I*- Parte Geral, II- Coisas, 3rd ed (Coimbra: Almedina, 2005), 276; Carvalho Fernandes, 'Terceiros para Efeitos de Registo Predial', 57 *ROA* (1997) 1283 et ff; Santos Justo, *Direitos Reais*, 5th ed (Coimbra: Coimbra Editora, 2017), 74-76; Pereira Mendes *Código do Registo Predial Anotado e Comentado*, 17th ed (Coimbra: Almedina, 2007), 143; José Alberto Vieira, *Direitos Reais* (Coimbra: Coimbra Editora, 2008), 297.
178. *See* Orlando de Carvalho, 'Terceiros para Efeitos de Registo', *BFD* (1994): 97 ff; Pinto Duarte, *Curso de Direitos Reais* (Lisboa: Principia, 2013), 166; Paulo Henriques, 'Terceiros para efeitos do artigo 5.º do Código do Registo Predial', *BFD* 79 (2003): 443–445.
179. Article 7 CRegP.
180. Article 4(2) CRegP.
181. Article 4(1) CRegP.
182. Article 5(1) CRegP.

165. The definition of *'third parties'* gave rise to a strong debate in Portugal. Decree Law 533/99, of 11 December, introduced by Article 5(4) of the CRegP, providing that third parties are those who acquire from the same person, totally or partially incompatible rights over the same thing. Therefore, if the owner sells the same property to two different acquirers, whoever registers first becomes the new owner. Preference among the successive buyers depends on the order of entrance of their respective titles in the Land Registry. Some authors consider that in such a case registration might have an acquisitive function.[183] In fact, if *A* sells an immovable to *B* who does not register his/her acquisition) and to *C*, who registers his/her acquisition, *C*'s acquisition becomes enforceable against *B*. Registration will allocate an enforceable right to *C*, whereas he/she had acquired from a transferor who was no longer the owner at the moment of the conclusion of the contract, according to the general rules of the Civil Code.[184] Whereas, the transferor, *A*, had lawfully transferred ownership over the house to *B*, but since he/she has not registered his/her acquisition, his/her right is not enforceable against third parties.

183. Oliveira Ascensão, *Direito Civil, Reais*, 5th edn (Coimbra: Coimbra Editora), 366; Santos Justo, *Direitos Reais*, 5th edn (Coimbra: Coimbra Editora, 2017), 66; Menezes Leitão, *Direitos Reais* (Coimbra: Almedina, 2019), 288; José Alberto Vieira, *Direitos Reais* (Lisboa: Coimbra Editora, 2008), 289.

184. In Portugal, a contract for the transfer or creation of property rights, unless otherwise provided, will cause transfer of property immediately upon its conclusion. A contract to transfer the property or other real right is an acquisition title and does not need to be followed by the delivery of the goods which are the object of the contract, or registration, in order to produce the acquisitive effect. Cf. Article 408 CC.

Chapter 4. Limited Interests

166. As a general principle, real rights entitle their holders with a direct and immediate power over the goods. Holders of limited real rights always enjoy goods to a lesser extent than owners, since they entitle their holders to exercise only *certain* powers over another's goods. A real right of enjoyment gives the holder the power to use someone else's property and in certain cases the power to enjoy it (e.g., taking the fruits that the property produces). As I have mentioned in Chapter 1, taking into account its object, it is possible to distinguish rights that rest solely on immovable goods (e.g., easements) from the rights that may indistinctly fall on movable and immovable goods (e.g., usufruct).

§1. Usufruct

I. Concept, Constitution and Statutory Provisions

167. The legal regime of the usufruct is to be found in Articles 1439 to 1483 of the CC. Article 1439 of the CC defines 'usufruct' as a real right that entitles the usufructuary to use the property and to take its fruits without impairing its form or substance. A usufruct can be created by contract, by last will, by adverse possession (*usucapio*), or by legal provision.[185] For a usufruct to be enforceable against third parties, it must be embodied in a written deed, executed by a notary or a certified official (Article 875 of the CC), and registered against the title deeds of the servient property.[186] All the provisions mentioned above are mandatory.

II. Subjects and Object

168. Subjects of the usufruct are the bare owner and the usufructuary. The bare owner, who is the owner of the goods encumbered with the usufruct is legitimated to transfer and encumber its bare ownership (e.g., through constitution of a mortgage or an easement). The holder of a right of usufruct is the usufructuary, which may be either a natural person or a corporate body. When the usufruct is constituted in favour of a corporate body it is subject to a maximum deadline of thirty years.[187]

169. With regard to the object, this right may fall on movable and immovable goods, a collection of goods (e.g., an inheritance) or quotas of co-ownership. A usufruct in rights may also be possible,[188] provided they are neither inherent to the person nor inalienable. The possibility of a usufruct over an object consumable by use

185. Article 1449 CC.
186. Article 2(1)(a) CRegP.
187. Article 1443 CC.
188. Article 1439 CC.

is expressly admitted.[189] In this case, the obligation of restitution of the usufructuary at the deadline of its enjoyment will comprise the value assigned to the goods which are the object of usufruct. When goods have not been valuated before the delivery, an equal quantity of the same kind and quality (*tantundem eiusdem generis*), or its current price by the time the right ends, shall be returned to the bare owner.

III. Content

170. The usufructuary has the right to use and administer the property and to enjoy the fruits thereof. However, he/she must exercise his/her right according to the standards of a *bonus paterfamilias*, complying with the economic destination of the property and without impairing its form and substance.[190] Therefore, even if a certain degree of freedom is allowed in the exploitation of the property, the usufructuary's power to alter the property is restricted. As a result, the traditional academic opinion is that the usufructuary's power to alter the property is restricted to improvements which do not transform its economic destination.[191] The usufructuary would not be entitled to convert a house into a warehouse or a farm into a hotel. Recently, Menezes Cordeiro[192] provided a novel interpretation of the provision by suggesting that the usufructuary has to respect the economic destination of the property, but does not necessarily have to maintain it, if it will be possible to restore the economic destination of the property on termination of the usufruct. Therefore, the usufructuary is entitled to transform a garage into a restaurant, if it is possible to return to the *status quo ante* (from an economic viewpoint). Only if restoration of the economic destination were not possible would the usufructuary disrespect the economic destination of the property. Oliveira Ascensão regards Article 1446 of the CC as a default rule, which can be modified by an agreement between the owner and the usufructuary, allowing the usufructuary to change the economic destination of the property.[193]

171. The usufructuary has the right to use and enjoy the fruits of the property. A usufructuary is entitled to the natural and civil fruits of the farm. Plantations that are destined to be felled are considered fruits and the usufructuary is therefore entitled to cut an appropriate amount of wood and clear undergrowth in the ordinary course of husbandry.[194] The usufructuary must exploit the plantation in the same way as was done in the past or according to the customs prevailing in the community.[195]

---

189. Article 1451 CC.
190. Article 1446 CC.
191. Cf. *inter alia,* Carvalho Fernandes, *Lições de Direitos Reais*, 6th edn (Lisboa: Quid Iuris, 2009), 345.
192. Menezes Cordeiro, *Tratado De Direito Civil Português I-* Parte Geral, II- Coisas, 3rd edn (Coimbra: Almedina, 2005), 654.
193. Oliveira Ascensão, *Direito Civil*, Reais, 5th ed (Coimbra: Coimbra Editora,1993), 475.
194. *See* Decisions of the Supreme Court of 8 July 2003 [Process: 03A2080], available at http://www.dgsi.pt/jstj.nsf/954f0ce6ad9dd8b980256b5f003fa814/3ab239cd0729452f80256dc90030770f?

As a general rule, the usufructuary only acquires natural fruits on actual collection of the fruits.[196] It is therefore accepted that the moment of the collection of the fruits (*jure corporis*), rather than the moment of sowing the seeds (*jure seminis*), is crucial. As a result, the estate of the usufructuary is only entitled to fruits already collected on expiry of the usufruct. After termination of the usufruct, the standing crops are the property of the owner. However, in order to treat both parties fairly, the bare owner is obliged, on termination of the usufruct, to reimburse the usufructuary for the cost of production of the crop up to the value of the standing crop.[197]

In cases other than those involving natural fruits, civil fruits are shared according to the duration of the usufruct (pro rata *temporis,* Article 213(1)(2) of the CC); they are divided between the bare owner and the usufructuary in proportion to the duration of each right. The usufructuary can thus collect the rent for the duration of his/her usufruct. This will also be the case if the usufruct expires six months before the lease expires. The rent for the last six months would accrue to the bare owner and not to the estate of the usufructuary.

172. The usufructuary is obliged to manage the property and to maintain it in a proper state of repair. According to Article 1472(1)(2) of the CC, the usufructuary is responsible for ordinary repairs, namely those repairs costing less than two-thirds of the annual net rent that can be collected from such property (e.g., if a central heating becomes defective, the paint of the building flakes off, the fences of a farm become dilapidated).[198] If any major damage to the building could be traced back to the usufructuary's omission to undertake ordinary repairs, he/she should be liable for the cost of the major repairs to the wall. By contrast, any extraordinary repairs (e.g., replacement of the central heating) are the responsibility of the bare owner; the usufructuary only has a duty to warn the owner about these. However, if the need for repairs can be traced to inefficient or careless management on the part of the usufructuary, the latter is responsible for such repairs. If the owner refuses to execute extraordinary repairs or if he/she postpones their execution, the usufructuary can execute the repairs and claim the cost from the bare owner. These expenses have to be reimbursed even before termination of the usufruct.[199]

In general, the usufructuary is not liable for ordinary wear and tear[200] except where it is caused by his/her fault.[201] At the outset of a usufruct, the usufructuary is

---

OpenDocument; of 4 February 2010 [Process: 3370/05], available at http://www.dgsi.pt/jstj.nsf/954f0ce6ad9dd8b980256b5f003fa814/5b058e047a29c5e5802576c5004f5e58?OpenDocument.

195. Article 1455 CC.
196. Article 213 CC.
197. Article 1447 CC.
198. Decision STJ of 2 February1991 [Process: 079975], available at http://www.dgsi.pt/jstj.nsf/954f0ce6ad9dd8b980256b5f003fa814/3106493bc91366bb80256f9e0038a2a9?OpenDocument.
199. Article 1473(2) CC.
200. If the usufructuary does not return the property in a proper condition, the owner can claim for damages (Decision of the Court of Appeal of Porto, of 30 Mars 2003 [Process: 0030331], at http://www.dgsi.pt/jtrp.nsf/56a6e7121657f91e80257cda00381fdf/c8df2a1c0107c2b1802568ea00446d1f?OpenDocument.
201. Article 1452 CC.

under a duty to prepare, in collaboration with the owner, an inventory of the various things included in the usufruct, and the condition and value of each item.[202]

173. The usufructuary is entitled to transfer his/her right in terms of the usufruct indefinitely or for a fixed term to a third party, subject to restrictions imposed by his/her title and the law. He/she remains liable for damages caused to the property by the person to whom he/she transferred his/her right.[203] According to the general principle *nemo plus iuris in alium transferre potest quam ipse habet*, the usufructuary is not allowed to transfer more rights than he/she has. As a result, he/she is unable to transfer his/her right or create servitudes or burdens which endure for longer than his/her usufruct.[204] The rights of any third party will therefore expire along with expiry of the usufruct. The usufructuary is entitled to burden his/her usufructuary interest with a mortgage which would also be extinguished on termination of the usufruct. However, when the usufruct is terminated by renunciation, acquisition of ownership of the property by the usufructuary or assignation of the rights of the usufructuary to the owner, the mortgage remains effective until the usufruct expires for another reason.[205]

The usufructuary is also entitled to create a sub-interest with regard to his/her usufruct in the form of, for example, a lease or a loan for use.[206] Since the usufructuary cannot burden the property for a term exceeding that of the usufruct, the lease (Article 1051(b) CC), or the loan for use (Article 1130(1) of the CC), will normally expire when the usufruct expires. However, the bare owner may demand the leased property or the property on loan only six months after expiry of the usufruct in the case of urban property and at the end of the agricultural year in the case of agricultural property.[207] However, in two exceptional cases the sub-interests will not expire together with the usufruct, namely where the usufructuary acquires the bare ownership of the property or where the usufructuary renounces the usufruct. In the latter cases, the sub-interest will remain until the usufruct expires for another reason, or the initial agreed duration comes to an end.[208]

174. Since a usufruct is an economic asset, it can be attached in execution proceedings against the usufructuary and can be included in his/her insolvency assets.[209]

---

202. Article 1468 CC.
203. Article 1444 CC.
204. Article 1460(1) CC.
205. Article 699 CC.
206. Article 1444 CC.
207. Article 1053 CC.
208. Article 1052 read with Article 1130(2) CC.
209. Decision of the Court of Appeal of Lisbon, of 10 Mars 1995 [Process: 0007481], available at http://www.dgsi.pt/jtrl.nsf/33182fc732316039802565fa00497eec/3c3574408bd07c31802568030002d829?OpenDocument, and Decision of the Appeal of Porto, of 22 January 2001 [Process: 0051482], at http://www.dgsi.pt/jtrp.nsf/56a6e7121657f91e80257cda00381fdf/ad5d1bb3c3b6bee580256a1f00562141?OpenDocument.

175. These rules are not mandatory; they can be changed by agreement between parties.[210]

IV. Extinction and Liquidation

176. The usufruct cannot exceed the lifetime of the usufructuary. If the usufructuary is a company, an association, or a charity, the usufruct cannot endure for more than thirty years.[211] A usufruct will automatically terminate on the death of the usufructuary; on expiry of the term for which it has been granted or where the usufructuary acquires ownership of the property in question. Renunciation by the usufructuary,[212] non-use of the property for a period of twenty years and complete destruction of the property will also bring the right to an end. According to Article 1476 of the CC, the right of usufruct terminates: if the usufructuary dies or when the duration expires; if the usufructuary acquires the bare ownership of the property; if the usufructuary does not use the property during twenty years; if the property is totally destroyed;[213] if the usufructuary renounces the right.[214]

177. Moreover, the usufructuary has a duty to return the property without impairment of its substance. He/she therefore has a duty to replace plantation trees if cut and the other trees if they die.[215] In addition, the owner may request the usufructuary to provide security in case of damage to the property.[216] Under normal circumstances, the bare owner is not entitled to terminate the usufruct if the usufructuary exploits the property in a harmful manner (misuses the property). Only in cases of harmful conduct which seriously affect the value of the property will the bare owner be allowed to request the return of the property.[217] In such a case, the bare owner is obliged to hand over the net income of the property to the usufructuary every year.[218]

Improvements may be removed at the end of the usufruct, provided that it does not cause damages or material injuries to the property.

210. Article 1445 CC.
211. Article 1443 CC.
212. Article 1476 CC.
213. *See* Decision of the Supreme Court of 24 May 2011 [Process: 877/05], available at http://www.dgsi.pt/jstj.nsf/954f0ce6ad9dd8b980256b5f003fa814/7ee703b9a8130d93802578a3003a8b14?OpenDocument.
214. *See* Decision of the Supreme Court of 19 October 2004 [Process: 04A2288], available at http://www.dgsi.pt/jstj.nsf/954f0ce6ad9dd8b980256b5f003fa814/3106493bc91366bb80256f9e0038a2a9?OpenDocument.
215. Article 1453(2) CC.
216. Article 1468(2) CC.
217. Decision of the Court of Appeal of Lisbon, of 22 May 2001 [Process: 00115367], at http://www.dgsi.pt/jtrl.nsf/33182fc732316039802565fa00497eec/891533427811d9ed80256b990030dd5d?OpenDocument.
218. Article 1482 CC.

§2. Use and Habitation

I. Concept, Constitution and Statutory Provisions

178. The core of the legal regime of the right of use and habitation is to be found in Articles 1484 to 1490 of the CC. The right of use [*direito de uso*] entitles the usuary to use the property and to take its fruits, according to his/her needs and the needs of his/her family.[219] If the right of use is referred to a dwelling, it is called right of habitation [*direito de habitação*].[220] The needs of the usuary are set according to his/her social condition.[221] In the concept of family of the right holder, Article 1487 of the CC includes his/her married partner; his/her unmarried children; other relatives to whom the usuary owes maintenance; and employees living with him/her.

179. The right of use and habitation can be created by contract, by last will, or by legal provision.[222] In contrast to usufruct, however, it cannot be acquired by adverse possession.[223]

180. A right of use or habitation will be enforceable against third parties, if it is embodied in a written deed, and executed by a notary or a certified official (Article 875 of the CC), and registered against the title deeds of the servient property.[224] The above-mentioned rules are mandatory.

II. Content

181. The right of use entitles the usuary to use the property and to take its fruits to the extent necessary to meet personal and family needs.[225] Due to its close link with the person of the usuary (*intuitus personae*), the usuary cannot sell, donate, or create a mortgage or a further right in respect of his/her right of use.[226] Similarly,

219. Article 1484(1) CC. *See* Decision of the Supreme Court of 17 April 2008 [Process: 08B983], available at http://www.dgsi.pt/jstj.nsf/954f0ce6ad9dd8b980256b5f003fa814/069442df8bf8fb63802574320030bae8?OpenDocument.
220. Article 1841(2) CC.
221. Article 1486 CC.
222. Law 7/2001, of 11 May (as amended – last amendment by Law 71/2018, of 31 December) regulating the legal status of two persons, regardless of gender, who live together in a de facto union for more than two years, provides a special regime for termination of the relation on the death of one of the partners. It entitles the surviving partner a real right of habitation of the house, for at least five years (Article 4(1)).
223. Article 1485 CC.
224. Article 2 (1)(a) CRegP. *See* Decision of the Supreme Court of 8 May 2003 [Process: 1064/11], available at http://www.dgsi.pt/jstj.nsf/954f0ce6ad9dd8b980256b5f003fa814/a03dbc0d9705d1a280257b7100507e57?OpenDocument.
225. Article 1484(1) CC.
226. Article 1488 CC.

the usuary's right of use cannot be attached in execution proceedings and cannot be included in the usuary's insolvency assets.[227]

If the usuary takes all the fruits of a property or the holder of the right of habitation occupies the entire house, he/she is responsible for all ordinary repairs, administrative expenses and taxes levied on the property as if he/she were a usufructuary.[228] If the usuary needs only a part of the fruits or the holder of the right of habitation occupies only part of the house (e.g., he/she uses only the first floor of a two-floor building), his/her responsibility is proportionally reduced.

III. Extinction

182. The rules on the termination of a usufruct apply to the right of use and habitation.[229]

§3. Building and Planting Rights: The Superficies Right

I. Concept, Constitution and Statutory Provisions

183. The legal regime of the superficies right is to be found in Articles 1524 to 1542 CC.

The right of superficies entitles the holder to plant or maintain trees or plantations or to erect or maintain buildings on land belonging to another either for a fixed term or perpetually.[230] In Portugal, the grant of a right of superficies can take the form of an alienation of a building or trees separately from the soil.[231] The landowner receives the price (always in money) that can consist of a lump sum of money or multiples instalments (though it may also be granted rent-free), according to Article 1530 of the CC. Since DL 257/91, of 18 July, the right of superficies also entitles the holder to have a building below the surface of someone else land. Insofar as it allows someone to have a building on (or below the surface of) someone else land, *superficies* consists of an exception to *superficies solo cedit* principle. Thus, a superficies right provides a right to property which is transmissible *inter vivos* or *mortis causa*,[232] can be subjected to charges, or object of a public taking. When created by the State or other public authority the holder of the right may be subjected to specific obligations.[233]

---

227. Decision of the Court of Appeal of Lisbon, of 22 June 1989 [Process: 0002359], at http://www.dgsi.pt/jtrl.nsf/86e7be72073894728025687906e5bd8?CreateDocument, and Decision of the Court of Appeal of Porto, of 3 September 1999 [Process 9850162], available at http://www.dgsi.pt/jtrp.nsf/56a6e7121657f91e80257cda00381fdf/ee39416a1c38ad2c8025686b00670e44?OpenDocument.
228. Article 1489 CC.
229. Article 1485 CC.
230. Article 1524 CC.
231. Article 1528 CC.
232. Article 1534 CC.
233. Article 1527 CC.

184. The right of superficies can be created by contract, last will or adverse possession as well as by alienation of a building or trees on the property separately from the soil.[234] To create a right of superficies enforceable against third parties, a written deed containing the right must be executed by a notary or by a public official (Article 875 of the CC) and registered against the title deeds of the servient property (Article 2 (1)(a) of the CRegP).

185. The nature of the right of superficies remains controversial among Portuguese scholars. From a traditional point of view superficies can be seen as a limited real right that entitles the holder to build or plant on another's land, therefore acquiring the temporary ownership of the building or plantation, as an exception to the principle *superficies solo cedit*. On the contrary, a modern interpretation says that it is the right to maintain the separated ownership of a building or plantation on someone else land, which does not necessarily have to be construed or planted by the holder.

II. Content

186. The right of superficies entitles the holder to erect a building or to plant crops and trees (in the case of a farm) [*construir uma obra ou fazer plantações*] on another's property, perpetually or for a certain period of time. This also comprises the right to retain and use [*manter*] any existing building, crops or trees on the land.[235] Where the right of superficies entitles the holder to plant or maintain trees or plantations on land belonging to another, the *superficiarius* is not entitled to cut existing plantations, fruit trees, decorative trees, or shrubs. The position would be the same with regard to new trees and plantations planted by the holder of the right of superficies.

If however, the right to the trees and the plantation has been granted to him/her separately from the soil, it is commonly accepted that he/she has the same extensive rights as would have the owner of the property.[236] Therefore, the superficiarius would have full discretion to exploit the plantation in his/her best interest. However, the right would expire if the trees or plantation are destroyed and the superficiarius does not make an effort to restore it.[237]

If the right of the holder of a superficiary right pertains to an existing building, he/she would not be allowed to change the economic destination of the building. If it pertains to future buildings the superficiarius being considered to enjoy the same rights as an owner, would be free to convert a house into a warehouse (store) or a farm into a hotel.

234. Article 1528 CC.
235. Article 1524 CC.
236. Pires de Lima & Antunes Varela, *Código Civil Anotado*, 2nd ed, III (Coimbra: Coimbra Editora, 1987), 539; Oliveira Ascensão, *Direito Civil*, Reais, 5th ed (Coimbra: Coimbra Editora, 1993), 532.
237. Article 1536(b) CC.

187. Where the holder of a superficies right has the same extensive rights with regard to the plantation and the building as an owner, he/she is entitled to create a further sub-interest in respect of the property and to collect the income there from until his/her right expires.[238] The holder is entitled to sell or donate his/her time-limited right. The right of superficies is transmissible both *inter vivos* or *mortis causa*.[239] The owner of the soil has a right of pre-emption when the right of superficies is offered for sale.[240] The right of superficies may also be mortgaged (Article 688(1) of the CC) or burdened with a sub-interest similar to a lease. The expiry of the right of superficies will cause the extinction of the mortgage or the sub-interest (Article 1539 of the CC), according to the following principle: *resoluto jure dantis resolvitur jus accipientis*.

188. Since the right of superficies has economic value, it can be attached in execution proceedings against its holder and can be included in his/her insolvency assets.

III. Extinction

189. According to Article 1536 of the CC, the right of superficies terminates under any of the following circumstances: if the right holder does not conclude the building or the plantation before the deadline agreed to by the parties, or before the default deadline of ten years; if the building or the trees are destroyed and the right holder does not reconstruct the building or renovate the plantation; when the duration expires, if the right of superficies is temporary; if the right holder acquires the ownership of the land; if the soil disappears or becomes useless; or if there is a taking by a public authority.

When the right expires, the owner of the land acquires the ownership of the construction or plantation; he/she has only to pay compensation according to the rules of unjust enrichment.[241] Rules on fruits are laid down in the general part of the Portuguese Civil Code, so the solution is the same as for a usufructuary, as follows: according to Article 213 of the CC, the *superficiariu s*only acquires natural fruits on actual collection of the fruits (*jure corporis*). The estate of the *superficiarius* would only be entitled to fruits already collected on expiry of the superficies. Moreover, after the termination of the superficies, the (maintained or planted) trees are the property of the owner. However, in order to treat both parties fairly, the owner is obliged on termination of the superficies to reimburse the *superficiarius* according to the rules of unjust enrichment.[242]

If the superficies granted for a fixed term expires, for any reason, before the term ends, real rights created during the course of the superficies remain effective. For

---

238. Articles 1539 CC and 213(2) CC.
239. Article 1534 CC.
240. Article 1535 CC. *See* Decision of the Supreme Court of 27 September 2011 [Process: 360/005], available at http://www.dgsi.pt/jstj.nsf/954f0ce6ad9dd8b980256b5f003fa814/ad954354250b5a458025791900303352?OpenDocument.
241. Article 1538(1)(2) CC.
242. Article 1538(2) CC.

example, if a mortgage was created over a superficiary right, which right would only expire in 2015, but expired in 2010 (e.g., because the *superficiarius* acquired the land), the mortgage still remains effective until 2015.[243] If, for any reason, execution proceedings have to proceed against the *superficiarius*, only the right of *superficies* will be seized and executed by the Court.[244]

IV. Rights of Additional Floors

190. Article 1526 of the CC states that construction on top of a building belonging to someone else is allowed, and it is subject to the legal regime of the right of superficies and to the restrictions deriving from apartment ownership legal regime. Once the new building is constructed, the legal regime of apartment ownership shall apply, and the constructor becomes the holder of the common parts of the building.

§4. Easements and Profits (The Servitudes)

I. Concept, Constitution and Statutory Provisions

191. Under Portuguese law,[245] a servitude (easement in appurtenance) is a real right created by the owner of a piece of land, the servient land [*prédio serviente*], to benefit the successive owners of another piece of land, and the dominant land [*prédio dominante*]. The distinctive feature of this institute is that the charge is imposed on an estate to serve the estate belonging to another holder. Under its scope, commodities can be future or eventual. The holder of an easement is entitled to a limited use of a piece of land, e.g. to pass through (positive servitude), or to prohibit certain acts on the servient tenement (negative servitude).

Similar to any other right in land, the right to servitude must be constituted by a formal deed or a certified private agreement (Article 875 of the CC) and registered (Article 2(1)(a) of the CRegP) in order to be effective as a real right and enforceable against third parties.

192. Under Portuguese property law, easements in gross [*servidões pessoais*], that is to say, to a personal benefit of another person, are not real rights. Restricted personal servitudes might be agreed upon by parties, but they will only have *inter partes* effects, according to the *numerus clausus* principle of Portuguese property law.[246] In contrast to a declaration of conveyance, the agreement to constitute a personal servitude can be made orally or in a written deed.

243. Article 1541 CC.
244. *See* Decision of the Supreme Court of 6 November 2007 [Process: 07A1564], available at http://www.dgsi.pt/jstj.nsf/954f0ce6ad9dd8b980256b5f003fa814/3b3e46e1949069f18025741a00426a4c?OpenDocument.
245. Article 1534 CC.
246. Article 1306(2) CC.

193. As regards easement, the Portuguese Civil Code establishes the distinction between legal and voluntary servitudes.[247] Legal servitudes are easements typified by law, but they do not constitute, per se, concrete real rights. In order to become effective, they have to be agreed upon by parties (the owners of the dominant and servient buildings), or if they do not reach an agreement, they can be created by a judicial decision or by an administrative order. The owner entitled to the servitude has a potestative right to claim, unilaterally, the constitution of the servitude. Legal servitudes are servitudes of passing through (Articles 1550 to 1556 of the CC)[248] and servitudes of waters (Articles 1557 to 1563 of the CC).[249] Under normal circumstances, the easement is enforced through a legal agreement between the affected owners, or through a decision by the judicial authority, when the owner of the servant state does not consent to the easement.

194. In contrast, voluntary servitudes are not typified by law. They can be agreed between parties in regard to an estate to provide the commodities, either future or eventual, to another estate.

195. The basic features of easements are as follows: (a) it is required that the two estates affected (dominant estate and servant estate) belong to different owners; (b) they are inseparable from the estate to which they belong, which means that they may not be transferred nor mortgaged separately from the dominant estate; and (c) they consist in a utility that the servant estate provides to the dominant estate.

II. Content

196. Positive easements are those in which the owner of the servant estate commits himself/herself to tolerate someone else's activity (e.g., passing through the property). Restrictive or negative easements are those in which the owner of the servant estate commits himself/herself to *non facere*, that is to say, not doing something that would be licit for him/her to do it would the easement not exist (e.g., not raising a construction, not raising it beyond a definite height). A negative easement is a burden with a negative content which is indissolubly linked to the estate that it

247. *See* Decision of the Supreme Court of 2 May 2012 [Process: 1241/07], available at http://www.dgsi.pt/jstj.nsf/954f0ce6ad9dd8b980256b5f003fa814/712dd16595942a92802579f7004dfb2f?OpenDocument.

248. *See* Decisions of the Supreme Court of 10 December 2013 [Process: 719/07], available at http://www.dgsi.pt/jstj.nsf/954f0ce6ad9dd8b980256b5f003fa814/f605e2afb6f92cb480257c3d0051191d?OpenDocument; of 21 Mars 2013 [Process 2173/07], available at http://www.dgsi.pt/jstj.nsf/954f0ce6ad9dd8b980256b5f003fa814/0d073bcc6936d9fc80257b420050f04a?OpenDocument, and of 24 October 2006 [Process: 06A2626], available at http://www.dgsi.pt/jstj.nsf/954f0ce6ad9dd8b980256b5f003fa814/c62a3678f6018204802572730052a581?OpenDocument.

249. *See* Decisions of the Supreme Court of 28 October 2014 [Process: 750/03], available at http://www.dgsi.pt/jstj.nsf/954f0ce6ad9dd8b980256b5f003fa814/83367b9d6b7dc14780257d8000382a95?OpenDocument, of 8 May 2013 [Process: 2915/06], available at http://www.dgsi.pt/jstj.nsf/954f0ce6ad9dd8b980256b5f003fa814/38823ab031a8db9280257b660033c8b6?OpenDocument; of 23 October 2008 [Process: 08B2004], available at http://www.dgsi.pt/jstj.nsf/954f0ce6ad9dd8b980256b5f003fa814/a36f72b5d106ca0b802574ec003a7db2?OpenDocument.

burdens. The holder may enforce the easement against anyone who becomes owner of the servant estate, who will see his/her ownership limited by the burden.

III. Extinction

197. According to Article 1569 of the CC, an easement terminates under the following circumstances: gathering of the two real estates on the estate of the same holder;[250] if the servitude is not used during twenty years; by *usucapio libertatis*, if the holder of the servitude renounces his/her right; at the time limit, if the servitude is time-limited. It should be considered that legal servitudes and voluntary servitudes acquired by *usucapio* can be declared unnecessary upon requirement to the judge of the holder of the servant estate.[251]

§5. Emphyteusis and Rent Charge

198. *Emphytheusis* [*enfiteuse*] on rural land was extinguished by DL 195-A/75,[252] of 16 March and *emphiteusis* on urban land was abolished by DL 233/76, of 2 April.[253] *Emphyteusis* was considered a partitioning of ownership, rather than a *ius in rem*. Rent charges, although known in Portugal since the Medieval period,[254] are not considered a real right anymore.

§6. Leasehold Interests

199. Lease is treated as a chapter in the title on Special Contracts in the book on Obligations of the Portuguese Civil Code. A lease is a contract whereby one party (landlord) grants another party (tenant) the use of property for a certain period of time, in return for payment of a rent. Thus, the essential terms of a contract of lease are the identification of the parties, the property to be leased, and the rent. A distinction is made between leases of movables and leases of immovables (tenancy contracts).

200. The general rules on leases (*locatio*) are found in Articles 1022 to 1063 of the CC. By default, they set forth the legal regime of leases over movables. The core of the legal regime of lease contracts concerning urban premises was re-inserted in

---

250. *See* Decision of the Supreme Court of 18 December 2013 [Process: 372/09], available at http://www.dgsi.pt/jstj.nsf/954f0ce6ad9dd8b980256b5f003fa814/bb635135e176feb580257c46003cfd15?OpenDocument.
251. *See* Decisions of the Supreme Court of 16 March 2011 [Process: 263/1999], at http://www.dgsi.pt/jstj.nsf/954f0ce6ad9dd8b980256b5f003fa814/c3fdf508349c28cf8025785a0035c2d5?OpenDocument, and of 5 May 2015 [Process: 273/07], at http://www.dgsi.pt/jstj.nsf/954f0ce6ad9dd8b980256b5f003fa814/2a0560e9b108788380257e3d003ca11f?OpenDocument.
252. Amended by DL 546/76, of 10 July.
253. Amended by DL 82/78, of 2 May; DL 73-A/79, 3 April; and DL 226/80, of 15 July.
254. *See* M. J. Almeida Costa, *Raízes do Censo Consignativo* (Coimbra: Atlântida, 1961), 18.

the Portuguese Civil Code (Articles 1064 to 1113) in 2006.[255] Articles 1092 to 1107 set forth special rules for residential premises. Articles 1108 to 1113 provide special rules on non-residential urban premises (tenancy contracts for commercial, industrial, and professional purposes).[256]

The legal regime of lease contracts concerning non rural premises is to be found in DL 294/2009, of 13 October.

201. Holding immovable goods under lease implies the right to use someone else's immovable goods, for a definite period, in exchange for a certain price. Under Portuguese Law, the lease is not a real right. Although the lease has some distinctive features, such as relationship on immediacy with the leased object, possessory protection,[257] and enforceability against the new acquirer of the property,[258] recent legislation has made it more similar to a personal right. Although tenants still have a protected position in Portugal, since the entering into force of Law 6/2006, of 1 February, tenants' rights have been levelled down almost to a mere personal right (e.g., with respect to duration, transmissibility and extinction of the contract.[259] The legal regime set in 2006 has been subject to several amendments (in 2012, 2014 and 2017). Recently, Law 12/2019, of 12 February, introduced the figure of harassment in tenancy contracts, and Law 13/2019, also of 12 February, set several measures in order to re-balance the contract in favour of the tenant.

The landlord does not need to be the owner of the leased property, and persons with the right to administer the property are capable of establishing leases with regard to that property (e.g., the holder of a usufruct or a superficies right).[260]

---

255. The New Tenancy Law [Novo Regime do Arrendamento Urbano], hereinafter NRAU, was introduced by Law 6/2006, of 27 February, and amended by Law 31/2012, of 14 August, Law 79/2014, of 19 December, Law 42/2017 and Law 43/2017 of 16 June, Law 12/2019 and Law 13/2019 of 12 February, with Corrections from 7 March and 4 April 2019. This new legal regime replaced the Tenancy Law Regime [Regime do Arrendamento Urbano – RAU], implemented by Decree Law 321-B/90, of 15 October, amended by the Decrees-Law 278/93, of 10 August, 257/95 of 30 September, 64-A/2000 of 22 April, and 329-B/2000 of 22 December. For a general overview on the new legal regime, *see* Maria Olinda Garcia, *Arrendamento Urbano Anotado – Regime Substantivo e Processual*. Coimbra: Coimbra Editora, 2014.

256. For a general overview, *see* Maria Olinda Garcia, *Arrendamentos para Comércio e Fins Equiparados* (Coimbra: Coimbra Editora, 2006). *See* Decision of the Supreme Court of 24 September 2013 [Process: 317/09], at http://www.dgsi.pt/jstj.nsf/954f0ce6ad9dd8b980256b5f003fa814/f67bc1ab83ee8c8a80257bf0005461cf?OpenDocument.

257. Article 1037 CC accords a tenant the same protection as a possessor, by extending to the tenant the remedies for disturbance or deprivation of possession.

258. While the precedent RAU was in force, some authors claimed that by entering into possession of the leased premises or land, the tenant would acquire a real or property right on the same, enforceable against the world. *See* Oliveira Ascensão, *Direito Civil*, Reais, 5th ed (Coimbra: Coimbra Editora, 1993), 519; Menezes Cordeiro, *Tratado De Direito Civil Português I*- Parte Geral, II- Coisas, 3rd ed (Coimbra: Almedina, 2005), 689.

259. Henrique Mesquita, *Obrigações Reais e Ónus Reais* (Coimbra: Almedina, 1990), 131 ff.

260. Nevertheless, the right of the landlord over the property is important with regard to the duration of the contact (Article 1051(c)). The lease will expire along with the principal right. *See* Decision of the Supreme Court of 14 November 2000 [Process: 00A3165], available at http://www.dgsi.pt/jstj.nsf/954f0ce6ad9dd8b980256b5f003fa814/1fca0a1103ebf63b80256ad80031555c?OpenDocument.

I. Urban Leases

A. *Concept, Constitution and Special Statutory Provisions*

202. The contract of lease must be in writing.[261] Registration is required to make leases of residential,[262] commercial, industrial, or professional purposes, lasting more than six years, enforceable against third parties.[263] Otherwise, a lease lasting less than six years does not need to be registered in the Land Registry to be enforceable against third parties.

203. Portuguese law, in general, does not allow leases for a term of less than one year and more than thirty years. A clause purporting to allow a 'lease for life' or a lease exceeding thirty years would be void but would not invalidate the entire contract. The term of the contract would simply be reduced to the thirty-year limit.[264] It is expected, soon, the approval of a new legal regime of tenancy for life (direito real de habitação duradoura).

A lease of urban dwellings can be time-limited [*contratos com prazo certo*]. Duration of the leasing must be expressed in the contract.[265] At the end of the agreed period, the contract is automatically renewed if neither of the parties gives notice of termination.[266] Landlords, however, are not entitled to give notice of the contract before three years after it is concluded. Only contracts for non-permanent or transitory uses (professional, touristic, or education) are not under automatic renewal. If parties do not set a time limit for the contract, it is considered to last for five years.

Duration of leases for commercial, industrial, or professional purposes is also freely agreed by parties. If the duration is not set in the contract, Article 1110(2) of the CC sets the default duration of five years.

B. *Content of the Right*

204. Under the Portuguese Civil Code, the landlord's main obligations are to deliver the property to the tenant and to ensure that it can be used in accordance with the purpose of the contract.[267] The landlord must tolerate such use and is not allowed to act in a manner that would prevent or restrict this.

If a building is leased, it must be delivered to the tenant in a good condition, unless the contrary is stipulated in the contract. There is a presumption in favour of

261. Article 1069 CC. *See* Decision of the Supreme Court of 17 March 2016 [Process: 2243/11], at http://www.dgsi.pt/jstj.nsf/954f0ce6ad9dd8b980256b5f003fa814/5ead7f067b47aeb580257f790053585c?OpenDocument.
262. If they are to endure more than six years.
263. Article 2(2)(m) of CRegP.
264. Article 1025 CC.
265. Article 1095 CC.
266. Article 1096 CC.
267. Article 1031 CC.

the landlord that the building was in good condition at the time of delivery if there is no document attached to the contract which describes the condition of the building at the date of transfer.[268]

The tenant's duties include a duty to allow the landlord to inspect the building, to take care of the property, and to exercise his/her rights with due diligence. The tenant must also allow the landlord to execute urgent repairs to the building.[269] As long as the tenant uses the property with the care of a *bonus paterfamilias* (Article 1043 of the CC) and in accordance with the purpose of the contract, he/she is not responsible for any damage caused to the property and need not repair, replace, or renew it before the property is returned to the landlord.

205. As regards the leasing of urban dwellings, the tenant is entitled to make alterations to the building to suit his/her comfort or convenience. However, in the absence of a stipulation to the contrary, these changes would have to be reversed on termination of the lease so that the building can be returned in its previous condition.[270] The landlord is responsible both for works of ordinary conservation (which include e.g., works of repair and cleaning, works required by public authorities, and works necessary to maintain the building fit for the purpose of the contract), and extraordinary conservation of the property (which include e.g., the repair of defects in the building, maintenance required as a result of damage caused by force majeure). It should be emphasized that the tenant is not allowed to conduct works in the building, except if authorized by the landlord or if that possibility is foreseen in the contract.[271] The tenant is also allowed to make urgent repairs, if the landlord does not act on time after notice has been given.[272] In such a situation, the tenant is entitled to compensation. Finally, the tenant is responsible for the repair of damage caused by his/her negligence or the negligence of persons for whom he/she is responsible.[273] The above-mentioned is also the default legal regime for urban leases for commercial, industrial, professional, and other purposes. The parties may, for example, agree, in a written deed, that ordinary and extraordinary repairs as well as improvements to the property [*benfeitorias*] are the responsibility of the tenant.[274]

206. The tenant is not entitled to grant anyone the total or partial use of the leased property or to cede his/her rights gratuitously or for consideration by subletting the property or lending it out for use except if permitted by the law or authorized by the landlord.[275] When authorized by the landlord or permitted by law, the tenant has a duty to inform the landlord within fifteen days that he/she has granted

268. Article 1043(2) CC.
269. Article 1038 CC.
270. Article 1072 CC.
271. Article 1074 CC.
272. Articles 1036 CC ex vi Article 1074(3) CC.
273. Article 1043 CC, *a contrario.*
274. Article 1111 CC.
275. Article 1038(f) CC. *See* Decision of the Supreme Court of 8 May 1984 [Process: 071455], available at http://www.dgsi.pt/jstj.nsf/954f0ce6ad9dd8b980256b5f003fa814/84f2381b59d5be1080256 8fc003a4b53?OpenDocument.

the use of the property to another.[276] Notification is required following the requirements set out in Article 9 of Law 6/2006.

The rent received from a sub-lease may not be more than 20% above the principal rent.[277] If a higher rent is contracted, the landlord is entitled to cancel the lease. The sub-lease will terminate with the expiry of the principal lease.

207. The commercial or industrial lease contract is considered an asset of the enterprise; as so it can be attached in execution proceedings and can also form part of the insolvency assets of the debtor.

Utilities concerning the use of the premise are to be paid by the tenant (e.g., consumption of water, gas, electricity, heating), according to Article 1078(2) of the CC. In Portugal, water, electricity, gas, and telephone companies conclude individual contracts directly with tenants, upon exhibition of the tenancy contract.

C. Emptio Non Tollit Locatio

208. The position of a tenant is governed by the maxim '*emptio non tollit locatum*' contained in Article 1057 of the CC. This maxim provides that sale does not supersede lease. As a result, any person acquiring the rights of the landlord will succeed to the rights and obligations of his/her predecessor and would thus have to allow the tenant, without prejudice to the registration provisions, to enjoy his/her lease for the remaining period.[278] Although the maxim refers specifically to sales, it is considered to cover all kinds of alienations such as legacies, donations, or the constitution of a usufruct.

209. Residential leases for a term of less than six years do not require registration for their validity. Therefore, if concluded in written form before the conveyance of the property to C, these contracts will be enforceable against C. Both residential leases for a term of more than six years and leases of premises for commercial, industrial, or professional purposes require registration for their enforceability. These leases are, therefore, only enforceable against third parties, if they were registered prior to the conveyance. Any other factors, such as knowledge or occupancy, are not relevant.

---

276. Article 1038(g) CC.
277. Article 1062 CC.
278. *See* Decisions of the Supreme Court of 26 June 2012 [Process: 159/2006], at http://www.dgsi.pt/jstj.nsf/954f0ce6ad9dd8b980256b5f003fa814/54c278990a9f198980257a2f00497486?OpenDocument; and of 29 January 2014 [Process: 45/06], at http://www.dgsi.pt/jstj.nsf/954f0ce6ad9dd8b980256b5f003fa814/18436972292c331b80257c7500520188?OpenDocument.

210. It should be emphasized that the tenant has a pre-emption right if the landlord sells or gives *in payment*[279] (datio in solutum), the premise rented and the contract is already over than two years.[280]

D. Registration

211. A property subject to a lease in favour of a tenant may be attached and sold in execution by the executing creditors of the landlord.[281] If the lease contract was concluded before the attachment of the property, the general rule of Article 1057 of the CC applies, as follows: the purchaser will acquire all the rights and obligations of the landlord with regard to the property. Thus if the property is encumbered with a valid (registered or unregistered) lease, the purchaser will be bound to recognize it and to allow the tenant to exercise the lease for the remainder thereof. As a result, the tenant's right prevails over the right of the purchaser, unless the lease was concluded *after* the executing creditor executed against the property.[282]

212. Under Portuguese law, property rights are graduated according to the principle: *prior in tempore, potior in iure*. It means that it is possible to create a prior mortgage over the property and several posterior personal servitudes, for example, a usufruct, a real servitude. However, according to the above-mentioned principle, in a sale in execution, the personal servitude would not prevail. Since the ranking of the tenant's right depends on prior registration, the fact that the personal servitude was registered after the registration of a mortgage on the property means that the personal servitude of the tenant will not prevail against the prior mortgage.

It should be noted that mortgages constitute one of the few cases in Portuguese law where registration is necessary for the validity (as opposed to the enforceability) of a real right.[283] If registered, Article 686 of the CC grants the mortgage creditor a priority right with regard to the proceeds of the sale, subject to special privileges that rank above the mortgage or real rights registered before the mortgage.[284] There is no rule against the constitution of a personal servitude or a second mortgage on property which is already burdened with a mortgage. If a conflict arises, however, the first mortgage creditor has priority with regard to the proceeds of the sale (of all property and not only of the bare property). Further, in such a situation, the personal servitude would expire, according to Article 824 of the CC. This provision sets forth that if the property is sold in execution, only the real rights of use registered before the constitution of a mortgage or attachment of the property remain valid. The holder will then have the right to compensation for termination of

279. *Datio in solutum* takes place when the debtor – in order to be released from an obligation – makes a different performance than the one initially agreed upon, with the consent of the creditor (Articles 837 to 840 CC).
280. Article 1091 CC.
281. Whereas the lease contract is not included in the attachment assets.
282. Article 819 CC.
283. In general, registration has declarative value, it renders the registered rights enforceable against third parties.
284. This applies only to real rights registered after the registration of the mortgage.

his/her right, but this credit will arise after the right of the mortgage creditor.[285] Under normal circumstances, the price obtained in a sale in execution would not be enough to pay this compensation.

213. I would like to mention that a personal servitude created over the property after the attachment is not enforceable against the execution proceedings. If the owner has created a lease over the property and then a creditor attaches the property, the regime is similar to the one described above. Because, according to Article 1057 of the CC, *emptio non tollit locatum*, the above applies in relation to sale in execution. On the contrary, a lease created over the property after the attachment is not enforceable against the execution proceedings.[286]

214. As regards a lease created after a prior mortgage on the property, the solution is slightly different. The question whether a lease contract is enforceable against a mortgage creditor, who has registered a prior mortgage on the property, has led to a strong debate in Portuguese case law and academic literature. Portuguese law does not prohibit the owner of mortgaged property to conclude an enforceable lease over the property.[287] If the owner registers a mortgage in favour of a creditor and then duly concludes a lease contract with a tenant, it is contested whether the lease in favour of the tenant would be enforceable against the mortgage creditor. Article 824(2) of the CC states that on sale in execution of the property, real rights of use [*direitos reais de gozo*] over the property would remain valid if they were registered *before* the registration of the mortgage or the attachment of the property. As a result, it is clear that a right of usufruct registered after the registration of the mortgage would expire. However, since a lease is not one of the recognized real rights in Portuguese law, it does not necessarily follow that a lease concluded after the registration of a mortgage would likewise expire. However, doctrine and case law have disputed this conclusion by determining that Article 824(2) of the CC which states that rights expire after a sale in execution also refers to leases. The Supreme Court of Justice[288] concluded that the fact that the lease is not a real right does not prevent its analogous inclusion in Article 824(2) of the CC. In sum, the tenant's rights will

285. If A had created two mortgages (in favour of *B* and *C*), instead of a mortgage and a personal servitude, the situation would be different. If *B* attached the property, *C* (and all the holders of security rights) would also be called to the execution. The judge would then graduate the credits according to their priority. The property is sold not subject to the mortgages. The creditors will be granted, instead, a share of the proceedings resulting from the sale, according to their priority rank. If the price received is enough to pay to *B*and to *C*, they will have their credits satisfied. If not, only the prevalent mortgage creditor will be paid.

286. Article 819 CC.

287. However, it can be agreed upon in the mortgage contract. This question is very important in Portuguese law where a lease is commonly considered as a strongly protected right as is evident from the fact that a lease may only be terminated by the landlord in very limited circumstances. The granting of a lease over property may greatly decrease the value of the property.

288. Decisions STJ, of 15 February 2005 [Process: 04A4786], available at http://www.dgsi.pt/jstj.nsf/38f33c44b0c8358280256879006bc013?CreateDocument, and of 5 February 2009 [Process: 08B4087], available at http://www.dgsi.pt/jstj.nsf/954f0ce6ad9dd8b980256b5f003fa814/257a6eda37894aa380257554005cb964?OpenDocument.

not prevail over the right of a mortgage creditor, except where the lease was concluded *prior* to the mortgage registration.[289]

E. Extinction

215. A lease will terminate on expiry of a fixed term [*caducidade*],[290] by mutual agreement [*revogação*] or by ordinary notice [*resolução*]. Ordinary notice is appropriate where the breach of an important contractual obligation destroys the relationship between the parties to such an extent that it is not just and reasonable to expect the other party to continue the relationship.[291]

216. Time-limited contracts [*contratos com prazo certo*] are automatically renewed, for successive periods (Article 1096(1) of the CC), if neither of the parties give notice of termination. The landlord cannot give notice before the contract has lasted at least three years.

217. An open-ended contract might expire based on specific notice [*denúncia*]. 'Specific' notice by the landlord might require a specific cause prescribed by law. It is allowed in cases where the landlord has an objective and legitimate interest in the termination of the lease contract (e.g., where the landlord needs the premises for himself/herself or his/her family or where he/she wants to rebuild or restructure the premises). Specific notice, *ad nutum*, by the landlord, will become effective five years later (which is the minimum duration for a time-limited contract). The tenant may give specific notice, *ad nutum*, by giving notice at least 60 or 120 days before termination, depending of the duration of the contract.[292]

218. The contract of lease does not expire when the landlord dies, according to the general rules on Successions Law.[293] If the tenant dies, the contract is transmissible to the partner or to another parent, according to the list provided in Articles 1106 of the CC or Articles 26, 27 and 57 of Law 6/2006, if the contract is prior to NRAU.

II. Rural Leases

A. Concept, Constitution and Special Statutory Provisions

219. The legal regime of tenancy contracts concerning rural premises (*Regime do Arrendamento Rural e Florestal*, hereinafter 'RARF') is to be found in DL 294/

289. A very recent Decision STJ of 27 November 2018 (Process: 1268/16.6T8FAR.EI.S2) has, however, took a different approach. Therefore, a new trend might be expected.
290. *See also* the Decision STJ of 11 December 2012 [Process: 655/06], at http://www.dgsi.pt/jstj.nsf/954f0ce6ad9dd8b980256b5f003fa814/f3ab9f1fa5f183cd80257b2800504ea7?OpenDocument.
291. Article 1083 CC.
292. Article 1100(1) CC.
293. Article 2024 CC.

2009, of 13 October.[294] It encompasses all tenancy contracts with agricultural, forestry, or other purposes related to agriculture, forestry or stock-farming. The lease of agricultural land, which covers the lease of a farm for the cultivation of crops or the farming of livestock (Article 1 of the RARF), pertains to the soil, the waters, the permanent vegetation on the soil, the buildings exploited either as a residence or for other agricultural purposes by the tenant.[295] The contract might also pertain to equipment, if parties agree upon.

220. A lease of agricultural property must be in writing. Within thirty days after conclusion of the lease, a copy of the contract thereof must be delivered to the Tax Office, which, in turn, must communicate it to the Regional Department of the Ministry of Agriculture and Fishery.[296] Agricultural leases need not be registered and no administrative fees are payable.

221. Agricultural leases must be concluded for a term superior to seven years. At the end of that period the contract is automatically renewed if neither of the parties give notice of termination.[297] Forestry leases may be concluded for a term of between ten and seventy years.[298]

B. Content of the Right

222. The tenant's duties include a duty to take care of the property and to exercise his/her rights with due diligence. He/she must also allow the landlord to execute urgent repairs to the building.[299] As long as the tenant exploits the property with the care of a *bonus paterfamilias* and in accordance with the purpose of the contract, he/she is not responsible for any damage caused to the property and need not repair, replace or renew it before the property is returned to the landlord. The tenant is allowed to make urgent repairs, if the landlord does not act on time after notice has been given.[300] Otherwise, the tenant is not allowed to make works in the building, except if authorized by the landlord or if that possibility is foreseen in the contract.[301] The tenant is not entitled to compensation.[302]

---

294. This Decree Law replaced the Rural Tenancy Regime set forth by Decree Law 385/88, of 25 October, amended by Decree Law 524/99, of 10 December, and the Forestall Tenancy Regime provided by Decree Law 394/88, of 8 November.
295. Article 4 RARF.
296. Article 6 RARF.
297. Article 9(3) RARF.
298. Article 7 RARF.
299. Article 22 RARF.
300. Article 23 RARF.
301. Article 23 RARF.
302. Article 23(5) RARF.

223. The tenant is obliged (and consequently responsible for the repairs necessary) to maintain the dwelling in the same condition he/she received it, with allowance being made for fair wear and tear.[303] It would be responsibility of the tenant to repair the fences if dilapidation was due to his/her fault. The tenant is also allowed to make urgent repairs, if notice was given to the landlord and he/she does not act on time.[304] In such a situation, the tenant is entitled to compensation.

224. The tenant is not entitled to grant anyone the total or partial use of the leased property or to cede his/her rights gratuitously or for consideration by subletting the property or lending it out for use except if permitted by the law or authorized by the landlord.[305]

225. The agricultural tenant is under an obligation to return the property in the same state as he/she received it.[306] Furthermore the tenant is not allowed to affect the productivity, substance, or the economic and social function of the property; and his/her processes of cultivation may not prejudice the productivity of the property.[307] The tenant cannot prevent the landlord from carrying out works necessary to ensure that the normal production of the land is maintained after termination of the lease.[308]

C. *Emptio Non Tollit Location*

226. Article 20 RARF sets forth that the contract does not expire with the sale of the rented premise. According to Article 31(2) RARF, if the landlord sells the premise, and the tenant has a contract already for a period over three years, the latter has a pre-emption right.

D. *Extinction*

227. A lease will terminate on expiry of a fixed term [*caducidade*], by mutual agreement [*revogação*], by ordinary notice [*resolução*], opposition to renewal [*oposição à renovação*] and specific notice [*denúncia*]. The contract does not expire when the landlord dies, according to the general rules on Successions Law.[309,310] If

303. Article 22 RARF.
304. Article 1036 CC.
305. Article 10 RARF.
306. *See* Decision of the Supreme Court of 27 May 2010 [Process: 112/06], available at: http://www.dgsi.pt/jstj.nsf/954f0ce6ad9dd8b980256b5f003fa814/1c1f88fd827ca9a28025776900504ce5?OpenDocument.
307. Article 17 RARF.
308. Articles 21 and 25 RARF.
309. *See* Decision of the Supreme Court of 10 October 2012 [Process: 1827/08], available at http://www.dgsi.pt/jstj.nsf/954f0ce6ad9dd8b980256b5f003fa814/7b6a3dd8b136230a80257a94004ff01d?OpenDocument.
310. Article 2024 CC.

the tenant dies, the contract is transmissible to the partner or to another relative, according to the list of Article 20 RARF.

Ordinary notice is appropriate where the breach of an important contractual obligation destroys the relationship between the parties to such an extent that it is not equitative and reasonable to expect the other party to continue the relationship. Article 17 RARF sets the grounds that might be argued by the landlord and by the tenant, respectively.

Rural tenancy contracts are automatically renewed (Article 19 RARF), if neither of the parties give notice of termination. A time-limited lease will terminate on the fixed term if the landlord or the tenant opposes the automatic renewal at least one year before termination.[311]

A contract might expire by based on specific notice [*denúncia*] by the landlord if he/she is an emigrant and provided that requirements set in Article 19 RARF are met, namely, be back to Portugal and intend to explore the premise by himself/herself. The tenant might give specific notice in case of abandon of the activity or if the premise does not allow the normal development of a rural activity, according to Article 19(5) RARF.

Article 31(1) RARF sets forth that after the contract expires, if termination is not his/her fault, the tenant has a pre-emption right in the celebration of a new contract.

§7. Licences

I. Nature and Types of Licences

228. As a special permission to use real property for a special purpose, Portuguese law foresees two contracts: the *commodatum* [*comodato*] and the *precarium* [*precário*].

229. The *commodatum* is a gratuitous contract by which one party lends property to another, subject to the obligation to return the property after use.[312] Writing is not required, but handing over the property is essential for the completion of the contract of *commodatum* (*real quod constitutionem*).[313] Some contracts will only become effective between parties thereto once the respective object has physically or symbolically exchanged hands. Such is the case with loan for use contracts, regardless of whether the loan involves a specific thing, a sum of money or other fungible goods.

230. A loan for use may be concluded for a fixed term or for a certain purpose. In the case of non-completion, the property may be reclaimed only on the basis of

311. Article 19(3) RARF.
312. Articles 1129–1141 CC.
313. *See* Decision of the Supreme Court of 6 November 2012 [Process: 629/06], at http://www.dgsi.pt/jstj.nsf/954f0ce6ad9dd8b980256b5f003fa814/63c44b22480bd1ba80257ab400546bc8?OpenDocument.

an objective and just ground, such as an urgent and unforeseen need for the property.[314] However, where the property is lent for an indefinite term, the contract is terminable at the will of the lender.[315]

Under a contract of *precarium*, the use of the property is revocable at the will of the lender. This term is also intended to describe the position of a person who remains in possession of a building, with acquiescence of the owner, after the extinction of the title that allowed him/her to use it (e.g., termination of the agreed period in a lease). Finally, similar to the position of the contracting party who has signed a free loan the precarious results when the obligation of returning the borrowed goods to the owner had not been subject to a definite deadline. Portuguese law, however, does not draw a sharp distinction between a party whose holding of the property is revocable at the will of the lender and an ordinary borrower for use.[316] Both contracts are governed by the same provisions.

Licences do not represent a burden for the property, nor may they be opposed before purchasers of the object so possessed. Moreover, they may not be asserted against the current owner.

§8. Restrictive Covenants

231. A restrictive covenant is a type of real covenant, a legal obligation imposed in a deed by the seller upon the buyer of real estate to do or not to do something. Such restrictions frequently are registered against title, '*run with the land*', and are enforceable on subsequent buyers of the property. In Portugal, as a general principle, contractual restrictions on the transfer of property are not accepted.

232. Transfer of property is constitutionally granted. Article 62 of the CRP expressly states that everyone is secured, in accordance with the Constitution, the right to private property and to its transfer during lifetime or by death. Article 1305 of the CC also includes the right of disposal of property at the core of property rights.

It is generally accepted that the holder cannot renounce the power of disposal and that such an agreement would not have any real effect, that is, enforceability against third parties. Therefore, in a situation where *A* sells an immovable to *C*, a restriction to sale agreed upon between *A* and *B* is not enforceable against *C*. Obligational

314. *See* Decisions of the Supreme Court of 1 March 2012 [Process: 689/09], at http://www.dgsi.pt/jstj.nsf/954f0ce6ad9dd8b980256b5f003fa814/5da4b55de52d7745802579f9004b1b16?OpenDocument, and of 16 December 2010 [Process: 1584/06], available at http://www.dgsi.pt/jstj.nsf/954f0ce6ad9dd8b980256b5f003fa814/8006f340bccd281880257800003ab57b?OpenDocument.

315. Article 1137(2) CC. *See* Decision of the Supreme Court of 16 November 2010 [Process: 7232/04], at http://www.dgsi.pt/jstj.nsf/954f0ce6ad9dd8b980256b5f003fa814/eb7744610c327ee8802577e3003cc5e0?OpenDocument.

316. Decisions of the Supreme Court of 16 November 2010 [Process: 7232/04.OTCLRS.L1.S1], available at http://www.dgsi.pt/jtrl.nsf/33182fc732316039802565fa00497eec/3c91aab2e2c0fcfe802576640040b3db?OpenDocument, and of 16 December 2010 [Process: 1584/06.5TBPRD.P1.S1], at http://www.dgsi.pt/jstj.nsf/954f0ce6ad9dd8b980256b5f003fa814/8006f340bccd28188025780000 3ab57b?OpenDocument.

effects, that is, effects between parties, are accepted only if the renunciation is merely temporary.[317] In that case, *B* would claim for damages.

It should be recalled that the Civil Code imposes some statutory restrictions to transfer of property rights. The right of use and habitation is not transferable; real servitudes and legal preferences are transferable only with the property.[318] The right of usufruct is not transferable *mortis causa.*

233. Under Portuguese law, restrictive covenants shall not be confused with negative easements. Negative easements are those in which the owner of the servient estate commits himself/herself to *non facere*, that is to say, not doing something that will be licit for him/her to do if the easement did not exist (e.g., not raising a construction, or not raising it beyond a definite height). It is a burden with a negative content and indissolubly linked to the estate that it burdens. On one hand, it results from the autonomy of the owner of a real estate (and is not imposed by the seller). On the other hand, the holder of the easement may challenge the easement before anyone who becomes owner of the servient estate, who will have his/her ownership limited because of the easement.

§9. Leasehold Interests and Chattels Real

234. Leasehold interests as an estate in real property held under a rental agreement, transmitted, is not known in Portugal. The same applies to chattels real, that is, as an interest in real estate.

---

317. *See* C. Mota Pinto (with Álvaro Moreira and Carlos Fraga), *Direitos Reais* (Coimbra: 1971), 111–113; M. J. Almeida Costa, 'Cláusulas de Inalienabilidade', in *Contratos: Actualidade e Evolução*, ed. Universidade Católica (Porto: Universidade Católica, 1997), 25–48. *See* also the Decision STJ, of 16 April 2013 [Process: 230/08], available at http://www.dgsi.pt/jstj.nsf/cde84ff44faf0d0680256879006bc016?CreateDocument.
318. Santos Justo, *Direitos Reais*, 5th ed (Coimbra: Coimbra Editora, 2017), 32–33.

Chapter 5. Security Interests

235. The goal of guarantee real rights [*direitos reais de garantia*], the Portuguese denomination for security interests, is securing a credit through the granting to its holder (the creditor) of a power to demand the mandatory sale of an immovable property (normally a debtor's property, but may also be a third party's property), in order to be paid, before/after creditors, with the money obtained in the auction. Guarantee real rights have an accessory nature in relation to the credit that they guarantee, which means that they cannot exist without a valid obligation that sustains them.

The following are the security rights over immovable property: the statutory preferences [*privilégios creditórios imobiliários*] (Articles 743 and 744 of the CC), the mortgage [*hipoteca*], the retention right [*direito de retenção*] (Articles 754 to 761 of the CC), and the rent assignation [*consignação de rendimentos*] (Articles 656 to 665 of the CC).[319]

319. Further in Part V, Ch. 1. Some authors consider the preference resulting from a judicial seizure as granting a security right. This opinion, however, is not dominant in Portugal.

Chapter 6. Joint Ownership

§1. Joint Ownership of Immovable Property

236. Statutory provisions for co-ownership [*compropriedade*] are contained in Articles 1403 to 1413 CC, which apply not only to co-ownership in immovable or movable property *stricto sensu*, but also to joint-ownership [*comunhão*] of any other real right other from property.

I. In General

237. Article 1403 of the CC says that there is co-ownership when the ownership or other right over an object belongs to several people. The co-ownership described by these rules is the so-called Roman or by quotas joint-ownership. It is characterized because every co-owner holds an aliquot part of the common object, which empowers him/her to obtain a portion of the object or its price, at the moment of extinction and division of the joint-ownership. Although the Civil Code does not expressly provide for it, the co-ownership may have a legal or a contractual origin. The legal co-ownership is applicable when definite circumstances foreseen by a legal rule happen (e.g., inheritors of a dead person have a joint-ownership in the inheritance until the division of it). The contractual origin results of a contract agreed by two or more parties (e.g., purchase of a building by two or more buyers).

238. Co-ownership shall be distinguished from joint-ownership, whereas in the latter every joint-owner holds an aliquot part of the common right. Joint-ownership is characterized twofold: first, it always has a legal origin; and second, joint-owners cannot ask for the division. As examples of joint-ownership, I can mention the spouse's property (in general, the indivision remains while parties remain married) and the mandatorily common parts in condominiums (which cannot be divided among the unit holders).

II. Use and Management

239. Every co-owner may freely use the common object, but in such a way that the other co-owners are neither affected in their interest in the object, nor deprived of the same use.[320]

In order to administrate and better enjoy the goods, majority agreements will be necessary, in view of the fact that the Civil Code does not speak of a majority of people, but that of quotas, which means that the co-owner or co-owners who hold(s) the major part of the goods will be able to adopt the decisions on its management.

320. Article 1406 CC. *See* Decision of the Supreme Court of 19 September 2013 [Process: 433/2001], available at http://www.dgsi.pt/jstj.nsf/954f0ce6ad9dd8b980256b5f003fa814/54170748eb3956be80257bf20039198e?OpenDocument.

However, if such an agreement so adopted was seriously damaging for the remaining co-owners, the interested parties might go to the judicial authority.

None of the co-owners, without consent of the others, may modify the common object, even in cases wherein the modification could imply advantages for all of them. The sale or other types of alienation of the common object/right also requires the unanimous consent of every co-holder, which may be express or tacit, previous or subsequent. Contrary to this, and in reference to individual quota and economic rights, every co-owner is able to transfer the common thing or burden it freely.

III. Expenses

240. Every co-owner has the right to oblige the others to contribute to the maintenance expenses of the common object and for it to be reserved in a state according to its agreed use. Each one of them must assume this obligation in proportion to his/her respective quota, although they are allowed to renounce his/her part of the object and therefore be exempted of the payment. This eventual renunciation will redound for the benefit of the other co-owners, always in proportion to their respective participation in the joint-ownership.

IV. Extinction

241. Co-ownership can be extinguished because of several reasons (e.g., destruction of the good), although the Civil Code mentions only the extinction that occurs due to the division of the common object (*actio comuni dividundo*).

According to Article 1412 of the CC, none of the co-owners is obliged to remain in joint-ownership, and every one of them may, at any time, request the division of the common object.[321] The validity of an indivisibility agreement is admitted by Article 1413 of the CC, which requires that the indivisibility does not exceed the term of five years, although an ulterior prorogation by means of a new agreement is allowed.

242. When the common object is divisible, the parts resultant from the division have to be proportional to the quota of every co-owner. If it is an indivisible object, co-owners may agree its assignment to one of them, who would then assume the obligation of compensating the rest proportionally. If an agreement cannot be reached, the object will be sold and the price divided among the co-owners.

321. *See* Decisions of the Supreme Court of 29 January 2008 [Process: 07B2373], available at http://www.dgsi.pt/jstj.nsf/954f0ce6ad9dd8b980256b5f003fa814/077453f214c08408802573e500372f0b?OpenDocument, and of 14 June 2011 [Process: 1147/06], at http://www.dgsi.pt/jstj.nsf/954f0ce6ad9dd8b980256b5f003fa814/bcb674a394840d2e802578cd002bde76?OpenDocument.

243. There are three ways to carry out the division of the common goods, as follows: by contract, the co-owners themselves make the partition by common agreement, or by the judge – when there is no agreement to make the division by any of the previous procedures, the co-owners may ask the judicial authority to intervene.[322]

§2. Apartment Ownership

I. In General

244. In Portugal, the dogmatic structure of apartment ownership [*propriedade horizontal*] has evolved on the basis of property concepts, rather than collective ownership or concepts derived from associations. It is generally accepted that the concept of apartment ownership consists of two components, namely, individual ownership of a unit [*fracção autónoma*], and joint-ownership of the land and structural parts of the building.[323]

In a multi-building scheme, the purchaser of a unit therefore does not only acquire ownership of the single unit/house, but he/she simultaneously acquires joint-ownership in the common property [*partes comuns*]. Article 1420(2) of the CC provides that none of these components can be disposed of separately. Therefore, owners cannot alienate their shares in the common property while retaining individual ownership of their units. Both components, individual and common property, are inextricably linked to each other, and form a twofold unity. In accordance with this, they can only be alienated, charged, or otherwise dealt with, as an entity.

245. As regards to the entitlement to rights and powers similar to ownership in units in multi-unit buildings, there are no effective alternatives to condominium in Portugal. Share block schemes would be lawful under the Portuguese legal system. However, they are not used in practice, mainly because they would only grant the acquirer a personal right. In a similar vein, tenancy contracts entitle the tenant to a personal right, which cannot be mistaken for a right similar to an ownership right. Gated condominiums (i.e., gated (security) villages or multi-unit schemes governed by home-owners' associations) are not known in Portugal. A similar understanding of condominium might exist in the institute of 'complex condominium'. However, it is modelled on a totally different theoretical tradition.

Recent developments in Portugal point rather to the direction of extending and adapting condominium regime to new and distinct schemes, where powers over a unit and the enjoyment in common of property and some facilities can be found. The significance of condominium is fairly widespread through, for example, shopping centres regulation, commercial and industrial parks, and tourism resorts.

322. Article 1413 CC.
323. Article 1420(1) CC.

II. Nature of the Right

246. Apartment ownership is a right over a given unit characterized by the individual ownership of an autonomous fraction of the building (an apartment, a garage, a store, etc.) along with joint-ownership of the land where the building was erected and other common parts. The legal relationship recognized by the Portuguese legal system is, therefore, a twofold relationship, set between the private ownership of the unit and joint-ownership of the common property. By default, the status of ownership is applicable to the individual part, whereas the status of co-ownership is applicable to common parts. Those statutes are, in both cases, subjected to the deviations imposed by law.[324]

247. Apartment ownership, however, cannot be sketched out so simplistically. Individual ownership and common ownership are, naturally, qualified by their integration into the condominium regime. On one hand, individual ownership differs from traditional land-ownership in that it is subject to restrictions inherent in apartment ownership flowing naturally from the structural and social interdependence of the apartment owners. On the other hand, the share of the collective ownership which an apartment owner acquires, together with the other owners with regard to the land and structural parts of the scheme, cannot be equated with the Civil Law notion of co-ownership. First, any ordinary co-owner may at any time demand partition of the common property,[325] whereas the common property under an apartment ownership regime is indivisible and can only be partitioned after termination of the scheme. Second, a traditional co-owner is entitled to dispose of his/her share in the common property, whereas the share of the collective ownership which an apartment owner acquires cannot be disposed of separately.[326]

248. Yet, condominium is often addressed as a group of individuals owning different units in the same estate. It can be argued that the Civil Code accords prime importance to the concept of private ownership of the units and regards joint-ownership as functionalized to the enjoyment of private ownership units.[327] This is suggested, mainly, by the location of condominium legal regime in Book Three (Property Law), Title Two (Ownership), and Chapter Five of the Civil Code. This point gains further emphasis because the layman who owns a unit, feels like an owner rather than a co-owner. Condominium is understood as a specific kind of ownership, where the owner of a unit (which comprises the cubic entity formed by its surrounding walls, floors and ceiling, together with certain adjoining parts such as balconies and certain non-adjoining parts such as parking spaces in the basement of the building) has to bear with restrictions derived from the common property. Whether restrictions imposed by Portuguese law would turn a condominium into a

324. Article 1422(1) CC.
325. Cf. Article 1410 CC.
326. Article 1420(2) CC.
327. *See* Oliveira Ascensão, *Direito Civil*, Reais, 5th edn (Coimbra: Coimbra Editora,1993), 464.

dualistic system, where ownership of an apartment and the co-ownership of the common property are of equal importance, remains a controversial question in the doctrine.[328]

III. Allocation of Shares and Rights

249. Each owner is the individual owner of his/her own unit (for residential, professional, commercial or other purposes), and a joint-owner in forced indivision of the common parts, that is, land and other elements, such as the following: the outside shell of the walls and other structural walls (Article 1421(1)(a) of the CC); the roof (Article 1421(1)(b) of the CC); entrance halls, stairways, corridors (Article 1421(1)(c) of the CC); and general installations for services such as electricity, gas, water, and heating (Article 1421(1)(d) of the CC). May be designated for common use: recreation hall and gardens (Article 1421(2)(a) of the CC); lifts (Article 1421(2)(b) of the CC); a residence for the caretaker or manager of the scheme (Article 1421(2)(c) of the CC); parking areas (Article 1421(2)(d) of the CC). Self-contained portions of a building or even separate buildings may be designated for common use, such as a laundry area, swimming-pool, storage facilities, a clubhouse, or a kindergarten. As a general rule, all the portions of the building or separate buildings that are not allocated in the title shall be considered common property.[329]

250. Shares in common property are created by the deed of division, which is the constitutive document.[330] Developers (or joint-owners initiating a project) are allowed discretion to decide the formula to allocate the shares, that is, the participation quota for the various units. In practice, developers set the quotas in relation to the following features of an apartment: the relative size; the selling price; its interior and exterior condition; its location; and the degree to which the common elements can be made use of. An equitable formula is usually reached. Nevertheless, it is commonly accepted by the Courts that the developer cannot discriminate in favour of apartments owned by himself/herself.[331] Article 1419(1) of the CC sets

---

328. *See* Mota Pinto (Álvaro Moreira and Carlos Fraga) *Direito Reais*, 274; Pires de Lima, Antunes Varela & Henrique Mesquita *Código Civil*, 2nd ed III (Coimbra: Coimbra Editora, 1987), 395; Henrique Mesquita *Direitos Reais,* Sumários das Lições ao Curso de 1966–67 (Coimbra: Coimbra Editora, 1967), 305; Menezes Cordeiro, *Tratado De Direito Civil Português I-* Parte Geral, II- Coisas, 3rd edn (Coimbra: Almedina, 2005), 639; Santos Justo, *Direitos Reais*, 5th ed (Coimbra: Coimbra Editora, 2017), 329 et seq; Carvalho Fernandes, *Lições de Direitos Reais*, 6th ed (Lisboa: Quid Iuris, 2009), 402; Sandra Passinhas, *A Assembleia de Condóminos e o Administrador na Propriedade Horizontal,*2nd edn(Coimbra: Almedina, 2002), 161.
329. Article 1421(2)(e) CC. *See* Decision of the Supreme Court of 19 May 2009 [Process: 1793/05], available at http://www.dgsi.pt/jstj.nsf/954f0ce6ad9dd8b980256b5f003fa814/cbee50abd5fb09b2802575bd003ed24a?OpenDocument.
330. Article 1418(1) CC.
331. Decisions of the Supreme Court, of 8 July 1997 [Process: 97A242], available at http://www.dgsi.pt/jstj.nsf/954f0ce6ad9dd8b980256b5f003fa814/7c95eb39409de1d3802568fc003b6c29?OpenDocument, and of 12 November 2009 [Process: 5242/06], at http://www.dgsi.pt/jstj.nsf/954f0ce6ad9dd8b980256b5f003fa814/aa61f4296b119f2580257673005adf62?OpenDocument.

forth that the constitutive title, where the participation quota of each owner is set, may only be modified with the consent of all co-owners. Hence, a unanimous agreement is required for a change on the participation quota to take place.

251. According to Article 1418(1) of the CC, in an apartment ownership scheme, the allocation of shares and rights is expressed as a percentage, or a *per* thousand proportion. The participation quota serves, first, as the numerical quantification of an apartment owner's share in the common property and in the benefits and profits flowing, for example, from the leasing of a common part of the building. Second, the participation quota is used to allocate the number of votes of each joint-owner in the general meeting.[332] Finally, it also serves as the numerical basis for determining the financial obligations in respect of maintenance and administration of the scheme, which include the contribution to a reserve fund.[333] An owner's share in the common property might also become highly relevant in the proceeds of the sale of the land upon dissolution of the scheme, of the compensation paid by an expropriation authority; and of insurance money paid out on destruction of the building. On the contrary, an apartment owner's share in the common property does have little significance in relation to an owner's wide powers of use and enjoyment of the common property.[334]

The allocation of shares in common property and of voting rights to the apartment owners are legally binding, and cannot be subject to special provisions set out by the developers or agreed upon by joint-owners. If the owner has a participation quota of 18%, he/she mandatorily has an 18% share of the common property and eighteen votes at the general assembly. It is considered to be representative of his/her proprietary rights.

252. According to Article 1422(2) of the CC, apartment owners are obliged to maintain the apartment in a good state of repair, and to use the apartment in accordance with its purpose and the destination of the building. Law 128/2014, of 29 August (amended by Law 62/2018, of 22 August), considers compatible with a residential purpose the allocation of the apartment for touristic accommodation. Activities which are harmful to the reputation of the building are prohibited. The constitutive title, as well as resolutions of the general meeting approved without opposition, might also prohibit acts and activities in the scheme.

Alterations to the apartment are also specially regulated by Article 1422(3) of the CC. As a general rule, improvements and alterations inside the apartment should not impair the outward or the structural integrity of the building. An apartment owner cannot change the architectural components or the external structure and appearance of the scheme, except if authorized by a resolution representing two-thirds of the total vote to alter the common parts or the exterior of the building, in line with the destination of the building. In any case, the owner is not allowed to jeopardize the stability and safety of the construction.

---

332. Article 1430(2) CC.
333. Article 1424(1) CC, and DL 268/97, of 25 October.
334. Article 1406(1) CC.

Law 32/2012, of 14 August, amended Articles 1425 and 1426 CC, in order to protect disabled people. They are now allowed to install a handicap stair lift, or a ramped access, provided that they communicate their intention to the manager.

IV. Charges

253. Article 1424 of the CC, which regulates the contribution of joint-owners to common charges of condominium, is a default rule. Article 1424(1) of the CC imposes the costs of maintenance, repairs, and enjoyment of the common property according to the value of the participation quota of each joint-owner. On the contrary, the performance of services might be shared proportionally, according to the quota allotted to each apartment, if agreed by a 2/3 majority of apartment owners, without opposition from the others.[335] Charges pertaining to collective services may be apportioned amongst apartment owners equally or on the basis of the objective utility that those services and installations may render for each particular apartment owner (e.g., charges with the management service can be divided equally among co-owners). On this basis, utility quotas for each apartment with regard to each item have to be worked out and allotted to each owner in the by-law of the scheme. Finally, Article 1424(3) and (4), provide that expenses with regard to the various staircases, lifts and those parts of the common property which only serve certain owners, have to be borne exclusively by them.

254. Even if the unit has been rented, the owner remains liable for the common charges before the condominium. Landlord and tenant, however, can agree among themselves that the current charges for the utilization and maintenance of common property and for the use of common services shall be borne by the tenant. The agreement shall be in written, shall specify the charges for tenant, and be signed by him. The landlord is in duty to communicate to the tenant, within one month, information about the exact amount of the charges he/she had paid to the condominium. The tenant shall pay it within one month after communication.[336]

V. Management

255. Portuguese law requires a by-law [*regulamento*] for any scheme of more than four units,[337] which shall impinge upon the use, maintenance and administration of common parties. It must be proposed by the manager and approved by a majority of owners present at a general meeting, representing at least half of the value of the building. According to Article 1432(4) of the CC, in a second meeting, a by-law can be validly adopted by a majority resolution, irrespective of the number

335. Article 1424(2) CC. *See* Decision of the Supreme Court of 12 November 2009 [Process: 5242/06], supra *341*.
336. Cf. Article 1078 CC.
337. Article 1429-A CC.

of owners present, if the majority of voters represents at least a quarter of the shares in the common property. Only if the general meeting does not approve a by-law, the manager is entitled to elaborate it.

By-laws usually contain provisions on the administration of the scheme (management rules), use and maintenance of common parts (conduct rules), and bind all occupiers of the building, visitors and future owners. They can be amended by the same majority as required for its enactment, and do not need registration for their enforceability. The minute of the general meeting where a by-law was approved is lodged with the manager.[338]

256. Sometimes by-laws are drawn up unilaterally by the developer and registered as part of the constitutive document.[339] In that case, they may determine the manner in which not only the common property but also individual units can be used and enjoyed. The Portuguese Civil Code allows the developer a fair amount of autonomy as to the content of by-laws, with due respect for public order provisions or imperative rules of the statute. A by-law attached to the constitutive title follows the same requirements as the title: it shall be made in a public deed and inscribed in the Land Registry Office, and it can only be amended by unanimous consent of the owners.[340] I have claimed that whereas these rules impinge upon the use, maintenance and administration of common parties, that is, the normal content of by-laws, they can lawfully be modified by the majority decision of the general assembly.[341]

Resolutions [*deliberações*] are internal rules regulating the use and maintenance of common goods and services; they are reached through majority vote (Article 1432(3) of the CC), at the assembly meeting. In the main, the community of owners has only regulatory powers over the common parts; it cannot collide with the private ownership of the apartment. Resolutions, along with by-laws and the constitutive title, shape the legal status of the condominium, and bind occupiers, their visitors, and future owners. The minutes of resolutions are lodged with the manager and do not require registration in the Land Registry office.[342]

257. There is no express requirement that by-laws and resolutions apply equally to all owners of units put to substantially the same purpose, but it should be accepted as a general principle. Case law normally controls the balance among co-owners through the institute of abuse of rights.[343]

338. Article 1436(m) CC.
339. Article 1418(2)(a) CC.
340. Article 1419(1) CC.
341. Sandra Passinhas, *A Assembleia de Condóminos e o Administrador na Propriedade Horizontal,*2nd edn (Coimbra: Almedina, 2002), 76.
342. Article 1436(m) CC.
343. Decision of the Supreme Court of 12 November 2009, *supra 341.*

258. Portuguese law assigns the management of the apartment ownership scheme to a body consisting of the apartment owners, the general meeting of owners [*assembleia de condóminos*], and an executive organ, the manager [*administrador*].[344] In Portugal, the management body does not have juristic personality.

259. The general assembly is the highest administrative organ of an apartment ownership scheme; it is entrusted with powers to adopt resolutions within the parameters set out in law and in the constitutive title.[345] Apartment owners automatically become members of the management structure as soon as the apartment is conveyed to them.

Whereas policy decisions are taken by all the members in general meeting, the daily management of the scheme is entrusted to a managing agent, who controls the day-to-day running of the scheme. Condominium owners might decide that they themselves will also act as managers (normally, in a turn basis). The manager, however, does not need to come from the rank of owners but may be an outsider.[346] A professional manager may be appointed to execute the resolutions of the general meeting and to supervise the day-to-day management and administration of the scheme.

260. The general meeting exercises its powers by means of formal resolutions passed at a duly constituted general meeting. Articles 1430(2) of the CC sets forth that votes are mandatorily allocated in accordance with the participation quota of the apartment. According to Article 1432(3) of the CC, owners, representing at least half of the shares in the common property, have to be present or represented before valid resolutions can be taken at a general meeting. If the required forum is not obtained at the first meeting, Article 1432(4) of the CC provides that a second meeting can be convened, and must take place within a week from the first. The second meeting can validly adopt majority resolutions, irrespective of the number of owners present, if the majority of voters represents at least a quarter of the shares in the common property. If only certain owners are charged with certain expenses, only those owners are allowed to vote on resolutions concerning such expenses.[347]

261. The following resolutions are to be are to be taken by owners representing at least half of the shares in the common property: resolutions approving and amending the by-law of the scheme; appointing and revoking the contract of the management; determining his/her remuneration; or setting the amount of the monthly charges to be paid by the owners. Article 1428(2) of the CC requires a more stringent majority for resolutions in case of destruction of the scheme. If destruction of the building affects less than three-quarters of its value, the general meeting

---

344. Article 1430(1) CC. *See* Decision of the Supreme Court, of 28 May 2015, [Process: 1340/08], available at http://www.dgsi.pt/jstj.nsf/954f0ce6ad9dd8b980256b5f003fa814/8608d8a1051f56a980257e53005a9026?OpenDocument.

345. *See* Decision of the Supreme Court, of 2 February 2013 [Process: 4612/05], available at http://www.dgsi.pt/jstj.nsf/954f0ce6ad9dd8b980256b5f003fa814/3cd12253b2c260b380257c350051fe23?OpenDocument.

346. Article 1435(4) CC.

347. Article 1424(3) CC.

might authorize the reconstruction of the building only through a resolution approved by the majority of owners representing the majority of the value of the building.

262. The following actions can be taken by a resolution representing two-thirds of the total vote: authorization to individual owners to alter the common parts or the exterior of the building, in line with the design of the building;[348] and improvements in the common parts of the building.[349] Simple majority resolutions representing the majority of the value of the building are enough to approve the installation of a lift or piped gas, if the building is composed of at least eight units.

A resolution representing two-thirds of the total votes, approved without opposition from anyone, might rule that charges pertaining to collective services may be apportioned amongst apartment owners equally or on the basis of the objective utility which these services and installations have for each particular apartment owner.[350]

263. Unanimity is required by Article 1419(1) of the CC for the modification of the constitutive title[351] as to the decision of *terminating* the scheme. However, such a decision can be approved by all the owners present at the general meeting, if they represent two-thirds of the shares in the common property. According to Article 1432(7) of the CC, the owners absent from the meeting shall approve the decisions within ninety days after communication of the decision. The consent of all joint-owners is also required to lease the common property or any portion thereof.[352] Joint-owners might give their agreement to the lease before or after the signature of the contract. In both situations (amendments of the constitutive title and lease of common property) Portuguese law provides for valid resolutions in the form of resolutions consented to in writing or signed by all the owners.[353]

264. Except for the situations mentioned above, resolutions are to be taken at a general meeting. Portuguese law does not accept the resort to the 'round robin' method (all the members of the management body signing a motion which contain the resolution) because it is assumed that all co-owners have the right to speak and to be heard in the meeting by the other owners, and to try to influence the opinion and the vote of the joint-owners. The general meeting is considered the right place for this.

The general assembly cannot approach the court for relief if it is unable to reach a valid resolution, since consent of the owners is deemed to be strongly linked with their proprietary rights.

The Portuguese legal regime contains no special provisions on the protection of the minority against majority decisions.

---

348. Article 1422(3) CC.
349. Article 1425 CC.
350. Article 1424(2) CC.
351. *See* decision of the Supreme Court of 11 February 2014 [Process: 8284/07], at http://www.dgsi.pt/jstj.nsf/38f33c44b0c8358280256879006bc013?CreateDocument.
352. Article 1024(2) CC.
353. *See* Sandra Passinhas, *supra*, 191.

265. The manager or administrator is appointed by a majority of votes. If the general assembly cannot reach an agreement upon the person to be appointed, any owner can approach the court to have a manager appointed.[354] Meanwhile, Article 1435-A provides for the appointment of a provisional manager where the appointee is prevented from or in default of executing his/her functions.

Only one manager can be appointed, but this can be a natural person or a legal entity. The law restricts a manager's tenure to periods of one year. Tacit or express renewal of this initial period is, however, provided for in Article 1435(4) of the CC. The manager's remuneration is also fixed by majority vote of the management body.

Although a manager is usually appointed for a specific period, he/she may be dismissed by a majority vote of the general assembly at any time before the expiry of such period. The manager may, in addition, be dismissed by the court on application by an interested party if irregularities or neglect of duty can be proved.[355]

266. Among his/her functions, the manager has to execute the decisions of the general meeting; ensure compliance with by-laws; manage the financial affairs of the association, *inter alia*, by proposing an annual budget, by opening a separate bank account and by collecting monthly contributions from the owners; represent the owners in litigation and other matters; maintain the common property and the common services in a state of good repair and in proper working order, respectively; take emergency measures to preserve the common property, if necessary; maintain all documents related to the scheme.[356] Recent legislation on energy efficiency (namely, implementing Directive 2012/27/EU of the European Parliament and of the Council of 25 October 2012 on energy efficiency), created new duties and responsibilities for the manager in this field.

267. Portuguese legal system distinguishes between the external role of a manager in transactions with third parties and his/her internal role in dealing with individual owners. When transacting with third parties, the manager is usually regarded as acting on behalf of the collectivity of owners. Owners are bound by transactions performed by a manager acting within his/her authority. As regards internal affairs with individual owners, it is generally accepted that the manager acts as an organ of the community of owners, not on behalf of the owners individually. As a consequence, a manager's mandate cannot be revoked by an individual owner,[357] and a manager can file a suit against an individual member on behalf of the collectivity of owners.[358]

354. Article 1435(2) CC.
355. Articles 1435(3) CC and 1056 CPC.
356. Article 1436 CC.
357. Article 1435(1) CC.
358. Article 1437(1) CC.

VI. Private Building Complexes

268. Until 1994, condominium schemes would only encompass units in one single building (although each unit could be utilized for residential, industrial, commercial, and professional purposes, or for parking garages). However, it did not prevent the extension of the apartment ownership regime to distinct schemes. Developers, first, adapted the condominium regime for shopping centres regulation. In Portugal, shopping centres are usually composed of: a hypermarket; a department store and a wide range of services, such as bank, travel agent offices, telecommunications shops, photography shops, parapharmacies, laundries and quick repairs shops, among others; the food court; free parking spaces; and an outdoor esplanade (a shopping centre is not necessarily an open-air retail complex). Developers have two options with respect to the ownership of shopping centres.[359] Either they sell the units to different entrepreneurs (plural ownership), or they retain ownership over all shopping, and rent the single units (singular ownership and plural tenants). Only in the former, a condominium scheme might be implemented. In the latter, however, a management company is usually appointed, which shall moderate the relationships between the owner and the tenants, and among the distinct multiple tenants, and promote the shopping centre's value over time. Developers normally assume the management of the shopping centre and create a by-law that regulates the powers and duties of the entrepreneurs. The concrete regime of a shopping centre, with respect to the relationships among the different entrepreneurs, and to the use of the building, the units, and equipment, is mostly in line with apartment ownership terminology and legal regime.[360]

269. Since 1994, Article 1438-A of the CC provides that the condominium scheme might be applied to a gathering of autonomous low-rise buildings or of multi-unit high-rise buildings.

In this context, apartment ownership would arise, first, in groups of houses linked by common parts of the land where the buildings were erected, or common property, equipment, or services. Such a scheme combines house-ownership, which is exclusive and offers maximum privacy, with common amenities (e.g., gardens, swimming-pool, laundry services, porter). This became the legal framework for the development of housing accommodation for a high social and economic status segment of population. The main advantage of applying the condominium legal regime to those schemes is that rules of the Civil Code establishing rights and duties of the owners and rules on administration of the condominium will be applied, dispensing with a case-by-case stipulation basis.

359. *See* Decision STJ, of 27 January 2010, in www.dgsi.pt, and of 9 March 2004 [Process: 03A4204], at http://www.dgsi.pt/jstj.nsf/954f0ce6ad9dd8b980256b5f003fa814/07c1f5a79fa058c980256e8400 2aa2a2?OpenDocument.

360. *See* Decision STJ of 30 Jun. 2009 [Process: 1398/03], available at http://www.dgsi.pt/jstj.nsf/95 4f0ce6ad9dd8b980256b5f003fa814/7dcc84cae6c5307d802575e7004e312a?OpenDocument.

270. DL 267/94 was also very important for the implementation of commercial and industrial condominiums,[361] shaped in multi-unit low-rise buildings. Developers started to construct the scheme according to the needs of the single companies and entrepreneurs (e.g., a large parking place and a security service), which rendered the units easier to sell. Entrepreneurs, however, would also obtain several advantages due to this scheme. Owners of units would obtain substantial savings in terms of services and supplies (e.g., cleaning services, security), and benefit from the prominence of firms in close proximity. Commercial (retail parks) and industrial condominiums (industrial parks) soon became very popular in Portugal. More recently, iParks, promoting, creating, and settling companies with a high technological orientation have been created. Enterprises who acquire a unit in an iPark might benefit from several facilities. The management body provides services such as the following: administrative support; legal, financial, and strategic consulting; support to marketing and external promotion activities; checking and maintenance of infrastructures and shared spaces; organization and coordination of training programmes for human resources; management of incubation processes; support to technology transfer processes; dissemination of any information concerning innovation, science, and technology; creation and maintenance of databases with strategic information concerning the businesses of resident companies; promotion of international congresses on any subject that might interest the resident companies; and the promotion of internal, regional, national, and international partnerships.

271. Since one single building is not required to a condominium scheme, the condominium legal regime might be adapted to all schemes where owners of single units enjoy common property or facilities. They will be provided with a centralized and efficient administrative management regime, along with a clear set of rules on the rights and duties of each holder. Nevertheless, in all situations where apartment ownership applies, it shall be adapted to the concrete situation. The law is not strict in determining which parts have to be held in common in a multi-building scheme. The several units might be linked by the land (if land is common) or by common parties, equipment, or services (if the land is subdivided into parcels). In a commercial scheme, for example, the outside shell of each unit is not mandatorily common property, which means that the owners of non-residential units might not require consent from other owners before using the outside walls for advertisement purposes.[362] Provisions on modernization of the building, termination of the scheme, reorganization of the physical boundaries between the units, the use of common parts (such as parking spaces and toilets by the clients), can be laid down in the constitutive title. There is a wide range for private autonomy in the modelling of a concrete regime of condominium.

These schemes have to comply with town planning requirements set forth in the Legal Regime on Urban Occupation (*Regime Jurídico da Urbanização e Edificação*, hereinafter 'RJUE').[363] The land must be zoned.[364] Ownership of roads,

361. Professional and services condominiums are mainly located in a single multi-unit high rise building in the city centre.
362. The units comprising the scheme must, however, be designed as a harmonious architectural entity.
363. DL 555/99, of 16 December, as amended (last amendment by DL 121/2018, od 28 December).

other infrastructures, and facilities must be transferred to the municipality.[365] The municipality, in turn, might assign to the owner's association the maintenance and upkeep of the infrastructures and facilities.[366]

272. Since DL 167/97, of 4 July, the apartment ownership regime has been extensively used to regulate the complex relationships which flow from multi-proprietary rights in holiday apartments, villages, and resorts.[367] As is well known, tourism is one of the core growth engines of the Portuguese economy, and the promotion, enhancement, and sustainability of tourism activities is a core strategic national policy. DL 39/2008, of 7 March, in force,[368] has adapted the apartment ownership legal regime to overcome the difficulties of multi-property in tourist facilities, and to ensure high quality structures and services in the tourism industry (which claims constant monitoring and improvements). Further, Article 53 expressly provides that condominium legal regime is the default regulation for the relationships amongst owners in a resort scheme.[369] It is not clear whether a hotel can be divided into a condominium. Some authors would give a positive answer to that question,[370] as long as rooms comply with Article 1415 of the CC, that is, they should be autonomous and have an independent access to common parts, in order to lawfully constitute a unit.

273. Since the concept of apartment ownership includes two components, namely, individual ownership of a unit, and joint (common) ownership of the land and structural parts of the building, it could be concluded that the apartment ownership regime does not apply to situations such as caravan parks, dockominiums, and graveyards, where individuals have only a personal, time-limited right to the exclusive use of a space. However, it has recently come to my knowledge that notaries have accepted public deeds of condominiums of parking areas. This change in perspective means that a parking space could be recognized as a thing (and therefore an independent unit) and could be the object of property rights (by allotting a separate description to it in the title). To accept such a scheme would bring into existence a diverse understanding of property, hence further developments are awaited.

---

364. Article 41 RJUE.
365. Articles 43, 44, and 57 RJUE.
366. Articles 46 and 47 RJUE. *See* Fernanda Paula Oliveira et al., *Regime Jurídico da Urbanização e Edificação Comentado,* 4th edn (Coimbra: Almedina, 2017).
367. The apartment ownership regime had already inspired regulation of time-sharing interests by Decree 275/93 of 5 August, as amended (last amendment by DL 245/2015, of 20 October).
368. As amended (last amendment by DL 80/2017, of 30 June).
369. *See* Decision of the Supreme Court of 16 October 2008 [Process: 08B3011], available at http://www.dgsi.pt/jstj.nsf/954f0ce6ad9dd8b980256b5f003fa814/8bc33107cbecb151802574e400487e45?OpenDocument.
370. *See* Sandra Passinhas, 'Empreendimentos Turísticos em Propriedade Plural', in *Empreendimentos Turísticos*, ed. Alves Correia (Coimbra: CEDOUA, 2010), 197; and Cristina Siza Vieira, 'Propriedade Plural e Gestão de Empreendimentos Turísticos', in *Empreendimentos Turísticos,* ed. Alves Correia (Coimbra: CEDOUA, 2010), 180.

§3. TIMESHARE

I. General Introduction

274. A timeshare [*direito real de habitação periódica*] entitles its holder, a consumer, to use an accommodation in an apartment-hotel, touristic village, or touristic apartment during certain periods of time, that is, on a time-sharing basis. This right is ruled by DL 275/93, of 5 August, and undergone a recent reform, through DL 245/2015, implementing Directive 2008/122/EC, of the European Parliament and of the Council, of 14 January 2009.[371]

The legal regime of time-sharing is defined by two aspects: the need to set the content and limits of the real property right (according to the *numerus clausus* principle in force in Portugal), and the aim of regulating the contract under which a consumer, for consideration, acquires the right to use one or more overnight accommodation for more than one period of occupation (according to the policy of consumer protection)[372] In fact, the regime is shaped by the overall need to ensure consumer protection, through transparence and information,[373] and to enhance the market's competitiveness, in order to have diversified and high quality offer of time-sharing products. All time-sharing rights are acquired by a consumer, who is a natural person acting for purposes outside that person's trade, business, craft, or profession to a trader, a natural or legal person who is acting for purposes relating to that person's trade, business, craft or profession and anyone acting in the name of or on behalf of a trader. It does not prevent the existence of exchange contract, that is, a contract under which a consumer, for considerations, joins an exchange system which allows that consumer access to overnight accommodation, in isolation or together with travel or other services. Strict rules on advertising, pre-contractual information, withdrawal along with detailed regulation of the contract are to be found. The legal regime is mandatory.

The minimum duration of the right is now of one year (which represents a major change, since it was earlier a period of fifteen years), and the period of the time-sharing is freely agreed upon between the parties (before 2011, the minimum and maximum limits were set at one week and one month per year, respectively). All rights must have the same duration.[374]

371. Directive 2008/122/EC of the European Parliament and of the Council of 14 January 2009 on the protection of consumers in respect of certain aspects of timeshare, long-term holiday product, resale and exchange contracts.
372. Decision of the Supreme Court] of 10 April 2014 [Process: 1246/10.9TJLSB.L1.S1], available at http://www.dgsi.pt/jstj.nsf/954f0ce6ad9dd8b980256b5f003fa814/682008ffe82fafdd80257cba00394077?OpenDocument.
373. For example, the seller must provide the potential buyer with a document describing in a clear, precise, and understandable manner, the tourist resort where the accommodation is located and the rights and duties of the buyer.
374. Article 3(3) of Decree Law 275/93.

II. Constitution of a Time-Sharing Scheme

275. Timeshare may pertain to a building, a building complex, or an area architecturally differentiated between them, provided that it is composed of a minimum of ten different independent accommodations. The legitimization to constitute this right corresponds to the owner or owners of the building, complex or area, by means of the granting of a public deed[375] and the subsequent registration.[376] The division of a tourist undertaking in time-sharing rights must be communicated to *Turismo de Portugal*.[377]

The constitutive document may be modified upon unanimous consent of all the time-sharing holders, who may have their right interfered with. Holders of a time-sharing right can approach the court for relief if the refusal is not justified.[378]

Article 9 Decree Law 275/93 sets forth that before the acquirer is bound by any contract, the trader shall provide the consumer, in a clear and comprehensible manner, with accurate and sufficient information, following a standard information form. That information shall be provided, free of charge, by the trader on paper or on another durable medium which is easily accessible to the acquirer.

Each right to a timeshare requires an autonomous registration with the relevant property registry [*Conservatória do Registo Predial*]. The Registrar shall display a certificate of each right of time-sharing.[379]

276. The transmission of the rights is done by means of a declaration of the parties in the Register and must be registered.[380]

III. The Contract of Acquisition

277. The right of exploitation is purchased through a contract that for the protection of the purchaser, must be expressed in writing. Article 9 sets forth that the contract is required to be in writing, on paper, or on another durable medium, and drawn up in the language or one of the languages of the Member State in which the consumer is resident or a national, at the choice of the consumer, provided it is an official language of the European Community.

The acquirer is given a period of fourteen calendar days to withdraw from the timeshare, without giving any reason.[381] The withdrawal period shall be calculated from the day of the conclusion of the contract; or from the day when the consumer receives the contract. During this period it is prohibited to make or receive any payment, including advance payments or deposits (Article 13-A).

Article 16(7) and (8), of Decree Law 275/93, provide that the exercise of the right of withdrawal by the consumer terminates the obligation of the parties to perform

375. Article 6 of Decree Law 275/93.
376. Article 8 of Decree Law 275/93.
377. Article 5 of Decree of Law 275/93.
378. Article 7 (1) and (2) of Decree Law 275/93.
379. Articles 10 and ff of Decree Law 275/93.
380. Article 12 of Decree Law 275/93.
381. Article 16 of Decree Law 275/93.

the contract. Where the consumer exercises the right of withdrawal, the consumer shall neither bear any cost nor be liable for any value corresponding to the service which may have been performed before withdrawal.

IV. The Content of the Right

278. The right entitles its holder to the power to enjoy, exclusively for a certain period every year, a tourist accommodation together with adequate furniture for the use of it. The timeshare is, by default, a right for life.

According to Article 21, the holder has the rights to use the unit during the period of the right;[382] to use the public installations, equipment, and services of the touristic undertaking; and to transmit his/her right.

The holder shall use his/her right as a *bonus paterfamilias*, according to the normal purpose of the tourist undertaking. He/she is not entitled to cannot carry out acts or activities prohibited in the constitutive title or in the house rules.[383] The owner is obliged to allow the manager access to his/her apartment, for the purpose of cleaning and maintaining it.[384]

Article 22 Decree Law 275/93 provides that the holder must pay the owner of the undertaking every year a certain amount allocated to the service company that takes care of the building's cleaning and maintenance (or to the owner, if he/she takes care of these activities) as settled in the constitutive title. This amount pertains to charges with use and exploitation of the undertaking, tax payments, and remuneration of the manager.[385]

V. Management

279. The management of the units and of the common use installations and equipment is in charge of the owner of the undertaking, who is entitled to transmit to a third party the exploitation of the undertaking.[386] However, the owner of the undertaking remains liable before the holders of the units for the good management and conservation of the undertaking.

382. In case of a *force majeur*, the holder has the right to an alternative lodging in a touristic undertaking of equivalent quality and in a local near.
383. Article 21(2) Decree Law 275/93.
384. Article 26 Decree Law 275/93.
385. Decision of the Supreme Court [Process: 692/05.4TBGDL.E1.S1] of 6 March 2012, at http://www.dgsi.pt/jstj.nsf/954f0ce6ad9dd8b980256b5f003fa814/098a0f921ffaed1d802579bb00511a80?OpenDocument.
386. Article 25(2) Decree Law 275/93.

280. Article 27 Decree Law 275/93 sets forth that works are the responsibility of the manager of the undertaking,[387] and shall not interfere with the rights of the holders. If the deterioration is the result of misuse of the unit, the time-sharing holder must pay for them. Modifications of the units by the owners require the consent of the timeshare holders in the general assembly.[388] The general meeting shall appreciate the management plan.[389]

387. A reserve fund to works of repair and maintenance of the undertaking must be created (Article 30). *See* Decision of the Supreme Court of 6 March 2012 [Process: 692/05], available at http://www.dgsi.pt/jstj.nsf/954f0ce6ad9dd8b980256b5f003fa814/098a0f921ffaed1d802579bb00511a80?OpenDocument.

388. Article 28 Decree Law 275/93.

389. Article 34 Decree Law 275/93.

Chapter 7. Neighbourhood and Urban Problems

281. The Portuguese Civil Code sets forth an entire chapter (Articles 1344 to 1384) to neighbourhood relations. In order to prevent problems related to neighbourhood, the law imposes a general set of limits to property rights. These limits are established in order to shape the content and function of property rights over immovable property. They are not considered easements if favour of the adjacent buildings. For example, Article 1360 provides that the owner of a building cannot open new windows or doors in a distance less than one and a half metres of a neighbour building. This restriction is considered a general limit of property rights over a building rather than an easement in favour of a neighbour. Each property right over a thing is shaped according to the concrete characteristics of the object and the regulation that impinge upon it.

282. The neighbouring restrictions to property rights are set forth according to the normal use of the land. The criterion is necessarily objective and abstract. If the owner of the land has special needs that require a specific and more stringent protection, such protection is obtained through the legal regime of personality rights. For example, if the owner of a building is a sick person, who needs to sleep early, he/she might get an injunction against the neighbour in order to stop a noisy activity, under personality rights protection. That protection is granted in consideration to the concrete needs of the individual, and might further restrict the use of an estate.

283. Article 70 of the CC provides that individuals are protected against any unlawful offence or threat of offence against their physical or moral personality. This regime does not require the existence of fault on the part of the agent; objective unlawfulness is sufficient. Regardless of any civil liability, the person threatened or offended may apply for adequate measures to prevent the threat from becoming actual or to attenuate the effects of an offence already committed.

The measures to defend personality may be preventive, decreed in light of the danger of the injury, or may be attenuating when the injury has already been committed. Article 70(2) of the CC entitles the person whose personality is threatened to demand measures adequate to the circumstances of the case to prevent this threat from materializing. These measures to defend personality follow a simplified procedure, set forth by Articles 878 to 880 of the CPC.[390] The special characteristics of the personality procedure do not allow the inclusion of a request for damages, which must be subject to a separate action in keeping with the common rules. In any case, the effectiveness of this injunctive relief is very high and, therefore, Portuguese courts make a very extensive use thereof.[391]

---

390. This procedure only applies to matters of urgency, and grants the judge very wide discretionary powers.

391. *See* the Portuguese report of Pedro Pais de Vasconcelos & Nuno Ferreira, in Gert Brüggemeier, Aurelia Colombi Ciacchi, and Patrick O'Callaghan, *Personality Rights in European Tort Law* (Cambridge: CUP, 2010), 153.

284. Article 65(2)(a) of the CRP provides that in order to ensure enjoyment of the right to housing, the state shall be charged with planning and implementing a housing policy that is embodied in general town and country planning documents and supported by urban planning documents that guarantee the existence of an adequate network of transport and social facilities.

285. The main regulation on Planning and Development is the above mentioned DL 555/99, of 16 December,[392] that lays down the Legal Regime on Urban Occupation [*Regime Jurídico da Urbanização e da Edificação*]. It establishes the basic legal framework in respect of the licensing of urbanization and construction works and the use of buildings. Law 31/2014, of 30 May,[393] provides the Land, Town and Country Planning Law *[Lei de bases gerais da política pública de solos, de ordenamento do território e de urbanismo*]. Finally, Law 19/2014, of 14 April, establishes the environmental general legal framework [*Lei de Bases da Política do Ambiente*].

286. The *ius aedificandi* or power to build, inherent to the owner's right, is defined (e.g., positive duties to building or not building) in both zoning laws and urban development plans approved in every municipality. The latter's main function is determining the land liable and the land not liable to be urbanized, as well as the manner in which the development process must be implemented.

Zoning may include regulation of the kinds of activities which will be acceptable on particular lots (such as open space, residential, agricultural, commercial, or industrial), the densities at which those activities can be performed (from low-density housing such as single family homes to high-density such as high-rise apartment buildings), the height of buildings, the proportions of the types of space on a lot, such as how much landscaped space, impervious surface, and parking must be provided.

I. Building works

287. The land/building use and occupation are mainly controlled by local authorities, such as Municipalities, although regional and central authorities are also involved in such control, in respect of certain matters/projects.

The local Municipality shall authorize the building works. Depending on the type of works and on the legal situation of the property, the procedure and its complexity can vary. As a result, we may have a building permit, or we may have a previous communication procedure to be followed.

During such procedures, different public entities will analyse specific issues and provide opinions, which in certain cases can be binding.

Municipalities can also request the assignment of parts of land and can subject the issuance of a permit to the realization of public infrastructures.

392. As amended.
393. As amended by Law 74/2017, of 16 August.

II. Use Permits

288. An authorization specifying the permitted use of the property shall be issued by the local Municipality.[394] Depending on the foreseen use and also on the type of project, other permits and authorizations may be required.

289. Article 65(2) of the CPR states that in order to ensure enjoyment of the right to housing, the state shall be charged with promoting the construction of low-cost and social housing (in cooperation with the autonomous regions and local authorities) and with encouraging and supporting local community initiatives that work towards the resolution of their housing problems and foster the formation of housing and self-building cooperatives.

290. DL 37/2018, of 4 May, set out a legal regime promoting access to a suitable dwelling of people that do not have financial resources for it.

291. DL 29/2018, of 4 May, foresees the legal regime of urgent housing [*Porta de Entrada*], and DL 308/2007, of 3 September,[395] rules a financial support for people aged less than 35 years-old on payment of tenancy contracts [*Porta 65 – Arrendamento para Jovens*].

292. In what respects financed tenancy contracts, in force are Laws 80/2014 and 81/2014, of 19 December.

293. Social housing is mainly owned and managed by Municipalities. According to official Statistics of Construction and Habitation, in 2015 there were 120.000 social dwellings. Public housing constitutes 2% of the housing in Portugal.

---

394. Building and use permits cannot be implied by long use. However, there are some specific cases where building and use permits can be implied if the competent authorities do not take any action within a mandatory time limit.

395. As amended (last amendment by DL 43/2010, of 30 April).

Chapter 8. Agrarian Problems

294. The soil systems of Portugal are usually sandy, arid, and acid, reflecting the soils of the Iberian Peninsula in general. Soil in the north can be rocky. Northern Portugal is better suited for agriculture than the south because of abundant rainfall, but with proper irrigation the south could support more intensive agriculture. In the northern mountains, pine, oak, poplar, and elm trees are prevalent. Vegetation is more varied in the central region and includes citrus trees and cork oak. The warm, dry south contains many areas of rough pasture, as well as abundant cork oak.

295. Portugal has as agricultural area of 34,600 sq. km, which represents 37.8% of the total land. It encompasses 10,500 sq. km of arable land; 5,850 sq. km of land under permanent crops; and 18,250 sq. km of land under permanent meadows and pastures.[396]

296. As regards the agricultural policy,[397] Article 93 states that the objectives of Portuguese agricultural policy shall be, among others, to increase agricultural production and productivity by providing agriculture with adequate infrastructures and human, technical, and financial resources; to promote the development of the rural world, the rationalization of the structure of land-ownership, and the access by those that work on the land to ownership or possession of the land itself and of such other means of production as they directly employ thereon; to ensure the rational use and management of the soil and other natural resources, and to maintain their regenerative capability; to encourage farmers to form and join associations and to directly work the land. The state shall promote an agrarian planning and reconversion and forestry development policy, in accordance with the ecological and social factors that structure Portugal.

297. Article 94 rules on the elimination of very large estates. It provides that the law shall regulate the resizing of farming units that are excessively large from the point of view of the agricultural policy objectives, and in the case of expropriation, shall provide for the right of each owner to the corresponding compensation and to the retention of an area sufficient enough to ensure the viability and rationality of his/her own farm.[398]

298. In contrast, Article 95 rules on the resizing of small farms. It sets forth that the state shall promote the resizing of farming units that are smaller than those suitable from the point of view of the agricultural policy objectives, particularly through

396. Data from 2008, according to UN Statistic Divisions, <http://unstats.un.org/unsd/environment/agriculturalland.htm>.
397. The participation of rural workers and farmers in drawing up the agricultural policy shall be ensured via the organizations that represent them (Article 98 CRP).
398. Expropriated land shall be handed over for either ownership or holding, as laid down by law, to small farmers – preferably family farming units, to rural workers' or small farmers' cooperatives, or to other forms of worker operation (without prejudice to an experimental period in order to determine whether the land in question is being used effectively and rationally).

legal, fiscal, and credit incentives for their structural or merely economic integration, particularly in a cooperative form, or by measures designed to join parcels of land together.[399] Law 111/2015, of 27 August, has modernized the legal regime of dimension and structure of land estates.[400]

299. Article 66 of the CRP, concerning the environment and quality of life, provides that everyone is entitled to a healthy and ecologically balanced human living environment and has the duty to defend it. In order to ensure enjoyment of the right to the environment within an overall framework of sustainable development, the state shall be charged with, for example, conducting and promoting town and country planning with a view to a correct location of activities, balanced social and economic development, and the enhancement of the landscape; creating and developing natural and recreational reserves and parks, and classifying and protecting landscapes and places, in such a way as to guarantee the conservation of nature and the preservation of cultural values and assets that are of historic or artistic interest; promoting the rational use of natural resources, while safeguarding their ability to renew themselves and maintain ecological stability, with respect for the principle of inter-generational solidarity; and, in cooperation with local authorities, promoting the environmental quality of rural settlements and urban life, particularly on the architectural level and as regards the protection of historic zones.

300. Article 96 of the CRP imposes the law to regulate the rental and other forms of use of non-owned land in such a way as to guarantee the farmers' security and legitimate interests. The legal regime of lease contracts concerning rural premises is to be found in DL 294/2009, of 13 October.[401]

301. The fee-farming [*aforamento*] and colony [*colonia*] systems are prohibited by Article 99(2) of the CRP. The colony used to be common in Madeira, but it was extinguished by DL 47937, of 5 September 1967.[402]

---

399. Article 1380 CC sets forth a pre-emption right in favour of the owner of adjacent land who does not comply with the rules regarding the dimensions of the national rural unit [*unidade de cultura*].

400. On the subject, *see* Implementing Order 219/2016, of 9 August, as amended by Implementing Order 19/2019, of 15 January.

401. This Decree Law replaced the Legal Regime on Rural Tenancy [Regime do Arrendamento Rural], set forth by Decree Law 385/88, of 25 October, amended by Decree Law 524/99, of 10 December, and the Forest Land Tenancy Regime [Regime do Arrendamento Florestal], provided by Decree Law 394/88, of 8 November. Further in Ch. 4, §6.

402. *See* Oliveira Ascensão, *Direito Civil, Reais*, 5th ed (Coimbra: Coimbra Editora), 649–652.

Part II. Movable Property and Personal Property/Chattels

Chapter 1. General Classification

302. The Portuguese Civil Code provides the regime of property rights over tangible things, whether immovable or movable. Property law in Portugal does not consider the distinction between 'Real Property' and 'Personal Property', but rather only admits the categories of movable property and immovable property, which structure the entire legal regime.

303. The Portuguese Civil Code does not set down a closed list of things to be considered as movable. On the contrary, Article 205 of the CC sets forth an open clause: by default, everything that is not listed as an immovable in Article 204 is considered as movable.[403]

The significance of the object of the right of property (or any other real right) being movable or immovable has already been pointed out. As a general principle, immovable property receives a more severe treatment, which is justified because traditionally, the same was considered more valuable.

Article 205(2) provides that movables subject to registration remain under the general regime of movable things, unless regulated otherwise.

403. *See* paras 105 to 118.

Chapter 2. Legal Interests

§1. General Introduction

304. In Portugal, the distinction between legal interests and equitable interests is not known. Under the Portuguese legal system all property rights over movable property are legal interests, in the twofold sense that they have a statutory origin, and that they have a general efficacy by which they become enforceable against third parties. Real rights entitle their holders to a direct and immediate power over a thing, and the holders' power is endowed with an *erga omnes* efficacy, the power to exclude others from the use or other benefits of the thing.

I. The Registry of Movable Goods

305. In Portugal, specific chattels such as ships (Decrees 42644[404] and 42645,[405] of 14 November 1959), airships (Decree 13357 of 27 April 1927 and Decree 20062 of 25 October 1930),[406] motor vehicles (Decrees-Laws 54/75 and 55/75, of 12 February),[407] and commercial establishments (Commercial Registration Code)[408] are subject to registration.

DL 277/95, of 25 October, aimed at establishing a single and general public system of registration of movable property. However, it has not yet been regulated, and therefore it is not yet implemented.

II. Possession of Movable Goods

306. Possession has always fulfilled a significant role towards acquiring the legal publicity of property and limited real rights on movable goods, since it is a means of proving the existence of these rights before third parties. While in the field of immovable goods possession performs a secondary function, as the legal publicity is mainly implemented through the recording of the rights in the Land Registry, in the sphere of movable property, because of its fewer probabilities of identification and individualization, publicity rests mainly on the possession.

The analysis made in paragraphs 128–130 about possession of immovable goods applies, *mutatis mutandis*, to movable property.

---

404. As amended by DL 290/84, of 27 August, and by DL 403/86, of 3 December.
405. *See* DL 323/2001, of 17 December, and Implementing Order 528/98, of 17 August.
406. *See* Menezes Cordeiro, *Tratado De Direito Civil Português I-* Parte Geral, II- Coisas, 3rd edn (Coimbra: Almedina, 2005), 143–146.
407. As amended. DL 54/75 last amended by Law 30/2017, of 30 May. DL 55/75 last amended by DL 201/2015, of 17 September.
408. DL 403/86, of 3 December, as amended (last amendment by Law 89/2017, of 21 August).

§2. Ownership

307. The definition of ownership, as provided in Article 1305 of the CC, applies also to movable things. Ownership can be defined as an individual right endowed with real efficacy and characterized as a result of its all-embracing content, that is, full powers of enjoying and disposing of a good, within the limits set out by law.

The term 'disposing of' encompasses the owner's power to alienate and encumber the object of ownership (*ius disponendi*). As for 'alienation', it must be understood to imply any kind of act by means of which property can be transferred from one person to another (e.g., sale, exchange, donation, contribution of goods to a company, last will), while 'encumbrance' means the constitution of any limited real right over a thing, whether it is a right of enjoyment (e.g., usufruct, right of use) or a right of guarantee (e.g., pledge). The owner may also transfer the goods by means of inheritance rules. The owner may also voluntarily renounce his/her right, either in favour of a specific person, in which case the renunciation will normally be done onerously, or without the aim of favouring any specific person, as is the case when the owner of movable goods abandons them, enabling those goods to become a *res nullius*.[409]

The characteristics of the rights of ownership, as described in Chapter 3 of the General Introduction, fully apply to movable goods.

§3. Limited Real Rights

308. Ownership over movable goods might be compressed by limited real rights. Limited real rights can be classified into three groups, as follows: rights of use, guarantee rights, and rights of acquisition. Rights of use entitle the holder with some power of use/enjoyment of someone else's goods, for example, a usufruct. Guarantee real rights, for example, a pledge, are constituted to ensure the fulfilment of an obligation. They grant the holder the power to demand the compulsory sale of another person's goods (the goods given as guarantee), as well as to apply the price so obtained in order to satisfy his/her right of credit. Real rights to acquire a property, which are effective against third parties, might be legally foreseen (e.g., the pre-emption right, that is, *rights* in rem to acquire real property, of the tenant[410] or the joint-owner)[411] or can be agreed upon in a contract.

309. Although limited real rights may pertain to both immovable and movable goods, and the applicable regulation is basically the same, some nuances must be taken into account, as follows:

There are some limited real rights that may only have as object immovable goods. It is so in the case of building and planting rights, habitation, as well as easements. On the contrary, other real rights have exclusively movable nature, as for example

---

409. *See* Articles 1318 and 1267(1)(a) CC.
410. Article 1091 CC.
411. Article 1409 CC.

the pledge. Finally, there are limited real rights that may have as object both movable and immovable goods (e.g., usufruct, use, and leases).

Within the group of real rights indistinctly applicable both to movable and immovable goods, statutory provisions differ depending on the right falling upon one or other kinds of things. It is, for example, in the case of leases. The ones whose objects are immovable goods are subjected to the special statutory provisions contained either in the Civil Code, in Law 6/2006, or in the Law on Rural Leases. On the contrary, the movable leases are merely subjected to the general Civil Code provisions (Articles 1022–1063 of the CC).[412]

Another instance would be of the guarantee rights, which are also subject to different legal rules depending on the [movable or immovable] nature of the goods they pertain to. Those nuances will be analysed in detail *infra*, Part V, Chapter 2.

I. Movable Limited Real Rights

310. Article 1439 of the CC defines 'usufruct' as a real right that entitles the usufructuary to use the property and to take its fruits without impairing its form or substance. A usufruct can be created by contract, by last will, by adverse possession (*usucapio*), or by legal provision.[413] For a usufruct over movable property to be enforceable against third parties, no special form is required. Only if a usufruct is created over a movable subject to registration, must the usufruct be registered to be enforceable against third parties.

311. The right of use [*direito de uso*] entitles the usuary to use the property and to take its fruits, according to his/her needs and the needs of his/her family.[414] The needs of the usuary are set according to his/her social condition.[415] Within the concept of 'family of the right holder', Article 1487 of the CC includes his/her married partner; his/her not-married children; other relatives to whom the usuary owes maintenance; and employees living with him/her.

312. The right of use can be created by contract, by last will, or by legal provision. Law 7/2001, of 11 May,[416] that regulates the legal status of two persons, regardless of gender, who live together in a de facto union for more than two years, provides a special regime for termination of the relation in the event of the death of one of the partners. It entitles the surviving partner to a real right of use of the content (furniture and accessories for use, comfort, and decoration) of the house, during a minimum period of five years.

412. *See* Part I, Ch. 4, §6.
413. Article 1449 CC.
414. Article 1484(1) CC.
415. Article 1486 CC.
416. As amended by Law 23/2010, of 30 October.

II. Leasehold Interests

313. The general rules on leases (*locatio*) over movable property are found in Articles 1022 to 1063 CC.[417] A lease is a contract whereby one party (lessor) grants another party (lessee) the use of movable property for a certain period of time, in return for payment of a rent. Thus, the essential terms of a contract of lease are the identification of the parties, the property to be leased and the rent.

A. In General

314. The lease grants its holder the right to temporarily use another person's goods, in exchange for a definite price. The lessee is obliged to pay the lessor a price –the rent – in exchange for the temporary use of the leased object.[418] The Civil Code states the principle of freedom in fixing the minimum length of the right, and it imposes no mandatory prolongation for the benefit of the lessee.

315. Under the Portuguese Civil Code, the main obligations of the lessor are to transfer the property to the lessee and to ensure that it can be used in accordance with the purpose of the contract.[419] The lessor must tolerate such use and is not allowed to act in a manner that would prevent or restrict it.

316. If a movable is leased, it must be delivered to the lessee in a good condition, unless the contrary is stipulated in the contract. Article 1043(2) of the CC provides a presumption in favour of the lessor that the good was in good condition at the time of delivery if there is no document attached to the contract which describes the condition of the property at the date of transfer.

The lessee's duties include a duty to allow the lessor to inspect the building, to take care of the property and to exercise his/her rights with due diligence. The lessor is also allowed to execute urgent repairs to the property.[420]

Article 1038(c) and (d) of the CC set forth that the lessee must use the goods diligently, according to the purpose for which they have been leased. The lessee is obliged (and consequently responsible for the repairs necessary) to maintain the property in the same condition he/she received it in, with allowance being made for fair wear and tear.[421] The lessee is obliged to preserve the leased object, and to return it at the end of the contract in the same state the object was in when the lease

417. Those Articles also set forth, by default, the legal regime of tenancy contracts over immovable.
418. Article 1038(a) CC.
419. Article 1031 CC.
420. Article 1038 CC.
421. Articles 1043(1) and 1044.

began.[422] As long as the lessee exploits the property with the care of a *bonus paterfamilias* (Article 1043 of the CC) and in accordance with the purpose of the contract, he/she is not responsible for any damage caused to the property. Therefore, the lessee is not in charge of repairing, replacing, or renewing it before the property is returned to the lessor.

Repairs necessary to maintain the object must be paid by the lessor. The lessee must communicate to the lessor, as soon as possible, the need to carrying out those repairs. Otherwise, he/she will be liable for damages caused to the owner as a result of his/her negligence.[423]

317. According to Article 1038(f) of the CC, the lessee is not entitled to grant anyone the total or partial use of the leased property or to cede his/her rights gratuitously or for consideration by subletting the property or lending it out for use, except if permitted by law or authorized by the lessor. When authorized by the lessor or permitted by law, the lessee has a duty to inform the lessor within fifteen days that he/she has granted the use of the property to another.[424] Notification is required but it does not demand a specific form. Failure to notify entitles the lessor to terminate the contract.

Article 1062 of the CC provides that the rent received from a sub-lease may not be more than 20% above the principal rent. If a higher rent is contracted, the lessor is entitled to cancel the lease. The sub-lease will terminate with the expiry of the principal lease.

318. Article 1046 of the CC implicitly allows the lessee to carry out works to improve the leased object. If the improvements aim at preventing the loss or destruction of the good, the lessee has the right to compensation. If the improvements increased the value of the thing, these improvements may be withdrawn by the lessee at the end of the contract, provided that no damage will be caused to the leased object.[425] Otherwise, the lessee has a right to compensation according to the rules of unjust enrichment. Improvements that are not necessary or useful, but are voluptuous, cannot be withdrawn nor can they provide any right to compensation.[426]

319. The position of a lessee is governed by the maxim '*emptio non tollit locatum*' enshrined in Article 1057 of the CC. This maxim provides that sale does not supersede lease. As a result, any person acquiring the rights of the lessor will succeed to the rights and obligations of his/her predecessor and would thus have to allow the lessee, without prejudice to the registration provisions, to enjoy his/her

---

422. The lessee is obliged to preserve the leased object, and to return it at the end of the contract in the same state the object was when the lease started (Article 1030(i) CC). The lessee suffers the burden of proving that the object was already impaired when received by his/her, since the Civil Code assumes that the object has been delivered to him/her in a good condition (Article 1043(2) CC).
423. Article 1038(h) CC.
424. Article 1038(g) CC.
425. Articles 216(3) and 1273(2) CC.
426. Articles 216(3) CC and 1275(2) CC.

lease for the remaining period. Although the maxim refers specifically to sale, it covers all kinds of alienations such as legacy, donation, or the constitution of a usufruct.

B. Finance Leasing

320. In Portuguese law, the legal regime of the contract of finance leasing is set by DL 149/95, of 24 June.[427]

By means of this 'leasing' contract, a company obliges itself to give another undertaking the use of goods (normally industrial vehicles and machinery) for a definite period of time, in exchange for a periodical fee.[428] At the end of the agreed period, the user must choose from among the following options: (a) to renew the contract laying down the payment of a smaller fee; (b) to return the goods to the leasing company; (c) to acquire the goods by a remaining price fixed in advance.[429]

§4. Intellectual Property Rights

321. The Portuguese Civil Code only provides the regime of property rights over tangible things, be either immovable or movable. Intellectual property rights are considered as intangible property, and their regulation is made in autonomous legislation.

322. Intellectual property rights are individual rights which entitle their holder to exercise the several powers and faculties legally endorsed and to exclude others from them. They are fundamental rights recognized by the Constitution.[430]

323. Intellectual property law, in Portugal, refers distinctly to copyright and industrial property rights. Article 1302 of the CC subjects both copyright and industrial property rights to special legislation and states that its provisions might be applied on a subsidiary basis to those rights when compatible with their nature and without prejudice to their special regimes. Legal literature does not provide a joint analysis of them, so I will treat them separately in the following sections.

---

427. As amended (last amendment by DL 30/2008, of 25 February).

428. *See* F. Cassiano dos Santos, *Direito Comercial* Português I (Coimbra: Coimbra Editora, 2007), 383–409, J. Engrácia Antunes, *Direito dos Contratos Comerciais* (Coimbra: Almedina, 2009), 516–520, and M. Pestana de Vasconcelos, *Direito das Garantias* 3rd ed (Coimbra: Almedina, 2019), 491 ff.

429. *See* Decision STJ, of 2 March 2010 [Process: 5662/07], available at http://www.dgsi.pt/jstj.nsf/954f0ce6ad9dd8b980256b5f003fa814/47970f4fe075344e802576da00451cdb?OpenDocument.

430. Article 42(2) CRP.

I. Copyright

324. Property rights of authors over their own texts were recognized in the Constitution of 1838 and first regulated by Decree of 8 July 1851.[431] The Civil Code of 1867 contained several provisions protecting literary and artistic works. Those rules were replaced by Decree 13725 of 27 May 1927, concerning the protection of literary and artistic works and establishing a permanent property right over those kinds of works. A new Code was approved in 1966, by DL 46980 of 27 April, in order to meet the principles of the Berne Convention of 1886 and the Universal Convention on Copyright, signed in Genève in 1952. In accordance with this, this Code re-established the time-limited protection of author's rights (fifty years after death) and recognized the exclusive right of authors to the economic exploitation of their works.

325. Actually, the core of the legal regime of copyright is to be found on the Copyright and Related Rights Code (*Código dos Direitos de Autor e Direitos Conexos*, hereinafter 'CDADC'), approved by DL 63/85, of 14 March.[432] The Code is complemented by several acts, for example, regulating software and databases, special rights (namely rental rights, lending rights and the right to broadcast via satellite and to retransmit by cable) as well as other matters, including the registration of literally works, the compensation for the use of reprography and other mass production processes, and the organization, functioning and control of the collecting societies in charge of the collective management of works and of subject matter of related rights. It should also be noted that most aspects of the material protection of copyright are currently determined within the European sphere.

326. Portugal is a signatory to most of the international conventions in the field of copyright. In addition to adhesion to the Paris Act of 1971 of the Berne Convention in 1911 Portugal is also part of the Universal Convention of 1956. In 2002, the adhesion to the Rome Convention of 1961 on the protection of artists, phonogram producers and broadcasting organizations, was formalized. Portugal is also a contracting party to the Agreement on Trade-Related Aspects of Intellectual Property Rights (TRIPS) and to the WIPO Treaties (WIPO Copyright Treaty and WIPO Performances and Phonograms Treaty).

A. The Scope of Protection

327. The CDADC protects intellectual creations in the literary, scientific and artistic fields, in whatever form, and independent of its disclosure, publication, use

431. For a general overview, *see* Cláudia Trabuco, 'Intellectual Property Rights', in *Portuguese Law – an Overview*, ed. C. Ferreira de Almeida, Assunção Cristas & Nuno Piçarra (Coimbra: Almedina, 2007), 216–217.
432. As amended (last amendment by 100/2017, of 23 August).

or exploitation. According to Article 2, reference to original works,[433] whatever their type, form of expression, merits, mode of communication or objective, includes, in particular: (a) books, pamphlets, magazines, newspapers and other writings; (b) lectures, lessons, addresses and sermons; (c) dramatic and dramatic-musical works and their production; (d) works of choreography or mime which are expressed in written or any other form; (e) musical compositions, with or without words; (f) cinematographic, television, phonographic, video and radio phonic works; (g) works of drawing, tapestry, painting, sculpture, pottery, glazed tiles, engraving, lithography and architecture; (h) photographic works and works produced by processes analogous to photography; (i) works of applied art, industrial designs, and works of design that constitute artistic creations, whether or not protected as industrial property; (j) illustrations and geographical maps; (k) plans, sketches and three-dimensional works concerning architecture,[434] town planning, geography or other sciences; (l) emblems or slogans, even if used for advertising, provided that they show originality; (m) parodies and other literary or musical compositions, even if inspired by the theme or subject of another work.

The protection granted to a work shall extend to its title, whether or not it is registered, provided that it is original and that it cannot be confused with the title of any other work of the same nature by another author which has previously been disclosed or published. Such protection shall not apply to the following: (a) titles consisting of the generic, necessary or habitual designation of the subject matter of works of a certain kind; (b) titles consisting solely of the names of historical, historic-dramatic or literary and mythological personages, or of the names of living persons.[435]

Titles of newspapers or other periodicals shall be protected, provided that the latter are published regularly, subject to due registration in the relevant section of the register of the governmental department responsible for social communications. The title protected may be used for a similar publication one year after expiry of the right to publication, communicated in any manner, or three years after cessation of publication.

328. CDADC distinguishes between published and disclosed works. A published work shall mean a work reproduced with the consent of its author, provided

433. The fundamental requirement for the defence of a work within the framework of copyright is its original nature. This means that the work must present a minimum level if creativity and individuality, which varies considerably from work to work. Article 3 CDADC lists a series of works that shall be deemed to be original works: *(a)* translations, arrangements, instrumentations, dramatizations, cinematographic and other transformations of a work, even if it has not been the subject of protection; *(b)* summaries and collections of works, whether protected or not, such as selections, encyclopaedias and anthologies which, by reason of the selection or arrangement of their contents, constitute intellectual creations; *(c)* systematic or annotated collections of texts of conventions, laws, regulations, decrees, administrative or legal decisions, or decisions by anybody or authority of the State or administration. The protection granted to these works shall not prejudice the rights recognized to the authors of the corresponding original work.

434. *See* Decision of the Supreme Court of 5 July 2012 [Process: 855/07], available at http://www.dgsi.pt/jstj.nsf/954f0ce6ad9dd8b980256b5f003fa814/d9a725015751bf4980257a3800313abd?OpenDocument.

435. Article 4 CDADC.

that copies are effectively made available to the public, taking into account the nature of the work. The use or disclosure of a work that does not constitute reproduction shall not constitute publication. A disclosed work shall mean a work which has been lawfully brought to the knowledge of the public by any means such as the performance of a dramatic, dramatic-musical or cinematographic work, the performance of a musical work, public recitation of a literary work, transmission or broadcasting, construction of an architectural work and exhibition of an artistic work.

329. Intellectual property rights are intangible goods, which require embodiment of substance and form. Article 10(1) CDADC provides for carriers of works. Since it is incorporeal, copyright in a work shall be independent of the right of ownership in the material objects used for its fixing or communication.

B. Attribution of Copyright

330. Unless otherwise specified, copyright shall belong to the intellectual creator of the work. Copyright shall be recognized independently of registration, filing, or any other formality.[436] Any person who has in any way, either totally or partially, subsidized or financed the preparation, conclusion, disclosure, or publication of a work do not thereby obtain any of the powers derived from the copyright, unless there is written agreement to the contrary.

331. The code establishes and regulates some special cases of entitlement. According to Article 14 of the CDADC, copyright in a work carried out on commission or on behalf of another person, either in fulfilment of official duties or under an employment contract, shall be determined in accordance with the relevant agreement. In the absence of any agreement, it shall be deemed that ownership of copyright in a work carried out on behalf of another person belongs to the intellectual creator. Where the name of the creator is not mentioned in the work or is not shown in the customary place, it shall be deemed that the copyright remains the property of the person or entity on whose behalf the work is carried out.

332. As provided in Article 16 of the CDADC, a work is of joint authorship, when it has been disclosed or published under the names of all or some of the co-authors, whether or not it is possible to distinguish their individual contributions.[437]

Copyright in a work of joint authorship as a whole shall belong to all those who collaborated therein and the joint exercise of this right shall be subject to the regulations governing joint ownership. Unless parties agree otherwise and in writing, the indivisible parts belonging to the co-authors of the work shall be deemed to be of equal value. Authors of a work of joint authorship hold several rights, namely, any

436. Article 11 CDADC.

437. An aleatory work of art in which creative contributions by one or more performers were originally envisaged shall be considered a work of joint authorship.

of them may request the disclosure, publication, exploitation, or modification of the work of joint authorship; any disagreements shall be settled according to the principles of good faith.[438]

333. As regards collective works carried out by a single or collective entity and has been disclosed or published in its name, Article 19 CDADC provides that copyright shall belong to the single or collective entity[439] that has organized and directed its creation and in whose name the work has been disclosed or published. Where it is possible to distinguish the individual contributions of some or all of the authors in a collective work, the provisions on individual contributions to works of joint authorship cited above shall apply.

334. A work incorporating all or part of a pre-existing work with the consent, but without the collaboration, of its author shall be deemed to be a composite work.[440] The rights pertaining to a composite work shall belong exclusively to its author, without prejudice to the rights of the author of the pre-existing work. Copyright law also provides specific solutions for broadcast works,[441] cinematographic works;[442] phonographic and video graphic works;[443] and works of architecture, town planning, and design.[444]

C. Duration

335. Article 31 of the CDADC provides that copyright shall lapse seventy years after the death of the creator of the work, even in the case of works disclosed or published posthumously. Copyright in works of joint authorship, as a whole, shall lapse seventy years after the death of the last surviving author. Unless otherwise provided, copyright in collective works or in works originally attributed to a collective entity shall lapse seventy years after the first disclosure or publication. With regard to individual contribution that can be distinguished, the duration of copyright attributed to each author in works of joint authorship or in collective works shall be in conformity with the duration of seventy years.

Article 33 foresees that the duration of protection of anonymous works or works lawfully disclosed or published without any author being indicated shall be seventy years following disclosure or publication. Where the use of a name other than the author's own leaves no doubt as to the author's identity or if his/her identity is

438. Article 18(1) CDADC.
439. Newspapers and other periodicals shall be deemed to be collective works and the copyright therein shall belong to the respective enterprises.
440. Cf. Article 20 CDADC.
441. Article 21 CDADC.
442. Articles 22–23 CDADC.
443. Article 24 CDADC.
444. Articles 25 and 26 CDADC.

revealed within the period referred to in the preceding paragraph, the duration of protection shall be that granted to works disclosed or published in the author's own name.[445]

336. The dates of lapsing referred are calculated from the first day of the year following that in which the period of protection ended. A work shall fall into the public domain upon expiry of the periods of protection of copyright.

D. The Content of Copyright

337. Copyright shall include economic rights and personal rights, termed moral rights.[446]

In the exercise of economic rights, the author shall have the exclusive right to dispose of his/her work, to exploit it, to use it, or to authorize its total or partial exploitation or use by a third party. The author has the right to exploit the work economically, either directly or through a third party. The law confers upon the author the right to choose the processes and conditions of use of the work and establishes a non-exhaustive list of possible forms of economic exploitation. Among these forms, are the right to produce, the right to distribute, rent, and publicly lend material copies; the right to communicate the work to the public; and recent uses allowed by information technology networks. The exclusive economic right of the author is circumscribed by several limitations in order to promote social interests, such as the promotion of public information, research, education, and culture, or to safeguard rights and liberties of other individuals, such as the freedom of expression and the right to private life. The Code enumerates several free uses, which are not subject to the author's consent, even though some of them entail payment of a fair compensation to the holder of the right.[447]

A copyright encompasses both personal elements, connected with the author's personality, and economic elements, related to the exploitation of the work's economic potential. The moral rights of the author are independent from the economic rights, and remain within the author even after the transmission or extinction of the latter rights.[448] Independently of economic rights, and even after their transfer or lapse, the author shall enjoy moral rights in his/her work, in particular the right to claim authorship and to ensure its authenticity and integrity. Independent of his/her

445. The Directive 2011/77/EU of the European Parliament and of the Council, of 27 September 2011, amending Directive 2006/116/EC, on the term of protection of copyright and certain related rights, has been implemented by Law 82/2013, of 6 December.

446. *See* Decision of the STJ of 17 November 2011 [Process: 103/04], available at http://www.dgsi.pt/jstj.nsf/954f0ce6ad9dd8b980256b5f003fa814/1bbd6fc9368417c68025795a0051d548?OpenDocument.

447. *See* Cláudia Trabuco, 'Intellectual Property Rights', in *Portuguese Law – an Overview*, ed. C. Ferreira de Almeida, Assunção Cristas & Nuno Piçarra (Coimbra: Almedina, 2007), 220–221. *See* Decision of Suprem Court of 29 April 2010 [Process: 3501/05], at http://www.dgsi.pt/jstj.nsf/954f0ce6ad9dd8b980256b5f003fa814/e4b42bb734c51b9e8025771f004ef43f?OpenDocument.

448. *Ibid. See* Decision of the STJ of 23 September 2013 [Process: 5509/09], available at http://www.dgsi.pt/jstj.nsf/954f0ce6ad9dd8b980256b5f003fa814/309b569aabe29d5680257bf30038c89d?OpenDocument.

economic rights, and even if they have been transferred or assigned, during his/her lifetime the author shall enjoy the right to claim authorship of his/her work and to ensure its authenticity and integrity by challenging any mutilation, distortion, or other modification thereof and, in general, or opposing to any act that might jeopardize to his/her honour and reputation. This right shall be perpetual, inalienable, and imprescriptible and shall continue after the death of the author in accordance with the CDADC. The author of a disclosed or published work may at any time withdraw it from circulation and may terminate its use in any form, provided that he/she has justifiable moral reasons. Nevertheless, he/she shall compensate the interested parties for damages.

E. Transfer and Assignment of the Economic Content of Copyright

338. Powers granted for the enforcement of moral rights may not be the subject of either voluntary or compulsory transfer or assignment.

The original owner of the copyright, as well as his/her successors or transferees, may authorize use of the work by a third party, or transfer or assign all or part of the economic content of the work's copyright. The authorization referred to must be in writing, and shall be considered non-exclusive and for consideration. The written document must specify the authorized form of disclosure, publication, and use, as well as the relevant conditions of duration, place, and remuneration. Simple authorization granted to a third party to disclose, publish, use, or exploit a work in any way shall not imply transfer of copyright in the work.

339. According to Article 44 of the CDADC, the total and permanent transfer of the economic content of copyright requires public deed, or a certificated private document, identifying the work and indicating the relevant remuneration.

340. The law also regulates the partial transfer or assignment of copyright. Such contracts shall consist of a written document bearing signatures witnessed by a notary. The transfer deed shall show the rights that are the subject of the provisions and conditions for their exercise, namely, the duration and place of exercise and, where payment is involved, the amount of the remuneration. Where the transfer or assignment is temporary and no duration has been laid down, it shall be considered that the maximum duration shall be twenty-five years in general and ten years in the case of works of photography. The exclusive right granted may lapse after a period of seven years if the work has not been used.

341. Copyright may be the subject of legal or voluntary usufruct,[449] may be offered as security,[450] and may be the subject of seizure or attachment.[451] In cases of attachment, where the purchaser of copyright in an unpublished work decides to publish it, the right to revise the proofs, to correct the work and, in general, the

449. Article 45 CDADC.
450. Article 46 CDADC.
451. Article 47 CDADC.

moral rights, shall not be affected. If the author retains the proofs without justification for a period exceeding sixty days, the printer may proceed without the revision.[452]

Article 50 of the CDADC provides that unpublished manuscripts, sketches, drawings, paintings, or sculptures, whether signed or not, shall be exempt from seizure and attachment when they are unfinished unless the author offers them or consents thereto. Where the author, by his/her direct acts, shows his/her intention to disclose or publish the works referred to above, the creditor may obtain seizure and attachment of the corresponding copyright.

An author who has transferred an original work of art that is neither a work of architecture nor applied art, his/her own manuscript, or copyright in his/her own work, has the right to a participation of 6% in the remuneration for each subsequent transaction. This right is perpetual, inalienable, and imprescriptible.[453]

F. Use of Works

342. An author shall have the exclusive right to enjoy and use his/her work, either in whole or in part, including, in particular, the right to disclose, publish, and exploit it economically in any direct or indirect form within the limits set by law. From the economic point of view, the guarantee of the pecuniary benefits resulting from such exploitation shall constitute the basic objective of legal protection.

Article 68 provides that exploitation and, in general, use of the work can be implemented, according to its type and nature, in any form whether currently known or not. The author shall, *inter alia*, have the exclusive right to carry out or to authorize the following, either by himself/herself or by his/her representatives: (a) publication, either by printing or by any other method of graphic reproduction; (b) performance, recitation, execution, exhibition, or display to the public; (c) cinematographic reproduction, adaptation, performance, execution, distribution, and projection; (d) fixing or adapting any apparatus used for mechanical, electric, electronic, or chemical reproduction and public performance, transmission or retransmission by such means; (e) diffusion by photography, telephotography, television, radio, or by any other process for reproducing signals, sounds, or images, as well as public communication by loudspeaker or analogous instruments, whether by wire or not, in particular, by Hertzian waves, optical fibre, cable, or satellite, when such communication is carried out by an organization other than the original one; (f) direct or indirect appropriation in any form such as the sale or rental of copies of the work reproduced; (g) translation, adaptation, arrangement, instrumentation, or any other transformation of the work; (h) use in another work; (i) total or partial reproduction by any means; (j) construction of an architectural work according to a plan, whether or not it is a repetition.

The owner of the copyright shall have the exclusive right to decide freely upon the procedures and conditions of the work's use and exploitation.

---

452. Article 61 CDADC.
453. Cf. Article 54 CDADC.

343. Powers related to the administration of copyright may be exercised by the holder of the copyright himself/herself or through his/her duly authorized representative. National or foreign associations and organizations established for the administration of copyright shall carry out this function as agents of the respective copyright owners, either because the author is a member thereof or is registered as a beneficiary of their services.

344. Article 75 provides a list of lawful uses of a work that do not require the consent of the author, such as the following: regular selections of press articles in the form of press reviews; fixing, reproduction, and public communication by any means of short excerpts from literary or artistic works when their use in news stories is justified for information purposes; partial or total reproduction by photography or by an analogous process of a work that has previously been made available to the public, provided that such reproduction is carried out by a public library, a non-commercial documentation centre or a scientific institution, and also provided that such reproduction and the corresponding number of copies are not for public use and are limited to the requirements of such institutions' activities; inclusion of quotations or summaries from another author's work, whatever their type or nature, in support of one's own opinions or for purposes of criticism, discussion, or teaching. Such use is subject to the indication of the author's name, the work's title, and other identifying features, and in certain situations to the payment of equitable remuneration to the author. In any case, the works reproduced or quoted shall not be liable to confusion with the works in which they are being used and the reproduction or quotation shall not be so extensive that they prejudice interest in such works.

Article 81 allows the reproduction of the following: (a) one copy, for purposes of exclusively scientific or humanitarian interest, of works not commercially available or impossible to obtain, for the period necessary for their use; (b) for exclusively private use, provided that it does not harm normal exploitation of the work nor cause unjustified prejudice to the author's legitimate interests, and that the reproduction is not used for any purposes of public communication or commercialization.

II. Industrial Property

345. Decree of 16 January 1837, regulating the property of new inventions, was the first act concerning industrial property law in Portugal.[454] This law was replaced by a Decree of 31 December 1852, which was partially revoked by the Civil Code of 1867. Trademarks were first regulated in 1833. In 1894, industrial property was for the first time assembled in a single legal statute. The first Industrial Property Code dates of 1940 (Decree 30679 of 4 August 1940), and was replaced by the 1995 Industrial Property Code (DL 16/95, of 24 January). The essential principles and rules concerning industrial property law were, them, to be found in the Industrial

454. For a general overview, *see* Cláudia Trabuco, 'Intellectual Property Rights', in *Portuguese Law – an Overview*, ed. C. Ferreira de Almeida, Assunção Cristas & Nuno Piçarra (Coimbra: Almedina, 2007), 222–223.

Property Code (*Código da Propriedade Industrial*, hereinafter 'CPI'), approved by DL 36/2003, of 5 March. A new Code was approved by DL 110/2018, of 10 December.[455] Portugal was one of the founders of the Paris Convention for the Protection of Industrial Property of 1883. In 1994, Portugal ratified the specific annex of the Agreement that created the World Trade Organization (WTO), which established relevant mechanisms aiming at the effective enforcement of intellectual property rights.

A. *The Scope of Protection: Function and Effects*

346. Private rights protected by the Industrial Property Code can be divided into two major categories: the protection of innovations, and the protection of signs and business goodwill.[456] The CPI defines the following as industrial property: patents, utility models, topography of semiconductors models, designs or models, trademarks, awards, trade names and insignias, logotypes, appellations of origin, and geographic indications.

According to Article 1 of the CPI, the function of industrial property is to guarantee fair competition by awarding private rights over technical processes of production and the development of wealth. As a general principle, the granting of industrial property rights entails a mere legal assumption of the requirements for granting them. Registration of awards guarantees the veracity and authenticity of ownership and guarantees their owners exclusive use for an indefinite time. Registration of trademarks, logotypes, appellations of origin, and geographical indications, are grounds for refusal or annulment of company names that may be confused with them, if the applications for authorization or alteration are submitted later than the applications for registration.[457]

Article 6 of the CPI sets forth that the rights emerging from patents and utility models and registrations of topographies of semiconductor products, designs or models, trademarks, and other distinctive trade signs are subject to attachment and seizure and may be attached or subject to other legal forms of confiscation of property.

B. *Transfer and Licences*

347. Article 30 of the CPI provides that the rights emerging from patents, utility models, registrations of topographies of semiconductor products, designs or models, and trademarks can be transferred free of charge or against consideration. If a

455. Implementing Directive (EU) 2015/2436 of the European Parliament and of the Council of 16 December 2015 to approximate the laws of the Member States relating to trade marks, and Directive (EU) 2016/943 of the European Parliament and of the Council of 8 June 2016 on the protection of undisclosed know-how and business information (trade secrets) against their unlawful acquisition, use and disclosure.

456. *See* Cláudia Trabuco, 'Intellectual Property Rights', in *Portuguese Law – an Overview*, ed. C. Ferreira de Almeida, Assunção Cristas & Nuno Piçarra (Coimbra: Almedina, 2007), 224.

457. Article 4 CPI.

logotype or trademark contains the name of the holder's individual, business, or company of or the name of the applicant for registration or his representative, a clause is necessary for its transfer.

A transfer between living persons shall be proven by a written document. However, if the annotation of the transfer is requested by the transferring party, the recipient must also sign the document supporting it or make a statement accepting the transfer.

The same rights may also be subject to a total or partial exploitation license, free of charge or in return for payment, in a certain area or throughout the country for the whole of their duration or for a shorter time. License contracts must be drawn up in writing, and shall be understood to be non-exclusive.[458]

Unless otherwise stipulated, a right obtained in an exploitation license cannot be transferred without the written consent of the holder of the right. If the grant of sub-licenses is not provided for in the license contract, they may only be granted with the written authorization of the holder of the right.

C. Extinction of Industrial Property Rights

348. According to Article 36, industrial property rights shall automatically expire when their duration terminates or on default of fees payment. Holders may renounce to their industrial property rights, provided that they so expressly declare to the National Industrial Property Institute.

D. Patents

349. Article 50 of the CPI provides that new inventions involving inventive activity can be patented if they have an industrial use, even if they apply to a product consisting of or containing biological material or to a process that produces, treats or uses biological material. Patents may be obtained for any inventions, be they products or processes, in all fields of technology. An invention is considered new if it does not form part of the state of the art. An invention shall be considered as involving an inventive step if, having regard to the state of the art, it is not obvious to a person skilled in the art; and it shall be considered as susceptible of industrial application if it can be made or used in any kind of industry or in agriculture.

New processes for obtaining known products, substances, or compositions may also be patented. The following are the exceptions: (a) discoveries, scientific theories and mathematical methods; (b) materials or substances already existing in nature and nuclear materials; (c) aesthetic creations; (d) schemes, rules or methods for intellectual acts, playing a game or doing business and computer programs, as such, with no contributions; (e) presentations of information.

---

458. An exclusive license is one in which the holder of the right renounces the faculty to grant other licenses for the rights covered by the license while it remains in effect. The grant of an exclusive exploitation license does not prevent the holder from also directly exploiting the right in the license, unless otherwise stipulated.

Inventions whose commercial exploitation is against the law or contrary to public policy, public health, or morality are not patentable and their exploitation may not be considered as such. The following are not patentable, among others: processes for cloning human beings, processes for modifying the germinal genetic identity of human beings, the use of human embryos for industrial or commercial purposes.[459]

The duration of a patent is twenty years from date of application.[460] While a patent is in effect, its holder may use the words 'patented [patenteado]' 'patent no. [patente n.º]' or 'Pat no.Pat n.º ' on the product.

1. Entitlement to the Right to Patent

350. As a general rule on the right to patent, the same shall belong to the inventor or his/her successors in title. If two or more persons have made an invention, any of them may apply for a patent on behalf of all. If an invention was made during the performance of an employment contract in which inventive activity is provided for, the right to the patent belongs to the company.[461] Otherwise, the company has a pre-emptive right to the patent in return for remuneration in keeping with the importance of the invention and may assume ownership of it or reserve the right to its exclusive exploitation, acquisition of the patent or the ability to apply for or acquire a foreign patent.

351. Anyone who is liable for obligations undertaken in relation to third parties or whose patent is expropriated in the public interest may be deprived of a patent. Any patent may be expropriated in the public interest on payment of fair compensation, if the need for dissemination of the invention or use by public bodies so requires (Article 105 of the CPI).[462]

2. Extent of Protection and Rights Conferred by a Patent

352. According to Article 97 of the CPI, the extent of the protection conferred by a patent shall be determined by the content of the claims, the description, and the drawings which serve to interpret them. If a patent concerns a process, the rights conferred by it shall cover the products obtained directly by the patented process.[463]

459. Article 52 CPI.
460. Article 100 CPI.
461. If the inventive activity is not especially remunerated, the inventor is entitled to remuneration. Article 60, on inventor's rights provides that if the patent is not applied for in the inventor's name, he/she has the right to be mentioned as such in the application and the patent. Only if he/she so requests in writing, may the inventor not be mentioned as such in any publications resulting from the application.
462. The CE is applicable, with the necessary adaptations.
463. CPI provides specific rules for patens on a biological material or on a process that enables a biological material to be produced.

353. A patent confers the exclusive right to exploit the invention anywhere in Portuguese territory. A patent also confers upon its holder the right to prevent others from manufacturing, offering, storing, commercializing, using, importing, or possessing a patented product for any of the aforementioned purposes without his/her consent.[464]

354. A patentee may oppose all acts constituting a violation of his/her patent, even if they merge with another patent with a later priority date, without being required to challenge titles or request annulment of patents with which this right merges. The rights conferred by a patent do not extend to the following: acts performed in private, rather than for commercial purposes; the preparation of medicinal products performed at the time and for individual cases on the basis of a doctor's prescription at pharmaceutical laboratories or acts relating to the medicinal products prepared in this way; acts performed exclusively for trial or experimental purposes, including experiments for supporting administrative processes required for the approval of products by the competent official bodies, though industrial or commercial exploitation of these products may not commence before expiry of the patent protecting them; use on board ships from other countries belonging to the EU or WTO of a patented invention in the hull, machinery, rigging, gear, or other accessories of the ship, if they temporarily or accidentally enter the waters of the country, provided that the said invention is used exclusively to serve the ship's needs; the use of a patented invention in the construction or operation of aircraft or land vehicles of other countries belonging to the EU or WTO or their accessories, if they temporarily or accidentally enter national territory; the acts set forth in Article 27 of the Convention of 7 December 1944 concerning international civil aviation if they pertain to aircraft(s) from another state to which the provisions of that article apply.[465]

According to Article 104, the rights conferred by a patent do not allow its holder to forbid acts related to the products protected by it after sale by the patentee or with his/her consent, in the European economic area (principle of exhaustion).

3. Conditions of Use

355. Article 107 provides that the patentee is obliged to exploit a patented invention directly or through an authorized person authorized and to dispose the results obtained in order to fulfil the needs of the national market.

464. *See* Decision of the Supreme Court of 20 May 2015 [Process: 747/13], available at http://www.dgsi.pt/jstj.nsf/954f0ce6ad9dd8b980256b5f003fa814/b09298597858c0ea80257e4b00540124?OpenDocument.
465. Articles 102–103 CPI.

356. Compulsory licenses may be granted for a certain patent, in any of the following cases: lack or insufficient exploitation of a patented invention;[466] dependency between patents;[467] reasons of public interest.[468] They shall be non-exclusive and may only be transferred with the part of the company or establishment that exploits them.

A compulsory license may only be granted if the potential licensee has made efforts to obtain a contractual license from the patentee on acceptable commercial conditions and the said efforts have not been successful within a reasonable period of time. It may be revoked without prejudice to the appropriate protection of the licensees' legitimate interests if and when the circumstances that gave rise to it cease to exist or are not likely to occur again. The competent authority may re-examine the continuation of said circumstances on a duly justified request. The patentee shall receive appropriate payment in each concrete case on the basis of the economic value of the license.

E. Utility Models

1. Entitlement to the Right to Utility Models

357. New inventions involving an inventive step can be protected as utility models, if they have an industrial application. An invention shall be considered new if it does not form part of the state of the art, and it shall be considered as involving an inventive step, if it meets one of the following requirements: (a) if it is not obvious to a person skilled in the art, (b) if it offers a practical or technical advantage for the manufacture or use of the product or process in question. An invention is considered as susceptible of industrial application if it can be made or used in any kind of industry or in agriculture The aim of utility models is to protect inventions by means of a simpler administrative procedure than that for patents. The same invention may be, simultaneously or successively, subject of a patent and utility model application.

Limitations as to the object of patents apply to utility models. Further, the following cannot be the object of a utility model: inventions whose commercial exploitation is against the law or contrary to public policy, public health or morality; inventions involving biological material; inventions involving chemical or pharmaceutical substances or processes.

The rules on patents concerning the entitlement of an industrial property right to apply to utility models.

The duration of a utility model shall be six years from date of application. In the last six months of the validity of a utility model, the holder may request its extension for two years. The duration of a utility model may not exceed ten years as of the date of submission of the respective application. While a utility model is in effect, its holder may use the expression 'Modelo de utilidade n.º' and 'MU nº.'

466. Article 109 CPI.
467. Article 110 CPI.
468. Article 111 CPI.

2. Extent of Protection and Rights Conferred by a Utility Model

358. The extent of the protection conferred by a utility model patent shall be determined by the content of the claims, and the description and drawings shall serve to interpret them. If a utility model concerns a process, the rights conferred by it shall cover the products obtained directly by the patented process.[469]

359. A utility model confers the exclusive right to exploit the invention anywhere in Portuguese territory.[470] If a utility model concerns a product, it entitles its holder to forbid others to manufacture, use, offer for sale, sell, or import the product for these purposes without his/her consent. If a utility model concerns a process, it entitles its holder to forbid others to use the process or use, offer for sale, sell, or import for these purposes the product directly obtained by this process.

The holder of a utility model may oppose all acts constituting a violation of his/her invention, even if they merge with another utility model with a later priority date, with no need to impugn titles or request annulment of utility models with which this right merges. The rights conferred by a utility model shall not exceed the scope defined by the claims and they do not cover acts performed in private and not for commercial purposes; and experimental acts involving the protected object.

2. Conditions of Use

360. The rules for patents apply to utility models.

F. Topography of Semiconductor Products

1. An Entitlement to Semiconductor Products and to Topographies of a Semiconductor Product

361. Article 153 of the CPI defines a 'semiconductor product' as the final or intermediate form of any product meeting all the following criteria: (a) it consists of a body of material including a layer of semiconducting material; (b) it has one or more layers composed of conducting, insulating or semiconducting materials and they are arranged in accordance with a predetermined three-dimensional pattern; and (c) it is intended to perform an electronic function, exclusively or in conjunction with other functions.

469. Article 144 CPI.
470. *See* Decision of the Supreme Court of 22 April 1999 [Process: 99B234], at http://www.dgsi.pt/jstj.nsf/Por+Ano/?SearchView&Query=FIELD%20DESCRITORES=%22PATENTE%22.

362. The topography of a semiconductor product is a set of related fixed or encoded images that represent the three-dimensional layout of the layers comprising the product, in which each image shows the layout or part of the layout of a surface of the same product in any stage of its manufacture.[471]

Only topographies of semiconductor products that result from the intellectual efforts of their creator and are not known in the semiconductor industry may be protected. Topographies consisting of elements known in the semiconductor industry may also be protected, provided that the combination of these elements, as a whole, fulfils the conditions in the previous paragraph. Protection granted to topographies of semiconductor products applies only to the topographies themselves and not to any concept, process, system, technique, or encoded information incorporated in them. Any creator of a final or intermediate topography of a semiconductor product enjoys the exclusive right to use this topography, provided that he/she meets the legal requirements, such as those regarding registration. Registration may not, however, occur two years after the first commercial exploitation, anywhere, of the topography or after the time limit of fifteen years from the date on which it was fixed or encoded for the first time, if it has never been exploited.

363. The duration of a registration is ten years from the date of application or the date on which the topography was first exploited in any location, if earlier. A registration of a topography of a semiconductor product expires as follows: ten years after the last day of the calendar year in which the registration application was formally submitted or the last day of the calendar year in which the topography was commercially exploited in any place, if earlier; if the topography has not been commercially exploited, fifteen years after the date on which it was fixed or encoded for the first time.

364. While the registration is in effect, its holder may use the upper-case letter 'T' with one of the following: T, 'T', [T], on semiconductor products manufactured through the use of protected topographies.

2. Extent of Protection and Rights Conferred by Semiconductor Products and by Topographies of a Semiconductor Product

365. According to Article 164 of the CPI, registration of a topography entitles its holder to its exclusive use throughout Portuguese territory, producing, manufacturing, selling, or exploiting the topography or objects in which it is used, with the obligation to do so effectively and in keeping with market needs. Registration of a topography also entitles its holder to authorize or forbid any of the following acts: reproduction of the protected topography; import, sale or distribution in any other form, for a commercial purpose, of protected topography of a semiconductor product in which a protected topography is incorporated, or of an article in which a semiconductor product of this type is incorporated, only to the extent that it continues to include a topography reproduced unlawfully.

---

471. Article 154 CPI.

Rights conferred by registration of a topography do not cover, e.g. the private reproduction of a topography for non-commercial purposes, or the reproduction for the purposes of analysis, assessment, or teaching.

3. Conditions of Use

366. The provisions on patents are, mutatis mutandis, applicable to topographies of semiconductor products.

G. *Designs or Models*

1. Entitlement to a Design or Model

367. Article 173 of the CPI provides that a design or model represents the appearance of a product[472] in whole or in part by virtue of such characteristics as lines, contours, colours, forms, textures, or materials used in the product itself and its ornamentation. A design or model shall be new if, before the application for registration or priority claim, no identical design or model has been disclosed to the public in Portugal or abroad. Designs or models are considered identical if their specific characteristics differ only in insignificant details. A design or model is considered to be distinctive if the overall impression that it gives to an informed user differs from the overall impression caused to that user by any model or design published prior to the date of the registration application or priority claim. Appreciation of distinctive character shall take into account the degree of freedom afforded to the creator to create the design or model.

New designs or models that are distinctive in character[473] shall have legal protection. Designs or models that are not entirely new but involve novel combinations of known elements or a different layout of elements already used in such a way as to endow their products with a distinctive character shall also have legal protection.

A design or model applied to or incorporated in a product constituting a component of a complex product is considered to be new and distinctive in character if it fulfils all the following criteria: it can reasonably be expected that even after being incorporated into the complex product, it will continue to be visible during the normal use[474] of the complex product; the visible characteristics of that component meet the requirements of novelty and distinctiveness of character.

The following are not protected by registration: (a) the visible characteristics of a product resulting exclusively from its technical function; (b) The characteristics

---

472. A product is any industrial or crafted article, including, *inter alia*, the components for assembling a complex product, packaging, presentation elements, graphic signs and typographic characters, but excluding computer programs. A complex product is any product composed of multiple components that can be removed from it for the purpose of stripping it, and replaced in it for the purpose of reassembling it.
473. *See* Articles 176 and 177 CPI.
474. Normal use shall be understood as any use made by the end user other than conservation, maintenance or repair.

of the appearance of a product that must necessarily be reproduced in their exact form and dimensions so that the product into which the industrial model or design is incorporated, or in which it is applied, be it mechanically connected to another product or inserted into, around or against the other product, so that both can perform their function.

368. The duration of registration shall be five years as of the date of application and it can be renewed for equal periods up to a maximum limit of twenty-five years.

369. While a registration is in effect the applicant may use on the products the expression '*Desenho ou modelo n.º* ' or the abbreviations *'DM n.º.'*

2. Extent of Protection and Rights Conferred by a Design or Model

370. Registration of a design or model confers on its holder the exclusive right to use it and prohibit its use by third parties without his/her consent. The use referred to in the previous paragraph particularly covers the manufacture, offer, commercializing, import, export, or use of a product in which this design or model has been incorporated or to which it has been applied, and the storage of the said product for the same purposes.

The rights conferred by registration do not cover the following: (a) acts performed in private and not for commercial purposes; (b) acts for experimental purposes; (c) acts of reproduction for the purpose of reference or for didactic purposes, provided that they are compatible with fair commercial practices, do not unduly jeopardize the normal exploitation of the design or model and that the source is mentioned; (d) equipment on board ships and aircraft registered in another country when temporarily passing through Portuguese territory; (e) the import of spare parts and accessories for these ships and aircraft; and (f) repairs to these ships and aircraft.

H. Trademarks

1. A Entitlement to a Trademark

371. According to Article 208 of the CPI, a trademark may consist of a sign or set of signs that can be represented graphically, namely words – including the names of persons, drawings, letters, numbers and sounds, the form of the product or respective packaging, provided they adequately distinguish the products and services of one company from those of others.[475] A trademark may also consist of advertising phrases for the respective products or services, provided that they are distinct in character, regardless of the protection conferred upon them by copyrights. The requirements of Article 209 are not met by the following: (a) trademarks

475. For a general overview, *see* J. Coutinho de Abreu, *Curso de Direito Comercial* I, 11th edn (Coimbra: Almedina, 2018), 354-394.

that are devoid of any distinctive character; (b) signs that exclusively consist of the form imposed by the nature of the product itself, the form of the product necessary for obtaining a technical result or the form that confers a substantial value on the product; (c) signs that are exclusively made up of indications that may serve in commerce to designate the type, quality, quantity, purpose, value, geographic origin, period or means of production of the product or the service, or other characteristics thereof; (d) trademarks that exclusively consist of signs or indications that have become common use in modern-day language or in the habitual and constant habits of commerce; (e) colours, except where they are combined with each other or with graphics, wording or other particular and distinctive elements.

Registration confers upon the holder the right of property and exclusivity of the trademark for the respective products and services for which it is designated. The state may likewise enjoy the right of property and exclusivity of the trademarks it uses, provided that it satisfies the legal provisions.

372. A collective trademark is defined as an association trademark or a certification trademark. An association trademark is a specific sign belonging to an association of natural or legal persons, the members of which use it, or intend to use it, for products or services related to the association's object. A certification trademark is a specific sign belonging to a legal person that controls the products or services or establishes standards to which the said products or services must adhere. This sign serves for use on products or services subjected to that control or for which the standards were established.

373. A registration lasts for ten years, beginning on the date of the respective grant. It may be indefinitely renewed for identical periods. During the registration's period of validity, the proprietor may use the words 'registered trademark', the initials 'R.T.' or also simply the symbol 'R' or ®.

2. Extent of Protection and Rights Conferred by a Trademark

374. Registration of a trademark confers upon the proprietor the right to prevent third parties from using an identical or similar sign without its consent in economic activities for products or services that are identical or similar to those for which the trademark was registered and which, as a result of the similarity between the signs and the affinity between the products or services, may give rise to a risk of confusion or association in the mind of the consumer.[476]

The rights granted by registration of a trademark do not entitle the proprietor to prevent third parties from using, in their economic activities, provided that it is carried out in conformity with the regulations and honest practices in industrial and commercial matters: (a) their own name and address; (b) indications relating to the

476. *See* Decisions of the Supreme Court of 9 September 2009 [Process: 118/09], at http://www.dgsi.pt/jstj.nsf/954f0ce6ad9dd8b980256b5f003fa814/87bf377d3022a5f78025762d00558222?OpenDocument, and of 11 January 2011 [Process: 627/06], at http://www.dgsi.pt/jstj.nsf/954f0ce6ad9dd8b980256b5f003fa814/24f456a7db37253a8025781700387af2?OpenDocument.

type, quality, quantity, purpose, value, geographic origin and period and means of production of the product or service or other features of the products or services; (c) the trademark, whenever this is required to indicate the purpose of a product or service, such as in the form of accessories or spare parts.[477]

375. Trademark registrations are transferable where a transfer would not mislead the public as to the origin of the product or service or as to its essential features. Whenever a transfer is partial, in terms of the products or services, a copy of the process should be requested, which will serve as the basis for an autonomous registration, including the title rights.[478] Trademarks registered to organizations that monitor or control economic activities are not transferable, except where allowed by a special legal provision.

376. The proprietor of a trademark registration may invoke the rights granted by the registration against a licensee that violates any clause or provision of the licensing contract, particularly relating to the contract's term of validity, the identity of the trademark, the nature of the products or services for which the license was granted, the demarcation of the license zone or territory or the quality of the products manufactured or services provided by the licensee.

I. Awards

377. Article 270 CPI defines awards as: (a) accolades of merit awarded by the Portuguese state or by foreign states; (b) medals, diplomas and pecuniary or any other prizes obtained at official or officially recognized exhibitions, fairs and competitions held in Portugal or in foreign countries; (c) diplomas and certificates of analysis, or praise, issued by state laboratories or agencies or organizations qualified for that purpose; (d) warrants of purveyor to heads of state, the government or other official establishments, both national and foreign; (e) any other accolades or demonstrations of preference of an official nature. Awards may not be applied to products or services other than those for which they were granted.

378. Awards of any type granted to manufacturers, traders, farmers and any other entrepreneur are their property. The use of legitimately obtained awards is permitted even if they are not registered, but only when registration has been carried out, the reference to them or copy of them can be accompanied by the designation 'Recompensa Registada' or the abbreviated forms 'R.R.' or 'RR' or 'RR'. Ownership of the awards is transferred with the legal formalities required for transfer of the assets to which they are an accessory.

477. Articles 249, 253 and 254 CPI.
478. Articles 256-257 CPI.

J. Logotype

379. Article 281 CPI sets forth that a logotype may consist of a sign or number of signs that can be represented graphically, namely by nominative or figurative elements or a combination of both. A logotype must be appropriate for distinguishing an entity that provides services or commercializes products. It can be used, for instance, in places of business, advertising, forms and correspondence.[479]

A registration remains in force during ten years, beginning on the date of the respective grant. It may be indefinitely renewed for identical periods. During the registration's period of validity, the proprietor may use the designation 'Logótipo Registado, 'Log. registado' or simply 'LR' on the logotype.

According to Article 295 CPI, logotype registrations are transferable where a transfer would not mislead or confuse the public. When it is used in an establishment, the rights resulting from a logotype application to registration or effective registration can only be transferred, be it a free or paid transfer, together with the establishment, or part of the establishment, with which the logotype is associated.

K. Appellations of Origin and Geographic Indications

380. A denomination of origin is defined by Article 299(1) CPI as the name of a region, of a specific place or, in exceptional cases, of a country, which serves to designate or identify a product: (a) originating from that region, specific place or country; (b) whose quality or characteristics are derived, essentially or exclusively, from the geographic environment, including the natural and human factors, and whose production, processing and development are carried out within the demarcated geographic area.[480]

According to Article 299(3) CPI, a geographic indication is understood to mean the name of a region, a specific place or, in exceptional cases, a country that serves to designate or identify a product: (a) originating from that region, specific place or country; (b) whose reputation, specific quality or another characteristic can be attributed to that geographic origin and whose production, processing or development is carried out within that demarcated geographic area.

Appellations of origin and geographic indications, when registered, are the common property of the residents or those established in the place, region or territory in an effective and serious manner and can be used indistinctly by those, within the respective area, who are engaged in any characteristic production branch, when authorized by the holder of the registration. Exercise of this right does not depend on the importance of the business operation or the nature of the products. An appellation of origin or a geographic indication can, consequently, be applied to any typical product from the place, region or territory that meets the traditional and customary, or duly regulated, conditions.

---

479. For a general overview, *see* Jorge Coutinho de Abreu, *Curso de Direito Comercial* I, 11th edn (Coimbra: Almedina, 2018), 345-353.
480. For a general overview, Jorge Coutinho de Abreu, *supra*, 394-398.

During the period of validity of a registration, the products for which the respective uses are authorized may bear the following references: (a) 'Denominação de Origem Registada or 'DO'; (b) Indicação Geográfica Registada' or 'IG'.

Registration of an appellation of origin or geographic indication confers upon the proprietor the right to prevent: (a) use by third parties, in the designation or presentation of a product, of any means that indicates or suggests that the product in question originates from a geographic region other than the true place of origin; (b) use that would constitute unfair competition as defined in Article 10*bis* of the Paris Convention, as modified by the Stockholm Revision of 14 July 1967; (c) use by persons not authorized by the registration holder.[481]

In the Portuguese Industrial Property Code, the effects of registration are determined for each exclusive right. The Code sets out a system whereby the right is only directly and exclusively attributed to the owner after registration.[482] The proof of those rights is made by titles corresponding to the different modalities of industrial property rights. However, registration of rights merely implies a presumption of the completion of the basic elements for attribution. The system of constitutive registration does not include rewards and geographic indications. These rights may be registered but this public act of registration pursues a different intent: it guarantees the authenticity of their corresponding titles and in both cases has a mere declarative effect.

§5. Acquisition of Property Rights over Movable Property

381. The Portuguese Civil Code sets forth in Book III, a chapter dedicated to the acquisition of property rights (Articles 1316 to 1343). The law does not distinguish between the acquisition of immovable and movable property. Article 1316 foresees as means of acquisition of property rights, among others, contract, heritance, *usucapio*, appropriation, and accession. Only appropriation is a specific way to acquire movable property. Special regulation exists for natural accession over movable things.

Further analysis of the acquisition of movable property will be made in Part III.

481. Article 306 CPI.

482. The Industrial Property National Institute, as mentioned, is the competent authority for the registering of industrial property rights, either with constitutive or merely declarative effects.

Chapter 3. Equitable Interests

382. Equitable interests are not recognized under Portuguese Property Law. The Portuguese legal system is very formal and title-based.

Chapter 4. Security Interests

383. Security interests over movable goods imply a direct bound of guarantee between specific goods in the debtor's patrimony and a definite credit. In the event of the debtor's non-fulfilment, security interests give the creditor the right to request the mandatory sale of the goods in which the security lies, as well as to apply the price so obtained to the satisfaction of his/her credit. Property may be followed by the creditor in satisfaction of the debt even if the debtor has, in the meantime, transferred the property to a third party.

The movable assets burdened by security rights must be earmarked and clearly specified in the constitutive deed – principle of specificity.[483] A global or general security right over all the movable assets of the security debtor is not allowed.[484]

Security rights held over movable assets are statutory preferences [*privilégios creditórios mobiliários*] (Articles 733 to 742 of the CC), the pledge [*penhor*] (Articles 666 to 685 of the CC), financial collateral arrangement [*penhor financeiro*] (DL 105/2004, of 8 May)[485] and the retention right [*direito de retenção*] (Articles 754 to 761 of the CC). *See* more detailed description in Part V.

483. Article 716(2) CC.
484. Article 716(1) CC.
485. As amended by Decree Law 85/2011, of 29 June, and DL 192/2012, of 23 August.

Part III. Acquisition of Property Rights

384. The modes of acquisition of property in Portuguese law are mainly foreseen in Article 1316 CC, which refers specifically to contract, inheritance, *usucapio*, appropriation, and accession.

Mechanisms that allow the acquisition of property (both ownership and limited real rights) may be divided into two groups, namely original and derivative ways of acquisition. Original acquisition of property occurs where an entirely new proprietary right has been created, that is, when the acquisition is without reference to a previous entitlement of another person.[486] The acquired right does not depend on a previous right, which might not even exist. When it does exist, however, the new right is not acquired because of it; rather, it is acquired despite of it (e.g., appropriation of movables, and the *usucapio*). Appropriation and *usucapio* are two forms of original acquisition.

385. An original acquisition by appropriation might occur in two situations. First, it exists where a new *res* has only recently come into existence. Second, it might occur when a *res nullius*– a movable thing without an owner, or a thing that previously was owned by someone, who has abandoned his/her property right in it – is seized in possession by a specific person who treats it as his/her property, with the effect that the law grants him/her a property right in the thing.[487]

Appropriation is a means of acquiring the right of ownership, which by its nature must be unqualified and unlimited, and since no one but the acquiring party has any right to the thing, the thing could not have been encumbered with any real property rights of others.[488]

The *usucapio* is a way of acquiring property based on the uninterrupted possession of an object for a certain length of time established by law, and exercised by a person other than the owner or holder of a limited right. *Usucapio* is a means to acquire both ownership and limited real rights.[489] The extension of the right only depends on the possession, as follows: *tantum possessum quantum praescriptam*. The possessor might acquire only a limited property right,[490] which means that the acquiring party did not obtain the thing in full property, but merely limited powers

486. *See* C. Mota Pinto (with A. Pinto Monteiro and Paulo Mota Pinto), *Teoria Geral do Direito Civil*, 4th edn (Coimbra: Coimbra Editora, 2005), 359 et seq.
487. Article 1318 CC.
488. *See* Ch. 5.
489. The right of use and habitation and non visible servitudes, however, cannot be acquired through usucapio.
490. *See* Ch. 4.

on it. There may be other proprietors who are able to exercise their rights in the thing against him. For example, the possessor might obtain a usufruct over an immovable property already charged with a servitude of passing through.

386. Derivative acquisition covers all situations where the proprietor has acquired a property right over an object that he/she has derived from a previous title holder. Where property is transferred from *A* to *B* the derivative acquisition of property is *translative* (e.g., when the owner sells a property to an acquirer). When a time-limited real right is created by the owner of the thing, the derivative acquisition is *constitutive* (e.g., if *A* creates a usufruct or a mortgage in favour of *B*. In the first situation, the acquisition is produced due to the transfer of the right by a previous holder (e.g., contract). No new property right is formed, but an already existing property right is taken, entirely, from a previous proprietor. In the second situation, on the contrary, the acquisition of the right must result from the constitution of a new limited real right.

Derivative acquisition always presupposes some other precedent conveyance. The existence of a previous right, and its extinction or restriction, is the ground of the acquisition by the new holder. The acquired right depends on the existence, extent, and nature of the previous right. Therefore, the *nemo plus iuris ad alium transferre potest quam ipse habet* principle (no one can transfer a greater right to another than he/she himself/herself has) applies.[491] Since the acquiring party has derived his/her property right from someone who already was entitled to that property, he/she might have to reckon with the existence of possible rights in rem of others, which already might have been vested in the acquired object (*e.g.*, if *A* creates a usufruct in favour of *B* over a property that he/she has already mortgaged in favour of *C*).

387. Some authors also mention the derivative acquisition that would result in a restitution of the thing, which is the restitutive acquisition. That would be the case when the owner of a thing that is burdened with a limited real right recovers full property. For example, when a usufruct expires and the bare owner re-acquires full property.

491. There are some exceptions to that principle. *See* Ch. 9, on acquisitions *a non domino*.

Chapter 1. Transfer of Property by Contract *Inter Vivos*

§1. General Introduction

388. The main structure of the Portuguese Civil Code follows the structure of the German *Bürgerliche Gesetzbuch* (BGB). Therefore, most of the rules concerning the formation of contracts are to be found in Book I of the Civil Code (Articles 217 to 294). Book II, on the Law of Obligations, encompasses a general part, which sets forth the rules regulating the content and effects of contracts, and a part dedicated to several contracts in special (Articles 874 to 1250 of the CC). The content of Books I and II is inspired by the Italian Civil Code of 1942, and to a lesser extent, by the *Code Napoléon.*[492] The most basic principle of Portuguese contract law is that of freedom of contract, expressly contained in Article 405 CC. This provision mentions the freedom to enter into a contract and to freely shape the content of a contract within the limits set forth by law.

389. A contract is said to have been concluded when a clear, sufficiently defined and firm or unequivocal offer is matched by a firm or unequivocal acceptance thereof. The contract must fulfil the following general validity requirements: (a) the mutual consent, freely expressed (*duorum vel plurium consensus*); (b) a determined object, whose traffic is not forbidden;[493] and (c) a licit cause, or in other words, an economic purpose legally admitted. Contracts will become effective between parties thereto as soon as they have been entered into.

390. As I have mentioned above, the Portuguese system of contractual acquisition of property is merely consensual, since a contract is enough for transfer of property (*consensus parit proprietatem*).[494] A contract for the transfer or creation of property rights, unless otherwise provided, will cause transfer of property immediately upon its conclusion.[495] A contract to transfer the property or other real right (i.e., sale, exchange, contributions of goods to a company, transaction) is an acquisition title and is not required to be followed by the delivery of the goods which are the object of the contract, or by registration, in order to produce the acquisitive effect.

Therefore, the delivery or *tradition* of the goods which are the object of the contract to the transferee and the payment of the price are obligatory effects of the contract of transfer. The transferee acquires the property or real right at issue even before performance of his/her contractual duties.[496]

---

492. For a general overview, *see* M. Lima Rego/ C. Ferreira de Almeida, 'Contract Law', in *Portuguese Law – an Overview*, ed. C. Ferreira de Almeida, Assunção Cristas & Nuno Piçarra (Coimbra: Almedina, 2007), 183. *See* also Menezes Cordeiro, *Tratado De Direito Civil Português I*- Parte Geral, 3rd edn (Coimbra: Almedina, 2005), 470–471.
493. Articles 280 and 398 CC.
494. The Portuguese system, however, is a causal one, since it requires a valid contract for the transfer of ownership.
495. Article 408 CC.
496. Article 879 CC.

391. The law provides specific exceptions to the immediate efficacy in rem of the contract of sale. According to Article 408(2) of the CC, when the contract of sale impinges upon future or unspecified things, the transfer of property will take place when the property becomes actual or specified. If the contract of sale impinges upon natural fruits, the transfer of property will take place after the collection. Finally, when the contract impinges upon fixtures, transfer of property will occur after separation.

392. Parties may determine that property over the goods sold will be transferable only at a specified later date. Article 409 of the CC allows parties to agree on the reservation of title. A 'retention of title clause' is a provision in a contract for the sale of goods, which states that the title to the good remains vested in the seller until certain obligations (usually payment of the purchase price) are fulfilled by the buyer. The main purpose of such clauses is to ensure that where goods are supplied on credit, if the buyer subsequently does not pay and defaults, the seller can repossess the goods. If the contract is over an immovable or a movable subject to registration, the clause has to be registered.[497] Otherwise, the clause is not enforceable against third parties.

§2. Contract of Sale

I. Statutory Provisions and Concept

393. General rules on the contract of sale are to be found on Articles 874 to 939 of the CC. Sale on consumer goods (both movables and immovables) is regulated by DL 67/2003, of 8 April.[498] Article 939 of the CC provides that the legal regime of the contract of sale is applied to all onerous contracts aimed at transfer of property. Therefore, the regime is applied *mutatis mutandis* to a contract of exchange.[499]

394. According to Article 873 of the CC, 'sale' is a contractual alienation of property or any real right upon an object that has direct and immediate efficacy. It should be emphasized that the CC categorizes as a sale the transfer not only of ownership but also of any real right. Therefore, if someone transfers a usufruct to someone on consideration, it constitutes a contract of sale. The contract of sale is a legal transfer of property from seller (or vendor) to buyer (or purchaser) for an agreed upon monetary value.

497. Cf. Article 2 CRegP.
498. As amended by DL 84/2008, of 21 May.
499. *See* Decision of the Supreme Court of 9 October 2007 [Process: 07A2761], at http://www.dgsi.pt/jstj.nsf/954f0ce6ad9dd8b980256b5f003fa814/171777f01a6d9159802573df00410a56?OpenDocument.

395. Since the Portuguese Property system is a consensual one, transfer of property results from the contract between a vendor and an acquirer.[500] *Traditio*, payment of the price or registration are not a requirement for property transfer.[501] Parties will have to perform the obligations under the contract, namely the duty to deliver the thing[502] and the duty to pay the price[503] at an agreed date.

396. Consideration is essential to the sale; Article 885 of the CC provides that the payment is due at the moment of the delivery and in the place where it shall take place, unless parties agree otherwise. Normally the acquirer enters into possession on occasion of the conclusion of the contract; however, as for the payment, entry into enjoyment may also be deferred or anticipated.

397. Legal treatment of the obligation to deliver is established within the set of rules referred to the sale contract.[504] Either the vendor, to obtain payment, or the acquirer, to obtain delivery of the thing, may apply to a court to enforce performance.[505]

398. Since property is transferred trough conclusion of the contract, the legislator imposes a specific default rule in order to reinforce the stability of legal traffic: the vendor, who has already delivered the thing, cannot rescind the contract by reason of breach if the acquirer does not pay the price.[506] The only remedy available to the vendor is to enforce payment.

399. The one that intends to transfer to another person the property upon an object must hold the ownership over it. The seller's lack of ownership makes the alienation title void, and constitutes an impediment for the acquisition of the right, because nobody may transfer something that he/she does not hold (*nemo plus iuris*). The seller, however, cannot argue the nullity against the good faith acquirer; similarly, the acquirer on bad faith cannot argue the nullity against the good faith seller.[507] Rules on liability are to be found in Articles 898, 899 and 900 CC. If, after conclusion of the contract, the seller acquires the ownership of the good, the contract of sale turns automatically valid and the transfer of property takes place.[508]

---

500. Should such transfer be subject to registration, however, it would only be enforceable vis-à-vis third parties once the transfer is registered.
501. Articles 408(1) and 879(a) CC.
502. Article 878(b) CC.
503. Article 879(c) CC. *See* Decision of the Supreme Court of 29 March 2012 [Process: 1470/09], at http://www.dgsi.pt/jstj.nsf/954f0ce6ad9dd8b980256b5f003fa814/89bae6cb5ce85d93802579d1005067f1?OpenDocument.
504. Article 882 CC.
505. Article 818 CC.
506. Article 886 CC.
507. Article 892 CC.
508. Article 895 CC.

II. Formalities

400. The principle of freedom of form in the matter of contracts applies in Portuguese law, as a default rule in the conclusion of a contract.[509] Contracts for the sale or transfer of an interest in immovable property must be executed through a public deed or through a private deed certified by a public authority.[510] A contract that lacks the required form (*ad substantiam*) is void.[511]

I will now devote some attention to the transfer of property rights over immovable property. In Portugal, transfer of immovable property can follow the traditional way of conveyance, be done through the *One Stop House Scheme*, or in an authorized credit institution.

A. *The Traditional Way of Conveyance*

401. According to the traditional way of conveying property, the title deed is normally drawn up at the Notary Office.[512] The sales contract is concluded in an oral hearing, usually at the notary's office, in the presence of both parties. At that time, the buyer might pay the purchase price to the seller (unless parties agree differently, the purchase price is paid immediately) and the seller might allow the buyer to come into possession. At the same time, the mortgage title might be signed, if that is the case. When payment is financed through a mortgage loan, the deed of sale and the deed of mortgage are usually signed in the same notarial deed, and the bank supplies the loan in that moment, even if the mortgage is not yet definitively registered.[513]

402. Under the traditional mode of conveyance, the original deed document is held by the Public Notary, and a copy is registered with the Central Registration Office. According to Article 8-B of the CRegP, the Notary must ensure registration

---

509. Article 219 CC.
510. Article 875 CC and Article 22(a), of Decree Law 116/2008, of 4 July. DL 116/2008 eliminated the requirement to execute public deeds for acts relating to real property. The sale and purchase of real estate can now be executed either by public deed or by privately executed contract, which must be certified by some authorized entities: lawyers, Chambers of Commerce and Industry; and paralegals [*solicitadores*]. These entities must ensure registration of the acts they have certified. Although intervention of notaries is no longer mandatory, in practice, contracts are still executed in a public deed, which is when banks are involved in providing financing secured by mortgages.
511. Article 220 CC.
512. It should be emphasized, however, that other entities have competence to convey property. What is referred in the text, applies *mutatis mutandis* to those entities.
513. The documents necessary for the public deed are as follows: the identification documents and Portuguese tax numbers of the parties (the tax number of a foreign purchaser is obtained prior to the act); the Property Tax Document *[Caderneta Predial]*, issued by the Tax Office of the area in which the property is located; the abstract of title *[Certidão do Registo Predial]* issued by the Land Registry; the use permit [*Licença de Utilização*] issued by the local Town Hall; certification of the payment of the tax over the transmission of real estates with consideration [*Imposto sobre Transmissões Onerosas de Imóveis]*, issued by the respective Tax Office. If there was an exemption of the tax, that must also be certified by document. If the acquirer is a consumer, the technical description of the building [*Ficha Técnica de Habitação]* shall also be presented to the Notary.

of the purchase in the Land Registrar (usually, a conversion of a provisional inscription into a definitive one, and maintaining the same rank). In contrast, the owner is required to apply for registration in the respective Tax Office [*Repartição de Finanças*].

B. *One Stop House Scheme [Casa Pronta]*

403. A fast-track home-buying system, the so-called One Stop House Scheme [*Casa Pronta*], was recently made available in Portugal. It aims at making the process of buying or selling a property simpler and faster, by eliminating formalities and allowing everything to be done at a single contact point. One Stop House Schemes are implemented in Land Registry Offices and in Registrars located in Citizen's Shops [*Lojas do Cidadão*].

In January 2007, the European Commission launched the foundations for an 'Action Programme to Reduce the Administrative Burden of Existing Regulation in the EU.' The 2007 Spring European Council ratified this Programme and set the goal of a 25% reduction in the administrative burdens on enterprises, to be achieved jointly by the EU and the individual Member States by 2012. Hence, the Council invited Member States to set comparable goals of their own at the national level. Portugal responded to this European challenge and committed itself to both: actively taking steps to pursue a programme called *Simplex*, aimed at reducing the administrative burdens on enterprises at the EU level, and achieving the same result at the national level. One of the measures adopted within the Simplex Program was the One Stop House Scheme (*Processo Especial de Aquisição, Oneração e Registo de Imóveis em Atendimento Presencial Único*), implemented by DL 263-A/2007, of 23 July (as amended).[514]

404. At the One Stop House users may, at the same time: pay the property transfer taxes;[515] conclude the contract of sale, the bank loan, and the mortgage; register their assets as required; request changes to their fiscal address; obtain from the municipal authorities drawings of the newly acquired property; request exemption from the municipal property tax, if that is the case;[516] submit the necessary data for registering the property or updating the data in the property register.

405. Although the One Stop House scheme was only foreseen for the sale of urban immovables, it was extended by Implementing Order 1126/2009, of the 1 of October, to contracts over rural immovables, and to the *datio in solution* (besides

514. Last amendment by DL 125/2013, of 30 August.

515. The *Imposto sobre Transmissões Onerosas de Imóveis* is a tax over the transmission of real estate with consideration. A document certifying payment or exemption of payment of the tax must be issued by the respective Tax Office.

516. Owners must pay Property Municipal Tax [*Imposto Municipal sobre Imóveis*].The amount due depends on the rate approved by the Town Hall.

the sale, the bank loan, and the mortgage). Since the Implementing Order 67/2010, of 3 February, the One Stop House Scheme can also be used for contracts of gift and exchange of immovable property.[517]

C. Sale in Authorized Credit Institutions

406. DL 255/93, of 15 July, establishes that authorized credit institutions can certify the sale and acquisition of a dwelling for residential purposes, when they finance the purchase. The contract of sale should be concluded in a private document, according to a sample approved by law. More recently, the Government is extending the One Stop House Scheme [*Casa Pronta*] to bank services by establishing '*One Stop House*' counters in banks' branch offices to provide the necessary assistance to individuals when the transaction requires a bank loan.

III. Defective Goods

407. The fact that the property has hidden or not visible defects *[defeitos ocultos*] does not contend with the transfer of property, but might have consequences that are worth mentioning.[518] I will distinguish three situations, as follows: a transaction between private individuals or between professionals; a transaction between a consumer and a professional; and a transaction from a seller who has also built the property to a third party.

A. Transaction Between Private Individuals

408. If a private acquirer had bought property to a non-professional seller, or a professional has acquired a property from another professional, Articles 913 of the CC provides the legal regime for the sale of defective things.[519] Therefore, if the property has a defect that causes a depreciation on it, or prevents the fulfilment of its function, or does not have the qualities granted by the seller, the acquirer has to give notice[520] of the defect within a year after the acknowledgement of the defect and within five years of the conclusion of the contract, if the property is immovable, or thirty days and six months, if the property is movable. If the buyer gives evidence of the defects affecting the quality of the property, he/she is entitled to the following legal rights against the seller: to have the property repaired[521] or

517. The Implementing Order 1167/2010, of 10 November, extended the One Stop House Scheme to the division of a building in apartment ownership.
518. Visible defects [*defeitos aparentes*] are presumed to be known, even if there was no examination of the thing.
519. Unless the contract is considered a commercial sale. In that case, Commercial Code applies.
520. Except if there was intentional fault on the part of the seller (Article 916 CC).
521. Article 914 CC.

replaced;[522] reduction of the price;[523] rescission of the contract;[524] and compensation for damages incurred (if the seller is responsible for the defect). If there is an intentional fault on the part of the seller, he/she has to compensate the acquirer for damages that he/she would have not suffered if he/she had not concluded the contract; if the sale was due to the acquirer's mistake, he/she is liable only for damages resulting from the contract [*danos emergentes*].[525] These rules are default in nature, therefore parties can agree otherwise.[526]

B. Transaction from a Professional to a Particular

409. If someone buys an immovable property from a professional (normally, a developer), special rules on consumer protection would apply. According to Article 5 of DL 67/2003, of 8 of April, in a *Business-to-Consumer* (*B2C*) transaction, the seller is responsible for the defects of the building, unless he/she proves conformity with the contract. Unless proved otherwise, any lack of conformity which becomes apparent within five years of delivery of immovable goods, or within two years in case of movable goods, shall be presumed to have existed at the time of delivery. Notice might be given by the owner within one year after acquiring knowledge of the defect and compensation might be claimed within three years after notice.[527] In case of movable goods, notice must be given within two months, and compensation must be claimed within two years. In the case of a lack of conformity, the consumer is entitled to have the goods brought into conformity free of charge by repair or replacement, to have an appropriate reduction made in the price or the contract rescinded with regard to those goods. Those rules are mandatory. Any contractual terms or agreements concluded with the seller before the lack of conformity is brought to the seller's attention which directly or indirectly waive or restrict the rights resulting from Decree 67/2003, is not binding on the consumer.

C. Acquisition from a Developer

410. If the acquirer is not a consumer and had bought an immovable property from a developer (the seller is also the builder of the house), Article 1225 of the CC applies. This provision sets forth that the seller is liable for damages, during five years, if he/she has also constructed, repaired, or modified the building. Liability exists if the building ruins totally or partially, or has defects, whether those defects

522. This duty does not exist if the seller did not know the defect of the thing.
523. Article 911 CC.
524. Article 905 ex vi 913 CC.
525. Articles 908 and 909 CC.
526. Article 912 CC.
527. Article 5-A(3) of DL 67/2003.

impinge upon the soil or the construction itself. Notice might be given by the owner within one year after acquiring knowledge of the defect and compensation might be claimed within one year after notice.[528]

IV. Restrictions to Sell

411. The law establishes several restrictions to transfer of property: the transfer made by and between spouses; transfer between (grand)parents and their (grand)children, transfer by tutors to children; and transfer of contested things.

Matrimonial law provides a series of restrictions to sale. Article 1682-A(1) of the CC provides that the sale of immovables (either joint or personal property) requires consent of both spouses, unless they are married in a system of separate assets. The performance of acts that imply the total or partial deprivation of the family home always requires the consent of both spouses, regardless of the proprietary status of the house. Article 1682-A(2) of the CC provides that one spouse cannot, without the consent of the other, sell, charge, lease, or lend the family house. The court may, upon petition from one spouse, grant permission for a conveyance if consent has been refused, or if for some other reason, it has not been possible to obtain (Article 1684(3) of the CC). Finally, Article 1714(2) of the CC forbids the sale of property between spouses. The rationale of this provision is to prevent the spouses from altering the matrimonial system chosen by them at the time of the wedding.

Article 877 of the CC forbids parents and grandparents to sale property to their children and grandchildren without consent of the others. The court may, upon petition, grant permission for a conveyance if consent has been refused, or if for some other reason, it has not been possible to obtain. The sale made without consent of the others is voidable, and invalidity can be argued by children or grandchildren one year after the knowledge of the contract, or if they are not capable, one year after the end of that incapacity.[529]

Articles 1937 and 1938(1) of the CC set forth a series of prohibitions on the transfer of minors' property by tutors. A valid transfer of property always depends on the authorization of the Court.

Finally, Article 876 of the CC forbids the sale of contested rights to judicial operators (lawyers, judges, public prosecutors, and judicial officials) of the Court where the judicial action is lodged.[530] Although the sale is void, only the seller is entitled to argue the invalidity.

528. Article 1225(2) CC.
529. About this legal provision, *see* A. Pinto Monteiro, 'Venda de padrasto a enteado', in *CJ* IV (1994), 5-15.
530. Article 579 ex vi 876(1) CC.

§3. DONATION

I. Concept and Statutory Provisions

412. Donation is defined in Article 940 of the CC as a contract by which a person transfers, gratuitously, an object (a good or a right) for the benefit of another person who accepts it. The one who does the attribution is called 'donor' and the attribution recipient is called 'donee'. As a contract, donation requires acceptance by the donee.[531] Donation is not an unilateral disposition of a thing by the donor; rather it is a contract, that requires acceptance in order to be concluded.[532]

Technically, donation also encompasses the assumption of an obligation. For example, parents might buy a car for their son or parents may assume the payment of the price of a car bought by their son – both cases would be considered a donation under Article 940 of the CC. The object donated may consist of both movable and immovable goods, provided they are already existent at the time the contract is agreed upon.[533]

II. Formalities

413. Donation of immovables goods must be stated in a notarial deed or in a written document recognized by a public official.[534] Donation of immovables, according to the general principle that the contractual transfer of property and real rights only requires to be based on a title, allows the immediate production of the alienation effect. The conclusion of the contract, by the union of the donor's proposal and the donee's acceptance, produces per se the acquisition of the donated thing or right,[535] without need of *traditio* or registration.

Donation of movable goods, on the contrary, might be stated in a private written deed, except if it is made through the delivery of the goods which are the object of the contract. In such a case, no further formalities are required.

III. *Actio Pauliana*

414. The donation of movable goods can objectively be prejudicial to a number of people, that is, creditors, which explains why lawmakers have enclosed some cautions regarding fraudulent conduct of debtors toward creditors.

---

531. *See*, however, Article 951 CC.
532. After completion of the donation, that is to say, after the donees acceptance or delivery of the movable good, the donation becomes irrevocable, except in some exceptional cases foreseen by Article 974 CC, due to donee ingratitude. The non-fulfilment of burdens by the donees also might give place to rescission of the donation (Article 966 CC).
533. Article 942(1) CC.
534. Article 947(1) CC.
535. *See* Decision of the Supreme Court of 25 June 2015 [Process: 26118/10], at http://www.dgsi.pt/jstj.nsf/954f0ce6ad9dd8b980256b5f003fa814/0a745a2c6e23d1df80257e6f00463e4e?OpenDocument.

Actio Pauliana is an action brought by a creditor seeking to set aside a contract made by him/her or his/her debtor that increases the debtor's insolvency, ruled in Articles 610 et seq. CC.[536]

IV. Restrictions to Donations

415. Article 953 of the Portuguese Civil Code sets forth several restrictions to donations, such as donations to tutors, managers of property, doctors and nurses (if the donor is their patient) and priests (if the donor is receiving spiritual comfort), and to the person with whom the donor has had an extramarital affair if he/she is married.[537]

§4. Other Contracts

416. The legal regime of the contract of sale constitutes the default regime for other onerous contracts. Exchange (a contract in which property is transferred from one party to the other in return for other property) and contribution of goods to a company[538] are examples of contracts governed, in whichever manner applied, by the provisions mentioned in Chapter 1, §2.

§5. Acquisition a *Non Domino*

417. The Portuguese law foresees some cases of acquisition a *non domino*. The protection results in preventing a vindication brought by the actual owner (*verus dominus*) against the third party from succeeding under certain conditions. His/her acquisition, despite being a *non domino*, is automatically produced provided he/she fulfils some requirements, strictly stated in legal provisions, basically having an onerous title and being in good faith. The goal of these legal provisions is to protect the third party who onerously and in good faith believed that the person who transferred him/her the object was the true owner of it, because of certain external signs that made presumable his/her ownership.

418. Article 291 of the CC sets forth that the declaration of the nullity of a contract upon an immovable or a movable subject to registration cannot prejudice the rights acquired on consideration, by individuals on good faith.[539] The acquirer is

536. An onerous contract is only subject to the revocatory action if the debtor and the third acquirer are in bad faith, that is, if they both are aware that their conduct of fraud disadvantaged the creditor (Article 612 CC).
537. Articles 2192 to 2198 CC *ex vi* Article 953 CC.
538. On the contribution of goods to a company, *see* Paulo de Tarso Domingues 'Article 25', in *Código das Sociedades Comerciais em Comentário*, I (Coimbra: Almedina, 2010), 423–440.
539. The acquirer is on good faith when, at the moment of the acquisition *(mala fides superveniens non nocet)*, he/she did not know, and was not supposed to know, the previous invalidity in the chain of acquisitions.

entitled to this protection three years after the conclusion of the sale. The registration of the acquisition must be prior to registration of the judicial procedure for declaration of nullity. For example, if *A* and *B* conclude a contract of sale of an immovable property, but they do not comply with the formalities required by law, the contract is void. If *A* sells the property to *C*, who is in good faith, *C* might be protected under Article 291, provided that the requirements of this provision are fulfilled.

419. Article 240 of the CC states that the simulated business – a business where parties agree on pretending a celebration of a business to mislead third people – is void. However, the nullity cannot be enforceable against third parties on good faith (Article 243 of the CC). If *A* and B conclude a contract of sale but disguise it of a donation (e.g., in *fraudem legis* to Article 877 CC), nullity is not enforceable against the seller's creditors.

420. Article 2076 of the CC protects acquirers on good faith that have acquired on consideration from apparent heirs (by common and general mistake), according to the principle *error comumunis facit ius*. In this situation, if the heir is on good faith, he/she is liable according to rules on unjust enrichment.

421. As I have mentioned in Chapter 3, §2, there are several constraints on the power of disposal of goods, derived from the marriage. Contracts concluded without the consent of the spouse, when required, are voidable. Article 1687(3), however, provides that the voidability of the contract over a movable good, concluded with a party in good faith, cannot be claimed against him/her.

422. Finally, the legal regime of the Land Registry also protects some acquirers a *non domino*. The Portuguese system is a causal one, since it requires a valid contract for the transfer of ownership, and consensual, since that contract is enough for transfer of property. Under the Portuguese legal system, registration is not necessary for the creation or transfer of a real right, except in the case of mortgages.[540] Therefore, if *A* sells a house to *B*, *B* acquires ownership. Ownership and real rights over property are validly acquired without the necessity of registering them. Facts subject to registration are still effective *inter partes* and may be invoked by their heirs.[541] However, if *B* does not inscribe his/her acquisition on the Registry, his/her right is not enforceable against third parties (those who acquire from the same person, totally or partially incompatible rights over the same thing, according to Article 5(4) CRegP). Since the function of the Land Registry in Portugal is to provide publicity to the legal status of the property, registration of the legal act that impinges upon property is only necessary for its enforceability [*oponobilidade*] against third parties.[542] However, if the owner sells the same property to two different acquirers, whoever registers first becomes, in fact, the new owner. In the above-mentioned situation, if *A* sells the same house to *C*, who registers his/her acquisition, *C*

540. Article 4(2) CRegP.
541. Article 4(1) CRegP.
542. Article 5(1) CRegP.

acquires a right enforceable against third parties, namely, against *B*. According to Article 408 of the CC, *B* had already acquired ownership of the house. Therefore, when *A* sells to *C*, he/she is selling something that he/she does not own anymore – and therefore, there is a *non domino* acquisition. However, since *A* is the last owner inscribed in the Land Registry, and since *C* has inscribed his/her acquisition, he/she is granted protection against *B*'s claims. The question whether good faith is required remains controversial in the doctrine. The debate is set among those who consider good faith as a general principle in the Portuguese legal system,[543] and those who consider good faith irrelevant in protection from registration.[544]

543. António Barreto Menezes Cordeiro, Do Trust no Direito Civil (Coimbra: Almedina, 2014); Menezes Cordeiro, *Tratado De Direito Civil Português I*- Parte Geral, II- Coisas, 3rd edn (Coimbra: Almedina, 2005), 276; Carvalho Fernandes, 'Terceiros para Efeitos de Registo Predial', *ROA* 57 (1997): 1283 ff; Santos Justo, *Direitos Reais*, 5th edn (Coimbra: Coimbra Editora, 2017), 70 et seq; Pereira Mendes, *Anotado,* 143; José Alberto Vieira, *Direitos Reais* (Lisboa: Coimbra Editora: 2008), 297.

544. Orlando de Carvalho, 'Terceiros para Efeitos de Registo', *BFD* 70 (1994): 97 ff; Pinto Duarte, *Curso de Direitos Reais* (Lisboa: Principia, 2013), 166; Paulo Henriques, 'Terceiros para efeitos do artigo 5.º do Código do Registo Predial', *BFD* 79 (2003): 443–445.

Chapter 2. Transfer of Property by Death

§1. General Introduction

423. Succession is the way someone assumes the legal position of someone else; it refers to rights and debts.[545] Within the domain of succession, Article 62(1) of the CRP guarantees the right to private property[546] and to its transfer in life or upon death. The aim of the constitutional legislation is to allow each individual the possibility of disposing of his/her patrimony as he/she would, which demonstrates a clear recognition of the freedom to bequeath as the expression of autonomy of will.

424. The most important source of Portuguese successions law is Book V of the Portuguese Civil Code (Articles 2024 to 2334). Portuguese successions law follows the individualist model of its Roman origins, albeit with strong concessions to the family model of Germanic origin, particularly in terms of the mandatory succession, the so-called *sucessão legitimária.*[547]

The last great reform of the Civil Code, embodied in DL 486/77 of 1 July 1977, represented a major alteration to the legal framework in force in order to match the new constitutional system brought into being by the 1974 Revolution, namely, the legal position of the surviving spouse or the higher relevance conferred upon the nuclear family.[548]

425. The succession is opened with the death of the deceased.[549] The estate devolves to the heir, provided that the latter accepts it; this acceptance may be tacit, or failing renunciation within the prescribed period of time. The time limit for accepting a succession is ten years from the time the heir becomes aware of the death and his/her entitlement to the inheritance.[550]

The competent authorities are the Court, the Notaries, and the Civil Registrar [*Registo Civil*].[551]

545. Derivative acquisition and succession may be distinguished using a metaphorical description. In a derivative acquisition, the property shifts from one owner to the other. In succession, the right does not move; is the new acquirer that will occupy the place of the former owner.
546. Inheritable estate is all private property without restriction; public assets are not eligible for transfer by private individuals.
547. *See* J. J. Abrantes, 'Law of Successions', in *Portuguese Law – an Overview*, ed. C. Ferreira de Almeida, Assunção Cristas & Nuno Piçarra (Coimbra: Almedina, 2007), 240.
548. Guilherme de Oliveira, 'Family and Succession Law in Portugal', in *International Encyclopedia of Laws: Family and Succession Law*, ed. Robert Blanpain (The Hague: Kluwer Law international, 2012), 213 ff.
549. Article 2031 CC.
550. Article 2059(1) CC.
551. According to Law 23/2013, of 5 March, as amended. Registers are the competent Portuguese authority to issue the European Certificate of Succession, according to Regulation EU 650/2012 of the European Parliament and of the Council of 4 July 2012 on jurisdiction, applicable law, recognition and enforcement of decisions and acceptance and enforcement of authentic instruments in matters of succession and on the creation of a European Certificate of Succession.

§2. Entitlement to Succession

426. Means of entitlement to succession recognized by Portuguese legal order are the law, the last will, and the contract.[552]

I. Legal Succession

427. Legal succession is supplementary [*sucessão legítima*] or mandatory [*sucessão legitimária*], depending on whether or not it can be overturned by the will of the author.[553] In Portuguese succession law, necessary or mandatory succession has substantial autonomy before legal and testamentary succession. It includes a portion[554] in favour of certain closest family members (spouse, descendants, and ascendants), the disposal of which is forbidden to the legislator. Both in mandatory and default legal succession, the spouse is in line for inheritance along with descendants, and in second place, when there are no descendants but there are surviving ascendants. In addition, the spouse is treated more favourably, since, in certain situations, he/she is entitled to a larger share than the other legal and necessary heirs,[555] and is entitled to have the family house allocated, without prejudice of the eventual restitution to the co-heirs.[556]

428. The rules governing inheritance establish five cases of legitimate successors in the following order: spouse and descendants; spouse and ascendants; brothers, sisters, and their descendants; other collateral relatives upon to the fourth degree; and the State. Collateral relatives have inheritance rights to the fourth degree in the collateral line.[557] In the absence of these, rights of succession are attributed to the State.[558]

552. Article 2026 CC.
553. Article 2027 CC.
554. Mandatory portion [*quota legitimária*].
555. Article 2139(1) CC.
556. Article 2103-A, 2103-B and 2103-C CC. *See* J.J. Abrantes, 'Law of Successions', in *Portuguese Law – an Overview*, ed. C. Ferreira de Almeida, Assunção Cristas &Nuno Piçarra (Coimbra: Almedina, 2007), 240 ff.
557. Article 2133 CC.
558. Article 2155 CC. Portuguese law does not confer any automatic inheritance rights on the surviving partner of a non-marital union, that is to say a non-registered de facto union. The latter can only become an heir if this is stipulated in a will. The surviving partner, however, has a right in rem of use of the family house for a period of at least five years, as well as a pre-emption right in the sale of the dwelling for the same period (Article 4(1) Law 7/2001). After the said period, the surviving member has the right to the lease of the property during use as the joint home. If the home was rented and the deceased partner was the tenant, the tenancy is transferred to the surviving partner (Article 5 of Law 7/2001 and Article 1006(1a) CC). The surviving partner has also several social benefits, such as survivor's allowance (Articles 3 and 6, of Law 7/2001), the right to benefits when death was a result of a work-related accident or occupational illness (Article 3(f) of Law 7/2001) and the right to pension for survivors of military personnel and for exceptionally meritorious services rendered to the country (Article 3(g) of Law 7/2001). Alimony and compensation for damages in the event of death are also foreseen in Articles 2020 and 496 of the CC.

There are certain rules governing the order of devolution upon death that are applied both to legitimate and to imperative succession:

Preference of classes: the successors within each class take preference over those of the following class (Article 2134). Preference of degree of relationship: within each class the closer relatives take preference over the more distant relatives (Article 2135). Succession per capita: the relatives within each class succeed per capita or in equal parts (exceptions stem from succession *per stirpes* and the division among full and half brothers and sisters – where the share of the former is double that of the latter, according to Article 2136).

429. The surviving spouse is a legal heir and is thus included in the first class of successors, except in cases where the author dies without descendants and leaves ascendants, in which case the surviving spouse is integrated within the second class. The partition of the inheritance between the spouse and the children is performed per capita, although the spouse's share cannot be less than one-quarter of the estate.[559] The descendants of the children who could not or did not wish to accept the inheritance are entitled to the succession in their representation and each receives that which their respective ascendant would have inherited.[560] In cases where deceased children or children who waived their rights have no descendants, their share of the estate is added to that of the remaining children.

430. The ascendants of the decedent only succeed when there are no descendants and they constitute, together with the spouse, the second class of successors. The ascendants are entitled to the entire estate if there is no spouse. If there is a spouse they are only entitled to one-third of the estate (while the spouse is entitled to two-thirds). Should any of the ascendants be unable or unwilling to assume the succession, the respective share will be added to that of the other ascendants and only in cases where there are no other ascendants will this share be added to that of the spouse.

In cases where there is no spouse and no descendants or ascendants, the brothers and sisters of the decedent are called or, in representation thereof, the descendants of these siblings (nephews and nieces). The entitlement of these successors varies in accordance with whether they are full or half-brothers or half-sisters; the share of each of the full brothers and sisters is equal to twice the share of each of the half-brothers and half-sisters.

In cases where there are no heirs in the preceding classes, the remaining collateral relatives, up to the fourth degree, are called. The closer relatives are accorded preference.

431. The State holds the title of legitimate successor (and may also be a testamentary successor) and it constitutes the final class of successors. The entitlement of the State depends on the non-existence of any of the foregoing classes of successors and this fact must be verified judicially through a special process, known as a 'settlement of estate in escheat in favour of the State' [*liquidação da herança vaga*

559. Article 2139(1) CC.
560. Articles 2039 ff.

em favour do Estado][561] only after liquidation of the estate, that is, settlement of liabilities, will any remainder be allocated to the State. The acquisition of the inheritance by the State as a legal successor is performed *ipso jure*, with neither the need to accept nor the possibility to decline the inheritance.[562]

II. Voluntary Succession

432. Voluntary succession can be testamentary or contractual. The general rule is a ban on succession agreements with the effect that, in principle, nobody can renounce the succession of a live person through a contract or dispose of his/her own succession of a third person. Therefore, contractual succession is only allowed under exceptional circumstances foreseen in Articles 1700 to 1706 of the CC. Such is the case for gifts (*mortis causa*) granted within marriages, which have been included in a prenuptial agreement. This agreement may involve the appointment of an heir or the nomination of a devisee or legatee in favour of either of the partners, performed by the other partner or by a third person, or in favour of a third person performed by either of the partners. Due to both the irrevocability and the bilateral nature of succession agreements, these are ranked second in the succession hierarchy, immediately after the mandatory succession and prior to the expressed will of the decedent in testament, which is a unilateral act and freely revocable.

433. Testamentary succession is based on the existence of a will. Testators enjoy the broadest powers with which to dispose of their property, if they do not have necessary heirs (i.e., those heirs to whom the law grants a certain reserved portion of the inheritance) in favour of family members or other people outside the family. Anyone who has not been declared incapable to do so by law can draw up a will.[563]

434. Portuguese law distinguishes between the appointment of heirs and the nomination of legatees. According to Article 2130 of the CC, an heir succeeds in all, or in a share of all, the assets of the decedent. A successor to the remainder of unspecified assets is also considered an heir. A legatee inherits specified goods or assets. Heirs and legatees are subject to different rules. In addition to the rules concerning the responsibilities for the debts of the estate (in contrast to heirs, legatees have only a limited responsibility regarding the charges from the legacy itself or in cases where the entire estate is distributed in legacies), the right of accretion, that is only fully recognized with respect to heirs (the only case where the right is conceded upon legatees is when they have been nominated regarding the same object).

561. Articles 938 to 940 CPC.

562. Article 2154 CC. *See* also Articles 38 and ff of DL 280/2007, of 7 August, as amended (last amendment by Law 82-B/2014, od 31 December).

563. Article 2188 CC.

§3. Restrictions to Transfer of Property by Death: The Necessary Heirs

435. Mandatory legal succession is based on an unassignable reserve [*legítima* or *quota indisponível*], which constitutes the part of the estate of the decedent that cannot be freely disposed of by him/her. This part is mandatorily reserved for the so-called *herdeiros legitimários:* the spouse, descendants, and ascendants according to the aforementioned order under legitimate succession.[564] Very recently, Law 48/2018, of 14 August, has considered lawful that, in a pre-nuptial agreement, spouses mutually renounce of the quality of mandatory heirs, in marriages celebrated under the regime of separation of assets. The effect of this agreement is, however, limited: although they are not necessary heirs, they still have the status of (default) heirs. Therefore, if the spouse does not want the other to succeed, a last will must be disposed.

436. The portion of each mandatory heir varies in accordance with his/her status within the defined order of succession. Thus, the portion of the spouse, when not dividing the estate among descendants or ascendants, is half of the estate.[565] However, according to Article 2159 of the CC, in cases where there are descendant children, the portion is two-thirds of the estate (the partition is performed per capita, while safeguarding the spouse's right to at least one-quarter of the unassignable share). The portion of the children, when there is no surviving spouse, is half or two-thirds of the estate depending on whether there was only one child, or two or more children.[566] The portion of the spouse and the ascendants, in cases of competition, is two-thirds of the estate.[567] The portion of the ascendants, when there is no spouse, is half or two-thirds of the estate, depending on whether the parents, the ascendants in the second and further degrees are called or not.[568]

437. Calculation of the unassignable reserve should take into account not only the value of the existing assets of the estate of the decedent on the date of the demise (*relictum*), but also the value of conferred assets (*donatum*),[569] as well as any expenses subject to restitution and debts of the estate.[570]

---

564. Articles 2157 and 2133(a) and (b) CC.
565. Article 2158 CC.
566. Article 2159(2) CC.
567. Article 2159(1) CC.
568. Article 2161(2) CC.
569. All gifts made by the decedent during life and post mortem can be contested by the legal heirs, as far as they offend their reserve. The process is defined by law, and the respective proceedings are subject to a limitation period of two years after the acceptance of the inheritance by the mandatory heir (Articles 2168 to 2178 CC).
570. Cf. Article 2162 CC. Restitution [*colação*] is, for the purpose of equality, reallocation of assets to the estate that were conferred upon descendants who wish to succeed the decedent and who on the date of the conferral were presumable mandatory heirs of the conferrer (Articles 2104 ff CC).

§4. Alienation of the Inheritance

438. Alienation of the inheritance can only take place after the acceptance and before the partition of the assets.[571] The heirs can jointly dispose of the inheritance as a whole, of certain assets of the inheritance, or of a share of the inheritance.

According to Article 2124 of the CC, the alienation of the inheritance, or of a share of the inheritance, is subject to the formal rules for the legal transactions involved.

The alienation of a share of an inheritance is subject to the pre-emption rights of the other co-heirs.[572]

§5. Administration, Liquidation, and Partition of the Inheritance

439. An inheritance is an autonomous estate [*património autónomo*] until it has been dissolved into the estate of the heirs and is liable for the debts of the testator and only for these debts (for which purpose only these assets are liable).[573]

An inheritance can remain undivided for a considerable period of time. Problems of administration can arise and the undivided estate should be jointly administered by the heirs or by the so-called head of household [*cabeça-de-casal*] on behalf of all.[574] In general, the powers of the *cabeça-de-casal* are limited to the ordinary administration, including the right to resort to judicial means for the maintenance or restitution of ownership. Beyond these powers, rights concerning the inheritance must be exercised jointly by all co-heirs.

571. *See* Rabindranath Capelo de Sousa, *Lições de Direito das Sucessões,* vol. II, 3rd ed, (Coimbra: Coimbra Editora, 2002), 63–71.

572. Article 2130 CC.

573. *See* Rabindranath Capelo de Sousa, *Lições de Direito das Sucessões,* vol. II, 3rd ed, (Coimbra: Coimbra Editora, 2002), 37–61.

574. Articles 2079 ff. *See* Decision of the Supreme Court of 14 January 2014 [Process: 332/11], available at http://www.dgsi.pt/jstj.nsf/954f0ce6ad9dd8b980256b5f003fa814/706805101f6db1e68025 7c670052085a?OpenDocument.

Chapter 3. Possession

§1. Possession

440. Under Portuguese law, possession requires a material element, the corpus, and an intellectual element, the *animus*. The corpus is the factual control over the property. The *animus* does exist when the factual control exercised by the possessor is an expression of a real right (ownership or a time-limited interest) over the property or a claim of right.[575]

A claim of right exists if the person believes he/she has rightful claim to the property, even if that belief is mistaken. A positive example is when someone acquires an immovable property through a simple private deed. Since Article 875 of the CC requires a public deed or a certified private deed to the contract of sale, the transaction is void, and there is no transfer of property. The acquirer, however, might not be aware of the nullity of the contract, and still have a claim of right.

A negative example would be a timber thief who sneaks into a property, cuts timber which is not visible from the road, and hauls the logs away at night. His/her actions, though they demonstrate actual detention, also demonstrate knowledge of guilt, as opposed to claim of right. The possessor must behave similar to the true owner or holder, in other words, he/she must do so in a way that externally shows the purpose of holding the goods as his/her own. It is not required that the possessor necessarily believes the goods or rights are his/hers, but only that he/she behaves as if they were so. When someone has factual control over a property but does not have *animus*, he/she is considered a holder [*detentor*] or a precarious possessor [*possuidor precário*] under Portuguese law.

441. Possession might have several characteristics. It might be under good or bad faith; violent or not; public or not; and ground on a title or not.[576]

Possession is under bad faith when the encroacher knows that the land he/she occupies is not his/her own; it is under good faith when the possessor has ignored the same;[577] it is public when it is of such character that would give notice to a reasonable person;[578] and it is pacific when the possessor has not taken the possession in a violent way.[579] Finally, possession is grounded on a title when that title would have transferred the property right if it were substantially valid, or if the transferor would have been the legal owner.[580]

---

575. Cf. Article 1251 CC. Possession is a factual state of exercising control over an object, whether owning the object or not. *See* Decision of the Supreme Court of 23 October 2007 [07A3050], at http://www.dgsi.pt/jstj.nsf/954f0ce6ad9dd8b980256b5f003fa814/706805101f6db1e680257c67005 2085a?OpenDocument.
576. *See* Decision of the Supreme Court of 20 March 2001 [Process: 00A4063], available at http:/ /www.dgsi.pt/jstj.nsf/954f0ce6ad9dd8b980256b5f003fa814/0738d38371cc1abe80256b0500562ba 6?OpenDocument.
577. Article 1260 CC.
578. Article 1262 CC.
579. Article 1261 CC.
580. Article 1259 CC.

442. Acquisition of possession can take the form of apprehension (taking an object not in someone's possession) or seizure (taking an object in someone's possession). It can also be obtained through a two-sided process of handing over the possession from one party to another. The transfer of possession of goods is called 'delivery'. In relation to land, it is common to speak of granting or giving possession.

§2. Adverse Possession

443. The *usucapio* is a way of acquiring ownership and other use of real rights, based on the uninterrupted possession of an object for a certain length of time established by law, and exercised by a person other than the owner or holder of a limited right. Article 1267(2)(d) provides that possession is interrupted when, by any cause, it is suspended for more than one year. The interruption is produced also when the owner sues judicially the possessor and he/she is summoned before the court,[581] or when the possessors' behaviour shows an express or tacit recognition of the owners' right.

444. Possession ad usucapionem must be public and peaceful.[582] Possession is peaceful when the possessor has not taken the possession in a violent way;[583] and possession is public if it is of such character that would give notice to a reasonable person.[584] The possessor shall not hide his/her acts of possession towards third parties and especially before the owner. He/she must act in such way that the owner can be aware of the possession when he/she visits his/her parcel of land. It is peacefully accepted that the owner has a duty of diligence and of taking care of property.

445. The duration of possession that will lead to *usucapio* varies according to the nature of the goods. In order to benefit from the adverse possession over immovables, the possessor normally must have possessed the property for at least twenty years.[585] The Portuguese Civil Code provides for short delays of fifteen and ten years[586] but these short terms are subject to two additional conditions, such as the following: (1) the possession is grounded in a title (that would have transferred property if it was substantially valid, or if the transferor would have been the legal owner)[587] which has been subject to registration; and (2) the possessor is in good

---

581. Article 323 CC *ex vi* Article 1292 CC.
582. Article 1297 CC.
583. Article 1261 CC.
584. Article 1262 CC.
585. For movable property, possession must have been longer than ten years (Article 1298(2) CC).
586. Two and four years for movable property.
587. By just title should be understood a contract allowing the transfer of ownership or any other limited real right, that is to say, there must be a contractual title that a priori is adequate to allow the acquisition. Only the lack of transferor's ownership or a material invalidity of the contract, such as error, could prevent the acquisitive effect. The one who has acquired goods from a non-owner may consolidate the acquired right owing to a lengthy period of possession.

faith, which means that he/she did not know and was not required to know at the moment of the taking of the possession that he/she was not the owner.[588]

446. The rights of adverse possessors are referred to as 'overriding interests' and they bind a purchaser even though they do not appear on the register. If the possessor can prove that he/she was in adverse possession for twenty years[589] before a third acquirer purchased the immovable, the third acquirer will not be able to recover possession of the property and the possessor will be entitled to be registered as owner. If the possessor had not accrued twenty years adverse possession when the transaction occurred, time will continue to run in his/her favour and the third acquirer will need to institute legal proceedings quickly if he/she wishes to recover possession.

If an owner sues the possessor to recover possession of the property, the possessor will make a counterclaim that the possessor had acquired the property by adverse possession.[590] A *reivindicatio* will not succeed if the possessor can prove that he/she was in adverse possession of the immovable for a continuous period of twenty years. In Portugal, acquisitive prescription can be invoked against a transferee for value, who relied on the contents of the register (*usucapio contra tabulas)*.

Since the possessor had successfully obtained title to property by adverse possession, he/she may, optionally, bring an action in court to 'quiet title' of record in his/her name. He/she might ask the Court to recognize that he/she is the owner of the house, and then have the judicial decision inscribed in the Land Registry.

447. Articles 89 et seq. CN provide a formal procedure – called *Escritura de Justificação Notarial*– that allows the possessor to have his/her acquisition settled in the Land Registry. It is a complex and public proceeding, under a Notary, which will provide the possessor a deed to register in the Land Registry Office.[591] However, if his/her right were challenged in Court by someone, the possessor would not benefit from the presumption of Article 7 of the CRegP (that he/she is the owner), and no reversal of proof would exist.[592] Therefore, the possessor would have to prove before the Court that he/she had acquired ownership of the property through adverse possession.

---

588. Article 1296 CC. *See* Santos Justo, *Direitos Reais*, 5th edn (Coimbra: Coimbra Editora, 2017, 175; Menezes Cordeiro, *Tratado De Direito Civil Português I-* Parte Geral, II- Coisas, 3rd edn (Coimbra: Almedina, 2005), 94; Oliveira Ascensão, *Direito Civil, Reais*, 5th edn (Coimbra: Coimbra Editora), 104; Menezes Leitão, *Direitos Reais* (Coimbra: Almedina, 2019), 133.
589. If a possessor did not acquire a immovable property, e.g., a farm, by virtue of a valid legal act conveying ownership (for instance, he/she simply moved into the farm), or, though he/she did enter into a valid legal act of acquisition with a third party, he/she did so in bad faith, because he/she knew the farm did not belong to the person conveying it, then he/she must possess the farm publicly, peacefully, and uninterruptedly for twenty years in order to acquire ownership of it and not be removed by the owner.
590. José Alberto González, *Direitos Reais e Direito Registal Imobiliário*, 4th edn (Lisboa: Quid Iuris, 2009), 270–271.
591. Article 116 CRegP.
592. Decision of the STJ (Uniformization Case Law) 1/2008, in *DR* of 31 March 2008.

Chapter 4. Accession

§1. General Introduction

448. According to Article 1325 of the CC, accession is a mode of acquiring property that operates when an object (called accessory object) is incorporated into another (principal or main object) in an indissoluble way, that is to say, in such a manner that the former cannot be detached or cannot be detached without impairment of the latter. The [continuous] accession is based on a general principle, which is usually in line with the Latin expression *accesorium sequitur principale*, according to which, when a permanent incorporation of an accessory object to a principal one occurs, the owner of the principal object makes his/hers the accessory one. As is obvious, this effect is regardless of the obligation to compensate to the accessory object's owner, depending on the circumstances of the incorporation.[593]

449. It is controversial whether accession to property is a mode of original acquisition.[594] Accession does not lead to the constitution of a new property right. In reality, only the object to which a property right is linked expands. When a house is built on a piece of land, the owner of that land automatically becomes, by accession, the owner of that house as well. But he/she has not acquired a separate new property right in it. The owner still has only one right of ownership, whose object now includes an additional component, for example, the house built on the land. It can be said that in accession there is a physical extension of the goods which are the object of the right of ownership.

450. Within the continuous accession, several species should be distinguished, because some cases of incorporation are due to natural forces (natural accession) and others due to human activity (industrial accession). The CC devotes Articles 1327 to 1332 to natural accession. As regards industrial accession, the Code uses for its classification the criterion of the nature of the goods affected by the union or incorporation of others. Therefore, Articles 1333 to 1338 are dedicated to the movable accession and Articles 1339 to 1343 deal with immovable accession.

§2. Natural Accession

451. The Civil Code regulates several cases of natural accession, mainly caused by the force of fluvial waters, lakes, and small lakes. On this issue, Articles 1328 ff state that the increase of land, gradually resulting due to the water current, belongs to the owners of the lands adjacent to the rivers banks. The alluvium is the gradual addition to land along a river, lake, etc., through the deposit of sedimentary material or the recession of water.[595] Article 1329 provides for avulsion, that is, the sudden and violent movement of soil, plants, or other objects, from one property to another,

593. Articles 1333 ff CC.
594. J. Castro Mendes, *Teoria Geral do Direito Civil*, vol. I (Lisboa: FDUL, 1978), 339 ff.
595. Article 1328 CC.

as a result of a flood or a shift in the course of a boundary stream. The owner of such things is entitled to claim their restitution within six months. Otherwise, the owner loses his/her right to the things and the owner of the land will acquire them through accession. The owner of the bed of a river also acquires the property over small river islands.[596]

§3. Industrial Accession

452. In industrial accession, incorporation is due to human activity; the object incorporated might be movable or immovable.

I. Movable Accession

453. A first instance of movable accession is the adjunction, which consists in the inseparable joining of two or more heterogeneous movable goods that belong to different owners. If the thing is incorporated in an indissoluble way or cannot be detached without impairing the movable, and the incorporator is in good faith, the owner of the object with higher value acquires ownership over all property. In such a case, he/she has the obligation to compensate the other owner or to give him a thing of equivalent value.[597]

If both things have the same value, owners can decide to bid in an auction between them, or to sell the thing in its new entirety and share the value of the sale.[598] In any case, the author of the incorporation is always obliged to keep the thing if the owner of the incorporated thing prefers to receive compensation.[599] If the thing can be detached without causing damage, and the incorporator is in bad faith, he/she is obliged to return the thing to its owner.[600]

454. If the thing cannot be detached without causing damage, the owner of the thing can prefer to keep it and to compensate the author according to the rules regarding unjust enrichment. Otherwise, the author is obliged to pay him the value of the thing and to compensate the owner for damages.[601]

A. Specification

455. It is necessary to mention the specification, understood as the creating of a new article out of someone' chattel by means of another person's labour. Although it is included among the legal provisions on accession, the specification causes no

596. Article 1331 CC.
597. Article 1333(1) CC.
598. Article 1433(2) and (3) CC.
599. Article 1433(4) CC.
600. Article 1434(1) CC.
601. Article 1334(2) CC.

incorporation, nor shall we speak of a principal object or an accessory one. What we are referring to is only the application of personal work on another persons' chattel. Articles 1336 and 1337 of the CC resolve the conflict between the person whose labour is involved and the chattel's owner, depending on the former acting in good or bad faith. When the person who has made the specification has acted in good faith, he/she may make the work his/hers, compensating its owner for the chattel's value. However, if the chattel's value is higher than the cost of the work, it is the owner who has the option of either keeping the new species after compensating the person the cost of the work, or asking for the compensation of the chattel's value. When the person who made the specification has acted in bad faith, the chattel's owner may make the new species his/hers without paying to him/her the cost of the work, except if the specification increased the value of the thing by more than one-third. If the value has increased by more than one-third, the owner shall pay the excess.

II. Immovable Accession

456. The owner of a land, who builds a work, or makes a planting or a seeding with materials, seeds, or plants belonging to another, acquires property over them if he/she pays the price and compensates the owner with their value and, when there has been bad faith, compensates – if caused – for the damages as well.[602]

Article 1340 sets forth that the owner of the materials, the plants, and the seeds who has built, planted, or sown in another's property might acquire the land provided that the following conditions are met: (a) he/she was in good faith, that is, did not know that the land belonged to another or if he/she was authorized by the owner of the land; (b) the value added by the works, plants and the seeding to the land is superior to the land's value;[603] and (c) he/she pays the value of the land.

If the value of the works, plants, and the seeding added to the land is not superior to the land's value, the owner of the ground where a third party has built, planted, or sown, will have the right to make his/hers the work, planting, or crops sown, compensating the necessary expenses to the person who made any of them.

If the owner of the materials, the plants, and the seeds/crops who has built, planted, or sown in another's property is in bad faith, the owner has the following rights: the right to claim the destruction of the work, plantation, or seeding; or the right to keep the work, plantation, or the seeding, compensating the owner according to rules regarding unjust enrichment. The owner of the ground does not have the power to oblige the person who built or planted to keep the ground for him/her, in exchange for the corresponding price, or to oblige the person who sowed the crops to pay a mandatory lease rent proportional to the time the ground was used.

602. Article 1339 CC. *See* Decision of the Supreme Court of 6 July 2006 [Process: 05A4270], at http://www.dgsi.pt/jstj.nsf/954f0ce6ad9dd8b980256b5f003fa814/04e55cbf4a42d2d1802571b10033d1d1?OpenDocument.

603. Under normal circumstances, only the value of works is superior to the value of the land.

457. Article 1343 foresees the situation of extra-limited constructions (i.e., the constructions that are mainly on one's own land and only in a small part on another person's ground). When something similar to this occurs, the CC provides a solution following the theory of reverse accession, according to which the principle *superficies solo cedit* must be reversed, with the result that the building is the principal object and the ground is the accessory object. The requirements for application of this solution are as follows: good faith of the builder; three months having passed without opposition from the other owner; the builder having paid the value of the land; and the builder having compensated the damaged caused to the neighbour.

Chapter 5. Appropriation

458. The appropriation is a way to acquire ownership (i.e., it is not suitable for limited real rights) upon movable property that is based on appropriation of goods without an owner (*res nullius or res derelicta*).[604] Appropriation is regulated in Articles 1318 ff CC. The Civil Code sets forth several rules respecting specific situations.

459. Article 1319 provides that wild animals can be the object of hunting and fishing, provided those activities are performed according to the requirements set forth by law.[605] Wild animals that are sheltered in a den and move to a den belonging to another person, belong to the latter if they cannot be recognized. If the animal can be recognized, the former owner might claim them.[606] If the animals were somehow attracted by the latter, he/she is obliged to return the animals. Otherwise, the owner will have the right to receive compensation equivalent to thrice the price.[607]

460. The owner of a swarm of bees has the right to capture them in a land belonging to another owner, but he/she is liable for damages.[608] If the owner does not chase the bees as soon as he/she knows that they have disappeared or if two days have passed, the latter owner is entitled to own them.[609]

461. According to Article 1323, whoever finds a lost animal or a movable good and knows who the owner is, ought to return it or give notice to the owner in an adequate way. If the owner does not claim the animal or the movable good within one year, the finder is entitled to appropriate it. The finder has the right to compensation for damages, and has *ius retentionis*.

462. A treasure is defined, for legal purposes, as a hidden and unknown deposit of money, jewellery, or other precious things, whose ownership is not definitively settled. According to Article 1324, if it is not possible to know who owns it, the treasure belongs to the owner of the estate where the treasure has been found. However, if the finding happened by chance, owing to a person other than the land's owner, half the treasure will belong to the finder and the other half to the estate's owner. The finder must give notice of the treasure or give notice to the public

604. As regards the requirement that goods liable to appropriation must be goods without an owner, this condition may be fulfilled because the goods have never had such an owner (*res nullius* by nature) or because they have abandoned the owner (*res derelicta*).
605. Hunting is regulated by Law 173/99, of 21 October, as amended (last amendment by DL 2/2011, of 6 January), and DL 202/2004, of 18 August, as amended (last amendment by DL 72/2018, of 11 April). Fishing is mainly regulated by Law 7/2008, of 15 February.
606. Article 1320(1) CC.
607. Article 1320(2) CC.
608. Article 1322(1) CC.
609. Article 1322(2) CC.

authorities, except if it is evident that the treasure was hidden for more than twenty years. If the finder does not comply with his/her duties, the State will subrogate on the rights over the treasure.[610]

463. DL 270/2001, of 6 October, establishes the specific regime for exploitation of quarries and mines.[611] A license to conduct research activities[612] and to explore mineral resources[613] is needed to open quarries and mines. The owner, or a person with whom he/she had celebrated a contract of research and exploration or only of exploration, is entitled to obtain such a licence.[614] This contract shall be made in a public deed and must specify the annual retribution to the owner.[615] Under Portuguese law, fruits are objects which a thing produces periodically, without impairing its substance.[616] Minerals and stones are not considered to be natural fruits. However, if the owner has celebrated a contract with a third person to explore a quarry, the usufructuary is entitled to collect the income from the mining or quarrying operations for the duration of the usufruct.[617] The consent of the bare owner is required, should the usufructuary wish to open new mines or quarries.[618] Otherwise, a usufructuary is entitled to only take stones from the soil to execute repairs and works for which he/she is responsible. A usufruct can be created over a concession to research activities and exploration of mineral resources. In such a case, the usufructuary has the right to exploit existing mines or quarries according to the practice of the owner.[619]

610. Article 1324(3) CC.
611. As amended by DL 340/2007, of 12 October.
612. Articles 20 ff of DL 270/2001.
613. Article 27 of DL 270/2001.
614. Article 10(1) DL of 270/2001.
615. Articles 12(2) and 14 of DL 270/2001.
616. Article 212 CC.
617. Article 1457(2) CC.
618. Article 1458 CC.
619. Article 1457(1) CC.

Chapter 6. Expropriation

464. Article 62(2) of the CRP sets forth that requisitioning or compulsory acquisition of property for public purposes shall be carried out only under the authority of law and on the payment of fair compensation. The legal regime of expropriation set in Expropriations Code (hereinafter 'CE') as approved by Law 168/99, of 18 September.[620]

§1. Compulsory Acquisition of Land

465. According to Article 1 of the CE, expropriation is a way to transfer a right of property by means of the deprivation of the goods being the object of the right, compulsorily decided by the competent administrative department. The expropriation must be justified by a public utility or a social interest,[621] and it requires the owner who suffers it to be paid an appraisal in exchange for the object of appropriation. The expropriating entity shall respect the rights and interests of the owner and other interested parties and respect the principles of legality, justice, equality, proportionality, impartiality, and good faith.[622]

466. The expropriation must impinge upon the property needed for the public purpose; however, future needs might be taken into consideration. Those needs shall be set according to a plan for the following six years.[623]

If the statement of public utility impinges upon a part of an immovable, or only a part of the immovable is needed for the purpose stated, the expropriation shall be partial. However, the owner can require the total expropriation of the land if the rest of the land rests with no economic interest, or if the diminution of the utility is not proportional.[624]

I. Public Utility

467. The entity expropriating shall try to attain an agreement of transfer of the goods needed for the purpose stated. In accordance with this, a concrete proposal of sale shall be endorsed to the owner and a proposal of compensation shall be endorsed to the tenant. According to Article 11 of the CE, the refusal or the non-answer of the endorsees on the agreement is a necessary prerequisite for the authority to require the statement of public utility.

---

620. As amended (last amendment by Laws 56/2008, of 4 September).
621. This declaration is considered to be implicit in projects of urban development and construction deemed priority (Article 93 CE).
622. Article 2 CE.
623. Article 3(1) CE.
624. Articles 3 and 55 and seq. CE.

A previous declaration of public utility, stated in Article 1 of the CE, is required. The resolution to require the declaration of public utility shall mention the following: the purpose to be attained, the goods to be taken, their owners, and other interested persons (such as tenants); the amount of the charges with the taking; and zoning restrictions.[625] The requirement shall be made to the competent Minister or to the Municipal Assembly. The declaration shall offer strong evidence that the land is needed for the purpose stated, and must be published in the Official Journal. Notice must also be given to the owner and other interested people. They shall also be notified when the public authority is to enter into possession of the property. If the expropriation is deemed to be urgent, the expropriating entity is immediately allowed to take possession of the land (Article 15 of the CE).[626]

II. Compensation

468. The CE provides for compensation to be paid for the property acquired. In the assessment of compensation, the prejudice to the owner as a result of expropriation should be considered, and not the gain obtained by the expropriating authority. It shall be the amount corresponding to the real and current value of the property, according to the effective and possible use as per a criterion of normal economic utilization, as on the date of the expropriation.[627]

469. Tenancy rights are autonomously considered for determining the amount of the compensation. An urban tenant for residential purposes has the right to choose between a new contract with location and rent similar to the previous one, or compensation in a lump sum of money. An urban tenant for commercial, industrial, or professional purposes has the right to compensation for reasonable expenses for relocation of place of business (including damages with the interruption of the activity). A rural tenant has the right to compensation for fruits and for improvements and also the right to be compensated by the damages resulting from the extinction of the contract.[628]

625. Article 10 CE.
626. The expropriation might also be considered very urgent, if it is grounded on reasons of public calamity, internal security or national defence. In such situations, the State or authorized Public Authorities are entitled to take immediately goods in possession. If possible, a folder *ad perpetuam rei memoriam* shall be organized in order to settle all the relevant elements for the process (Article. 16 CE).
627. Those provisions are applied, *mutatis mutandis*, to limited real rights (Article 32 CE).
628. Articles 30 and 31 CE.

III. Procedure

470. Within fifteen days after the publicity of the public utility declaration, the expropriating authority must propose the amount of compensation to the right holders. If no agreement is reached within that term, an arbitration administrative organization must then intervene.[629] This body must make a decision by majority and this decision must be notified to the owner, and the expropriating authority.

The expropriation process must then be sent to the Court, with a document attesting the deposit of the amount due as compensation. Within ten days, the judge allocates to the expropriating authority the property and the possession (if there is the case). Where the persons entitled to compensation are dissatisfied with the quantum awarded, they may oppose the arbitral decision by means of a judicial appeal, within twenty days after that communication.

IV. Reversal

471. The owner has the right to restitution of the property if the property is not allocated to the purpose stated within two years after the allocation. The same applies when the purpose stated ceases to exist. The reversal shall be required within three years. The right will, then, expire. Since that date until twenty years after the expropriation, the owner has a pre-emption right in the first alienation of the land.[630]

§2. Compulsory Acquisition of Movable Property

472. According to Article 91 CE, the expropriation of movable goods, when allowed by law (e.g., Law 13/85, 6 July, on cultural patrimony), shall initiate with the *ad perpetuam rei memoriam,* and by the taking into possession by the public authority. As regards the payment of compensation, the procedure described in above fully applies.

§3. Administrative Servitudes

473. Article 8 CE states the legal regime for administrative servitudes. They shall be needed for the achievement of the public purpose stated. The constitution of a servitude gives place to compensation when land cannot continue to be used as it used to be, globally considered; when the servitude prevents the use of the land; when the land losses its economic value. Compensation is set according to the general rules of the CE.

629. Article 38 CE.
630. Article 5(5) CE.

§4. Requisitioning

474. Requisitioning of property for public purposes is ruled on Articles 80 CE et seq. It is provided that in case of urgent need, and a national public interest, the State can require private land property (including business premises) to perform activities of clear public interest. Requisitioning cannot last for more than one year and entitles the owner to compensation. The goods or rights requested are acquired by the requisitioning entity or by a different organization as beneficiary of the request. The resolution of the Council of Ministers shall assess the urgency and the public interest at stake, according to the principles of proportionality and adequacy.

475. The owner has a right to compensation according to the duration of the requisition, the cost of the goods, their normal profit, the use made of, and the gain that the individual will not make. Compensation is settled by agreement, between the requisitioning entity and the owner, or if an agreement is not reached, by the minister competent. If owners are dissatisfied with the quantum awarded, they may challenge it by means of a judicial appeal.

476. The beneficiary entity of the request has several duties. It must pay the charges with the requisition; use the goods for the purpose set; to warm the owner if there is a defect on the good; remove all the improvements or material attached to the good; and to return the good at the end of the requisition. The beneficiary is liable for damages due to its fault.[631] The owner has the duty to deliver the good to the beneficiary, and do not disturb the use of it. If it is possible, and does not put at stake or disturb the requisition, the owner is entitled to continue using the good.[632]

§5. Confiscation

477. Articles 109 and 110 of the Penal Code provide for the confiscation of property in certain instances where the owner of the property has been involved in criminal activity. The property might have been used or aimed to be used for the practice of a crime, or might be a result of that crime (e.g., fake goods). Property by its very nature, or according to the concrete circumstances of the situation, must endanger security of people or public order, or might be used to the practice of new crimes. The judge might order the destruction of the property or take it out of the market.

In general, goods are not confiscated, if they do not belong to the agent. However, owners can also be confiscated if they have contributed to the practice of the crime; if they got benefits from the crime; or they have acquired the good after the commitment of the crime, knowing that the good had been used on it. Article 111 provides for confiscation of the benefits given or promised to the criminal agents. In this situation, third parties on good faith are protected.

---

631. Article 85 CE.
632. Article 86(1) CE.

478. Law 30/2017, of 30 May, implement Directive 2014/42/EU of the European Parliament and of the Council of 3 April 2014 on the freezing and confiscation of instrumentalities and proceeds of crime in the European Union. Law 83/2017, of 18 August,[633] on the prevention and repression of the use of the financial system for the purpose of money laundering and terrorist financing, implemented Directive (EU) 2015/849 of the European Parliament and of the Council of 20 May 2015 on the prevention of the use of the financial system for the purposes of money laundering or terrorist financing, amending Regulation (EU) No 648/2012 of the European Parliament and of the Council, and Council Directive (EU) 2016/2258 of 6 December 2016 amending Directive 2011/16/EU as regards access to anti-money-laundering information by tax authorities.

633. As amended by DL 371/2009, of 30 October, Law 46/2011, of 24 June, Decree law 242/2012, of 7 November, Decree Law 18/2013, of 6 February, DL 157/2014, of 24 October, and Law 62/2015, of 24 June.

Chapter 7. Insolvency

§1. General Introduction

479. The Insolvency and Corporate Recovery Code (hereinafter 'CIRE')[634] establishes a single main insolvency proceeding [*processo de insolvência*], without distinction being made between corporate recovery and insolvency. Creditors are required to assess the company's financial viability and decide jointly whether recovery or liquidation is appropriate, and in what terms. The debtor is considered to be insolvent when he/she is not able to comply with his/her obligations in due time. If the debtor is a company, it will be deemed insolvent when the aggregate value of its debt is higher than the value of its assets determined upon a fair assessment.

480. The main goals of the insolvency proceeding are: (i) the liquidation of the insolvent debtor's estate and the distribution of the proceeds amongst the creditors pursuant to the terms of the legal default regime; or (ii) to establish the terms of an insolvency plan in order to recover the insolvent company or to liquidate the insolvent debtor's estate, according to the rules settled by the creditors upon resolution. The insolvency proceedings may, after the insolvency's declaration having been issued by the court, lead to the immediate liquidation of the company or to the approval of an insolvency plan. This is determined by the creditors whose powers to determine the future of the insolvent company are significantly increased under the CIRE.

§2. The Proceeding

481. The insolvency procedure must be initiated in the court of the debtor's head office or domicile or, in the case of the insolvency of an unclaimed deceased estate, at the court of the deceased's domicile at the time of death. Application for a declaration of insolvency may also be made to the court in the location of the debtor's principal interests – this being defined as the place where he/she normally administers his/her affairs and which is recognizable as such by third parties.

After the declaration of insolvency, the company is controlled by the insolvency administrator. The administrator is entitled to perform all acts and carry out all transactions within the ordinary course of business in order to allow the continuation of the company's trading. He/she is also responsible for collecting the company's assets (and in doing so, he/she is entitled to bring up legal actions against the company's debtors), selling all the assets of the company and making all the arrangements in order to pay the creditors of the insolvent estate and of the insolvent debtor.

---

634. Approved by DL 53/2004, of 18 March, as amended (last amendment by Law 8/2008, of 2 March).

482. The directors and the shareholders of the company will maintain their functions and competencies. However, directors may not receive any remuneration being entitled to resign from their offices. Both directors and shareholders are obliged to: (i) provide all the relevant information requested by the insolvent administrator, by the creditors' assembly, by all of the creditors and by the court; (ii) attend, personally, the court if the judge determines that; and (iii) be cooperative with the insolvency administrator.

§3. Effects of the Insolvency on the Debtor's Patrimony

483. Unless provided otherwise, the estate of an insolvent party comprises all the debtor's assets on the date of declaration of insolvency by the court, together with assets and rights acquired by the debtor while proceedings are pending.

Non-attachable assets only form part of the estate if the debtor offers them voluntarily and if their non-attachable quality is not absolute.

484. The law draws a distinction between the insolvency debts and the debts of the estate. The former are claims on the insolvent party which arose prior to the declaration of insolvency. Claims which the creditor can prove to have arisen during the procedure are treated in the same way. Debts of the estate are those created during the process, and include, for example, costs of the proceedings and the administrator's remuneration.

485. As regards the debtor's assets, the effect of the declaration of insolvency is to deprive the debtor immediately – either directly or through his/her directors – of the power to administer and dispose of the assets comprising the estate. With effect from that moment, those powers are vested in the administrator, who takes over the role of debtor's representative for all matters of a financial nature relating to the insolvency. As a rule, acts undertaken by the insolvent party in breach of these arrangements are ineffectual.

486. The declaration of insolvency causes all the obligations of the insolvent party which are not subject to a condition precedent to become due for settlement.

§4. Claims

487. Unsecured creditors have to claim their rights in the insolvency proceeding within thirty days from the declaration of the debtor's insolvency issued by the court. Once this term has lapsed, unsecured creditors may still claim its credits through a lawsuit brought against the insolvent estate, the other creditors, and the debtor. This lawsuit must be filed within the term of one year after the declaration of insolvency. However, creditors who have been personally notified of the declaration of insolvency are not entitled to file this claim. Claims presented by unsecured creditors, whose rights have been acknowledged by the court, will be paid on a pro rata basis, depending on the value of the insolvent assets, and only provided that all the other debts of the insolvent estate, have been paid.

488. Secured creditors are usually notified of the declaration of insolvency since their credits are, in principle, registered at the relevant Registry Offices (Commercial or Land Registry). In view of this, they are only entitled to claim the amounts owed to them in the insolvency proceeding within thirty days from that declaration. In view of the above, creditors with security over real property owned by the debtor are first paid by the proceeds which arise from the sale of such assets. In the event that these proceeds are not sufficient to pay the full amount owed to the creditor, the outstanding amount will be treated as an unsecured claim. Even where a security was granted in favour of the creditor, 10% of the proceeds arising from the sale of the respective assets shall be used to pay the debts of the insolvent estate.

489. Set-off is permitted where the sums owed by the company to a creditor and owed by the latter to the company are mutual, both enforceable, due, and payable. Set-off is still permitted if the claims are expressed in different currencies provided that free and reciprocal conversion is permissible. Provided that the set-off criteria are met prior to the beginning of insolvency proceedings, both debtors and creditors are entitled to set-off their claims after the commencement of the insolvency proceedings. However, set-off will not be permitted as follows: (i) if the debt to the insolvent estate arose after the date of the declaration of insolvency; (ii) if the insolvency creditor acquired his/her claim from a third person after the beginning of the insolvency proceedings; (iii) in relation to debts of the insolvent company for which the insolvent estate is not liable; or (iv) between debts to the insolvent estate and subordinated claims against the insolvent estate

490. During the insolvency proceedings, the administrator will assess and quantify the claims against the debtor company. The creditors will be able to submit their claims by lodging them with the administrator. When filing their claims, the creditors should give details of the following: (i) the nature, amount (principal and interest), and due date of the claim; (ii) whether the claim is subject to any condition; (iii) whether it is a common, subordinated, guaranteed, or privileged claim; (iv) the existence of any personal guarantees of the claim and who the guarantors are; and (v) the applicable interest rate. A creditor is required to submit to the administrator a formal, written claim referred to as a 'proof of debt'. In general, all claims are provable, whether they be present or future, contingent or vested in the creditor and whether arising from contract, tort, breach of trust, statute or in any other manner. Rent and other payments of a periodic nature may be evidenced up to the date of the declaration of insolvency and thereafter as they fall due (unless they are payable as a debt of the insolvent estate in which case they are likely to be paid in full). Interest is only provable up to the last day of the time period for making claims.

491. After having paid the debts of the insolvent estate, the administrator may begin to make the payments to other creditors of the debtor according to the following order: (i) guaranteed creditors [*credores garantidos*] – which comprises secured claims and special preferred claims (e.g., claims of the employees); (ii) privileged creditors [*credores privilegiados*] – regarding generally preferred claims over the assets of the insolvent estate; (iii) common creditors [*credores comuns*] – regarding unsecured and unsubordinated creditors whose claims will be satisfied on a pro rata basis, depending on the value of the insolvency assets; (iv) subordinated creditors [*credores subordinados*] – the payment of these claims occurs after all of the other creditors of the debtor having been fully paid, in the order set forth in Article 48 of the CIRE, on a *pro rata* basis.

Part IV. Trust and Fiduciary Mechanisms

492. In Portugal, the institution of trust is unknown and the existence of two simultaneous titles of property on the same goods is not accepted.[635] The main reason set forth to support this idea is the *numerus clausus* principle in force in Portugal. However, the legal regime, in itself, would face several difficulties to encompass such an institution, as regards the publicity of property law, and the legal regime for succession law. The matter, however, remains controversial, both in doctrine[636] and, more recently, in case law.[637]

493. Therefore, I will devote my attention to institutions of fiduciary nature accepted by Portuguese law. Following the Roman categorization, I will distinguish between *fiducia cum amico* – that might have an aim of management – from *fiducia cum creditore* – that aims to guarantee the payment of a debt. Under the former category, I will also mention the fiduciary mechanism *mortis causa*, the *fideicommissum*.

494. As an operative concept, I will consider that a *fiducia cum amico* exists when the settlor conveys to the fiduciary an apparent property right upon one or more goods, so that the fiduciary might carry some kind of management activity

635. Portugal is not a party to the Convention Concerning the Law Applicable to Trusts and to their Recognition of 1 Jul. 1985. DL 264/90, of 31 August, authorized 'the incorporation and operation of companies, as well as the opening of branches by existing institutions whose sole object was trusts or offshore trust management' in the Madeira Free Zone, but only in Madeira Autonomous Region. This provision is, however, very restricted, both in material and in territorial scope.

636. M. João Vaz Tomé & Diogo Leite de Campos, *A Propriedade Fiduciária (Trust)*, (Coimbra: Almedina, 1999), 297–303, claim that the trust should be adapted to Portuguese legal framework and socio-economic reality. Pedro Pais de Vasconcelos, in *Contratos Atípicos* (Coimbra: Almedina, 2005), 277–285, claims for the actual validity of fiduciary contracts under Portuguese Law.

637. The Decision of the Court of Appeal of Oporto, from 10 May 2001 [Process 1942/06.5TBMAI.P1], available at http://www.dgsi.pt/jtrp.nsf/56a6e7121657f91e80257cda00381fdf/6ec62a306436caa2802578a10053e5c3?OpenDocument, in a totally innovative way, admitted as a general principle that fiduciary contracts, with a scope of guarantee, are valid under the principle of freedom of contract, as stated in Article 405 CC. In concrete, however, these contracts can be deemed as usurious and, thus, invalid. More recently, the Decision of the same Court of Appeal, from 28 November 2017 [Process 1050/06.9TVPRT.P1], available at http://www.dgsi.pt/jtrp.nsf/56a6e7121657f91e80257cda00381fdf/2a723bfa593117d380258213004d8366?OpenDocument&Highlight=0,trust took a different approach: the trust is not generally admitted in Portugal and does not overcome the *numerus clausus* principle. On a partial recognition, accepting a *inter parts* efficacy, the decision of the Court of Appeal of Évora, from 28 June 2017, available at: http://www.dgsi.pt/jtre.nsf/134973db04f39bf2802579bf005f080b/057542ff30e515bd80258154003d7d6c?OpenDocument&Highlight=0,trust.

regarding it. This fiduciary's management activity can lie in the mere custody of the goods, in their diligent administration (i.e., collecting fruits or rents), or in their alienation to a third party followed by a diligent management of the money received as a price.[638]

The *fiducia cum amico* is compatible with the fact that the fiduciary receives some kind of payment for its performance, perhaps by means of the permission to use the goods transferred to him/her under a fiduciary title, and/or to obtain the fruits or rents that they produce.

The interest to protect can be the settlor's interest, to whom the goods fiduciarily transferred (or those acquired instead of them) will have to be returned in the end, or it can be a beneficiary's interest, whom the settlor wants to favour, as is the case with the successory modalities of *fiducia cum amico*.[639]

The normal structure of a fiduciary relationship *cum amico* implies the conveyance of an apparent title upon one or more goods, the carrying out of the management according to which had been assumed in the *pactum fiduciae*, and the return of the object of the fiduciary operation once the management has been fulfilled.

495. There is a *fiducia cum creditore* when the fiduciary, a debtor, transfers to his/her creditor the fiduciary title upon one or more goods with the goal of guaranteeing the debt contracted with the latter. The debtor transfers the goods to his/her creditor with an additional agreement in accordance with which the creditor will return the goods to the debtor once the guaranteed debt has been paid. The fiduciary's title, exactly the same as in the case of the *fiducia cum amico*, is a temporary and functional one. However, unlike the *fiducia cum amico*, in the cases of *fiducia cum creditore* it is not in the settlor's benefit but in the fiduciary title holder's interest, since the fiduciary title holder is the creditor whose credit is intended to guarantee. The title upon the trusted goods, although a fiduciary one, gives the creditor the surety that the goods will not be the object of conveyance on the part of the debtor, in particular that the title will not be given as a guarantee in favour of other creditors.[640]

496. On the chapter dedicated to *fiducia cum amico*, I will analyse, mainly, the contract of mandate and the investment funds. As I will show, in the field of investment and management of securities, Portugal has incorporated systems of fiduciary management of securities and funds very similar to some kinds of trust. I will also

638. The purpose followed by the parties is settled in an internal arrangement agreed upon by the contracting parties, the *pactum fiduciae*. That agreement is normally a deed detached from the transferring contract and it establishes the obligations that the fiduciary assumes before the settlor.

639. The transfer of the fiduciary title upon the goods is not conceived to protect the fiduciary's interest, as occurs in the cases of *fiducia cum creditore*, but to protect the settlor's interest.

640. In normal conditions, that is to say, if the settlor-debtor pays the guaranteed debt, the fiduciary will be able to bring an action, based on the *pactum fiducia*, to obtain the return of the goods. This is a real action, since the settlor/debtor never loses the property upon the goods entrusted to the fiduciary.

mention the *fideicomissum*, as a fiduciary mechanism *mortis causa,* and the institution of foundations. On the Chapter dedicated to *fiducia cum creditore*, I will analyse the financial collateral arrangement [*alienação fiduciária em garantia*] and the sale with a *pacto de retro* [*venda a retro*].

Chapter 1. Administration of Property: *Fiducia cum Amico*

§1. Mandate

I. Concept and General Features

497. The mandate, with or without representation, is the legal instrument normally chosen to construct an express trust for the management of certain assets. Under Portuguese law, the mandate is a contract by which a party (mandatary) agrees to perform services for another (the mandator), for free or for consideration (Article 1157 CC).[641] By default, the powers granted by a mandate only include day-to-day management. If parties want to grant powers to dispose, sell, or mortgage property, the same must be expressed in the contract.[642]

498. The Civil Code clearly distinguishes the contract of mandate from the power of attorney. A mandate may or may not encompass powers of representation. If a mandate grants powers of representation, the mandatary acts on behalf of and in the name of the mandator. The powers of attorney are governed by Articles 262 to 269 CC, dealing with voluntary representation.[643] Both the power of attorney and the mandate are extinguished when the underlying relationship terminates.[644] As a general rule, both the power of attorney and the mandate are freely revocable.[645] Revocation and renunciation of the power of attorney will also lead to forfeiture of the mandate with representation.

499. When a mandate without representation is granted, the mandatary acts in his/her own name in dealings with third parties, and the legal effects of his/her actions are reflected on his/her own legal sphere. Afterwards, he/she is obliged to transfer and/or convey the effects of the mandate, that is, all rights, goods, money or other juridical objects, to the ownership of the mandator.[646]

641. The mandate is ruled in the special part of the Book of Obligations, more specifically Contracts (Articles 1157–1184 CC). The Commercial Code provides for commercial mandates – mandates to undertake commercial acts – and clearly distinguishes between mandates with and without representation, the latter known as ‘commission’ (Articles 231 to 277).
642. Article 1159 CC.
643. Powers of attorney are unilateral and may have an underlying mandate with representation or any other licit business.
644. Article 265 CC.
645. Articles 265(2), 1170 and 1171 CC.
646. Article 1181(1) CC. *See* Decision of the Supreme Court of 3 October 2002 [Process: 03B1585], at http://www.dgsi.pt/jstj.nsf/954f0ce6ad9dd8b980256b5f003fa814/0f5a48674d84278d80256df000 3bec5b?OpenDocument.

II. Rights and Duties of the Mandatary

500. The mandatary is engaged to act in the management of the affairs of the mandator. According to Article 1161 CC, the duties of the mandatary, with or without representation, include the following: (a) carrying out the acts included in the mandate according to the instructions of the mandator;[647] (b) providing information upon request of the mandator; (c) notifying the mandator of the execution of the mandate or, if the mandate is not executed, the reasons for non-compliance; (d) rendering accounts at termination of the mandate or when so required by the mandator; and (e) delivering and conveying to the mandator what has been received in the execution of the mandate or in its exercise.

III. Rights of the Mandator

501. The mandator is entitled to give instructions to the mandatary as regards the performance of the legal activity.

If the mandate was granted with representation, then by acting contrary to instructions, the mandatary is abusing the power of attorney. According to Article 269 of the CC, a contract executed by abusing the power of attorney is ineffective in relation to the mandatory provided that the abuse was known or should have been known to the third party. The mandator, however, may ratify the conveyance.[648] Ratification takes the form required for the power of attorney, and its effects are retroactive, without prejudice to the rights of third parties.

If the mandate was granted without representation, the mandatary acted *proprio nomine*. In such a case, the mandatary acquires the rights and duties resulting from the legal act. The mandator is, nevertheless, entitled to claim compensation from the mandatary for damages arising from the breach of the mandate.

IV. Extinction of the Mandate

502. Revocation without due cause of a professional mandate, or of one granted in the interest of both the mandatary and the mandator, gives rise to a claim for damages.[649] However, irrevocability of a power of attorney is expressly allowed when the power is executed in the mutual interest of the donor and the attorney. The same rule applies to the mandate when it is granted in the mutual interest of the mandator and the mandatary.[650]

---

647. In the absence of instructions, the mandatary shall act with the diligence and prudence of a bonus *paterfamilias*, in other words, as a prudent and competent manager.
648. Article 258 CC.
649. Article 265(3) CC. *See* Decision of the Supreme Court of 2 December 2013 [Process: 689/09], available at http://www.dgsi.pt/jstj.nsf/954f0ce6ad9dd8b980256b5f003fa814/9ee828afafcea93f80257c35004d22e3?OpenDocument.
650. Article 1170(2) CC.

V. Mandate Without Representation

503. A mandate without representation is granted without the underlying power of attorney.[651] Therefore, the legal effects of the acts of the mandatary are produced within his/her own legal sphere and, later, must then be transferred to the mandator. In fact, when a mandate without representation is granted, the mandatary acts in his/her own name, and the legal effects of dealings with third parties are reflected on his/her own legal sphere. Afterwards, he/she is obliged to transfer and/or convey the effects of his/her mandate, that is, all rights, goods, money, or other juridical objects, to the ownership of the mandator.[652]

504. This creates a well-known risk for the mandator in the case of insolvency or bankruptcy of the mandatary. Article 1184 of the CC protects the mandator against the personal creditors of the mandatary, who are not entitled to seize any of the goods that were acquired by the mandatary in execution of the mandate and are to be transferred to the mandator. In the case of goods whose transfer is subject to registration, the exemption is in force only prior to registration in the name of the mandatary. As a consequence of the publicity created by the registration, third party interests, including those of any creditors, become more relevant than those of the mandator. This regime of Article 1184 of the CC is of great importance and effectiveness with relation to trust-like situations.

§2. Investment Funds, Pension Funds and Securitization Funds

505. In the field of investment and management of securities, Portugal has incorporated systems of fiduciary management of securities and funds very similar to some kinds of trust. A fund is an autonomous estate, that belongs jointly to the investors, the unit holders, and is exempt from the creditors both of the fund and of the management company.

506. In principle, the professional administration of assets (portfolios) of third persons must be done by a portfolio management company. According to Articles 4-A(1)(c) and 8(2) of the Legal Framework of Credit Institutions and Financial Companies,[653] the administration of assets must be done exclusively by a special

651. According to the Portuguese report of Pedro Paes de Vasconcelos, in Michele Graziadei, Ugo Mattei, and Lionel Smith, *Commercial Trusts in European Private Law* (Cambridge: CUP, 2005), in common practice, management of assets, professionally or otherwise, is normally based upon a mandate with representation or merely a simple revocable power of attorney. It is neither normal nor frequent for ordinary people to trust the administration of goods to another person on the basis of a mandate without representation. There are, however, cases where goods are vested in third persons as fiduciaries (*fiducia cum amico*), who own them as proprietors with the aim of protecting the beneficiary from his creditors, from his own prodigality, or for some other reason. These cases of *fiducia cum amico* are usually kept secret or known only by a restricted number of people and/or inside the family.

652. Article 1181(1) CC.

653. DL 298/92, of 31 December, as amended.

kind of financial company, a management company [*sociedade de gestão de patrimónios*].[654] Management companies carry out the management of portfolios of assets on the basis of a written mandate granted by the client to the company, specifying the terms and limits of the management, and how discretionary it may be. Management companies are bound by several duties, including the following: to check the identity and legal capacity of the parties to contracts they enter into; the presentation of all contracts clearly and exactly so that no error or mistake may arise; non-disclosure of the identity of their clients, except where necessary for the conclusion of contracts; immediately informing clients about the details of contracts entered into on their behalf, unless otherwise agreed in the mandate (in principle, this should be done on the day of signing of the contract); and making best efforts for the fulfilment of contracts. All funds and transferable securities belonging to clients must be deposited in separate bank accounts opened in the names of the respective clients. These accounts may be opened in the name of the management company on behalf of the clients, provided that this is formally mentioned in each account.

507. The management must be conducted with regard to the client's interests in terms of the degree of the risk therein involved (Article 304 of the Securities Code [*Código dos Valores Mobiliários*]).[655] Portuguese securities law establishes the 'know your client rule', forcing the financial manager to inform himself/herself of the financial situation of his/her clients, their experience in terms of investment, and the goals of their investment decisions. Article 304 provides that financial intermediaries should conduct their activity so as to protect the legal interests of their clients and the efficiency of the market. In their relations with all the intermediaries in the market, financial intermediaries should observe the rule of good faith, in accordance with high standards of diligence, loyalty, and transparency. Insofar as is necessary for the compliance of its duties in providing service, the financial intermediary should be informed of the client's knowledge and experience as to the specific type of financial instrument or service offered or sought, and in addition, if applicable, as to the client's financial position and investment objectives. Financial intermediaries shall be subject to a duty of professional secrecy in the terms set out for bank secrecy. The principles and the duties referred in the following articles are applicable to the directors of the financial intermediary and the persons who effectively direct the business of the financial intermediary or the tied agent and the employees of the financial intermediary, tied agent or outsourcing entities, involved in the pursuing or supervising of financial intermediation activities or the operational functions that are essential for the provision of continual services under the conditions of quality and efficiency.

508. I will analyse the legal regime of the collective investment undertakings [*organismos de investimento colectivo*], of securitization funds [*fundos de titularização*], and of pension funds [*fundos de pensões*].

654. Ruled by DL 163/94, of 4 July, as amended.
655. DL 486/99, of 13 November, as amended.

I. Real Estate Investment Funds

509. The legal framework for real estate collective investment undertakings is now ruled by Law 16/2015, of 24 February (Undertakings for Collective Investment (UCI) Law [*Regime Geral dos Organismos de Investimento Coletivo*]).[656]

A. Concept

510. Real estate funds are collective investment undertakings, the sole objective of which is investment of capital obtained from unit holders, and the operations of which are subject to a principle of risk-spreading. Investment funds constitute standalone assets, belonging in joint-ownership to a group of natural persons or legal persons, known as unit holders. Investment funds are divided into equal parts, called participation units. Participation units with the same content constitute a category of investment unit.

511. As a general rule, funds are not, under any circumstance, liable for debts incurred by these unit holders, the participants, or by entities that under the terms of the law, are responsible for their management. Patrimonial autonomy is expressly foreseen in Article 13.

512. Investment funds may be open-ended or closed-ended. Open-ended investment funds are those which have a variable number of investment units. Closed-ended investment funds are those which have a fixed number of investment units. According to Article 62 of Law 16/2015, closed-ended investment funds may have a determinate duration. For closed-ended investment funds with a fixed duration, the period may not exceed ten years, however, the duration may be extended, for periods not greater than the initial period, provided that the shareholders' meeting votes in favour of same. The redemption of investment units by unit holders who have objected to the said extension is allowed. The participants who voted in favour of the extension may not request for the redemption of the respective investment units. Closed-ended investment funds with an indeterminate duration shall only be authorized under Article 62, 7, of Law 16/2015. Articles 211 and 212 set further regulation on this.

513. The Portuguese Securities Market Commission [*Comissão do Mercado de Valores Mobiliários*], hereinafter 'CMVM', is the main regulatory body in relation to investment funds. It is responsible for the authorisation of retail funds and for

656. As amended by DL 124/2015, of 7 July, as amended. Law 15/2015 has partially implemented Directive 2009/65/EC on undertakings for collective investment in transferable securities (UCITS) (UCITS IV Directive), as amended, as well as Directive 2011/61/EU on alternative investment fund managers (AIFM Directive), and sets out most of the rules relating to investment funds. Most of the new legal regime has entered in force on 26 March 2015.

supervision of their compliance with the rules and requirements set out in the applicable laws and regulations. Investment funds' management entities, as financial institutions, are subject to the supervision of the Bank of Portugal.

514. According to Article 210 of Law 16/2015, undertaking of collective investment for real estate are permitted to carry out the following activities: (a) the acquisition of property for rent or other forms of onerous use, (b) the acquisition of property for resale, (c) the acquisition of other rights on property, under the terms set forth by the CMVM in a regulation, with a view to the economic development of the said rights, and (d) improvements of their property.

515. Investment funds are also permitted to develop property construction and renovation projects, for one of the purposes described in items (a) and (b) of the previous paragraph, and within the limits defined for each type of investment fund.[657] The CMVM may, by means of a regulation, define the terms and conditions under which this activity can be carried on. Investment funds may acquire property, the consideration for which is deferred over time.

516. Article 149 of Law 16/2015 provides an extensive list of operations that are prohibited to undertaking for collective investment, namely the provision of guarantees. (Article 91 sets forth prohibitions to the activity of the management company.

517. Management companies must act in the sole interest of unit holders, when representing the management company itself or companies which it controls or is in a group relationship with. Whenever a management company manages more than one investment fund, it shall consider each one as a client, with a view to preventing conflicts of interests, and if these are inevitable, they shall be resolved in accordance with principles of equity and non-discrimination.[658]

518. Article 204 of Law 16/2015 provides that the assets of a real estate fund must comprise solely of property. The assets of investment funds may comprise property under right of ownership, superficies, or by means of other rights with similar content. The property held by real estate funds shall correspond to urban buildings or independent units of the same building Property may not be acquired under a system of co-ownership for real estate funds, except with regard to the co-ownership of property which is functionally linked to the use of independent units of the real estate fund. Real estate funds may acquire property under a system of co-ownership with other investment funds or pension funds, in which case an agreement must be drawn up, if applicable, on the establishment of apartment ownership, or on the distribution of income generated by the property.

---

657. The Supreme Court, on a decision dated of 13 November 2018 [Process 380/14.0T8VRL.G1.S2], available at: http://www.dgsi.pt/jstj.nsf/954f0ce6ad9dd8b980256b5f003fa814/471e4146d08d921d8025834a0033fc52?OpenDocument, considered that funds are to be considered as professionals for the purpose of consumer protection of the acquirer.

658. Article 73 of Law 16/2015.

519. The assets of an collective investment undertaking may also be comprised of investment units in real estate companies, provided as follows: (a) the object of the real estate company corresponds solely to one of the activities which can be directly exercised by investment funds; (b) at least 2/3 of the assets of the real estate company are comprised of property which can be directly integrated into the portfolio of the investment fund; (c) the real estate company does not own holdings in any other companies; (d) the real estate company has its statutory headquarters in one of the Member States of the EU or the OECD in which the investment fund is authorized to invest; (e) the accounts of the real estate company are subject to a system equivalent to that of investment funds as regards independent auditing and disclosure; (f) the real estate company agrees, in a contract with the management company of the investment fund, to provide all information subject to submission to the CMVM; (g) principles equivalent to the legal requirements applicable to investment funds shall be applied to property and other assets comprising the assets of the real estate company or acquired, used or disposed by it, in particular with regard to rules on valuation, conflicts of interests and information disclosure; (h) its shares are marketed in a regulated market or in a multilateral trading facility (for open-ended collective undertakings).

520. Article 208 of Law 16/2015 provides that the assets of a real estate fund may comprise liquidity. Liquidity shall be considered to mean bank deposits, deposit certificates, investment units from money market funds and securities issued or granted by a Member State of the European Union with a long-term book value of less than twelve months.

521. Articles 206 and 207, of Law 16/2015, also set specific rules concerning the portfolio of a collective investment undertaking.

B. *Constitution*

522. The constitution of real estate investment funds is subject to authorization by the CMVM. The proceedings are ruled by Articles 19 et seq. of Law 16/2015.

C. *Management Company*

523. According to Article 65 of Law 16/2015, the management of a real estate collective investment undertaking might be carried out by the undertaking itself or by a real estate fund management company (*sociedade gestora de fundos de investimento imobiliário*).[659]

Management companies have as their main company object the administration, on behalf of the unit holders, of one or more real estate funds. They may also do the

659. Management companies shall adopt the form of a public company, and the respective equity capital shall be represented by registered shares. Restrict exceptions are provided by Article 65 (2) to closed-ended investment funds.

following: (a) provide consultancy services related to real estate investment, including the carrying out of studies and analyses related to the property market; (b) carry out individual management of property portfolios, in accordance with the legal and regulatory provisions applicable to the management of portfolios on behalf of third parties. Management companies have as their main company object the administration, on behalf of the unit holders, of one or more real estate funds. They may also do the following: (a) provide consultancy services related to real estate investment, including the carrying out of studies and analyses related to the property market; (b) carry out individual management of property portfolios, in accordance with the legal and regulatory provisions applicable to the management of portfolios on behalf of third parties.

524. Management companies shall, in the exercise of their duties, act in the sole interest of unit holders. Articles 72 to 75 of Law 16/2015 provide that management companies, in general, shall be responsible for the practice of all acts and operations necessary or convenient to the proper administration of the collective undertaking, in accordance with criteria of a high level of diligence and professional competence, and independence.

525. Management companies are especially prohibited from carrying out the following operations: (a) issuing loans on their own behalf; (b) acquiring, on their own behalf, investment units in securities or property investment funds, with the exception of money-market funds; (c) acquiring, on their own behalf, other securities of any type, with the exception of public debt securities, equity certificates and bonds admitted to trading in a regulated market, when these bonds have been assigned at least an ‘A’ rating or equivalent, by a rating company registered with the CMVM or one that is internationally recognized; (d) granting credit, including the provision of guarantees, on their own behalf; (e) acquiring property, on their own behalf, which is not indispensable to their establishment and operations or to the pursuit of their company object.[660]

526. Management companies are permitted to subcontract another entity to perform part of its functions, according to Article 76 of Law 16/2015. Substitution of the management company is foreseen in Article 77.

D. Custodian

527. According to Article 120, the securities comprising the collective undertaking portfolio must be entrusted to one sole custodian.[661]

660. Article 91 of Law 16/2015.
661. The custodian must be a credit institution with its headquarters in Portugal, or, if it has headquarters in another Member State of the European Community, must be established in Portugal as a branch.

528. Article 121 of Law 16/2015 provides that the custodian is responsible, among others, for the following: (a) assuming a supervisory role and providing unit holders with a guarantee of compliance with the law and with the management rules and regulations of the collective undertaking, particularly as regards the investment policy and the calculations of the equity value of the investment units; (b) paying unit holders their quota of the results of the collective investment undertaking; (c) carrying out the instructions of the management company, except if these are against the law or contrary to the provisions of the management rules and regulations; (d) accepting deposits of the securities of the investment fund, or registering them; (e) ensuring that unit holders are paid when there are requests for the redemption of investment units.

529. The custodian is also responsible for the registration of investment units, according to Article 121, 1, b). Articles 121-A, B and C, 122 and 123 set out further specific duties for the custodian.

530. In the exercise of their duties, the management company and the custodian must act independently and solely in the interests of unit holders. Relations between the management company and the custodian shall be governed by a written contract, according to Articles 127 and 128 of Law 16/2015.

531. Liability of the custodian is set in Article 122. Recourse on the part of the custodian to the services of third entities shall not affect that responsibility.

E. Management Rules and Regulations

532. The management company shall draw up and maintain up-to-date management rules for each collective investment undertaking it administers, containing elements identifying the investment fund, the management company and the custodian, and also the rights and duties of unit holders, the management company and the custodian, the investment policy of the fund and conditions for its liquidation.[662]

533. The management rules and regulations must be made available to interested parties.

534. Amendments to the management rules shall be updated by the management company, according to Article 157, 2.

F. Liquidation

535. According to Article 42 of Law 16/2015, the extinction of an investment collective undertaking, the must immediately be communicated to the CMVM and

662. *See* Articles 159 and 216 of Law 16/2015.

published, together with an indication of the planned term for conclusion of the liquidation. The redemption of investment units should take place immediately.

536. Compulsory liquidation is foreseen in Article 42, 1, f), of Law 16/2015. The CMVM may revoke authorization to a collective investment fund whenever this is justified, in the interests of unit holders and the defence of the market, by virtue of the violation of the management rules and regulations or the legal and regulatory provisions.

G. On the Marketing in Portugal of Investment Units in Undertakings for Collective Investment in Real Estate, Having Headquarters or Being Administrated by Entities with Headquarters in a Foreign Country

537. The marketing in Portugal of investment units in undertakings for collective investment in real estate, having headquarters in or being administered by entities with headquarters in a foreign country, are ruled by Articles 196 and ff, and 229 and ff.

538. Articles 96 and ff rule the activity of foreign management companies.

II. Securitization Funds: Concept, Constitution and Statutory Provisions

539. Portuguese law allows receivables to be assigned to securitization funds [*fundos de titularização*] and/or to securitization companies [*sociedades de titularização*]. DL 453/99, of 5 November,[663] provides the legal regime for securitization (the legal requirements for granting credit for the effects of securitization and regulates the constitution and functioning of securitization funds, securitization) companies and the management companies of those funds. The securitization funds have no legal personality, and are managed by specialized management companies.

A. Concept

540. According to Article 9 of DL 453/99, securitization funds are autonomous assets, and belong jointly to a group of persons, individual and legal. Funds are exempt from the creditors of the fund's manager, from entities from which the loans comprising them have been acquired, or from the unit holders. Funds shall be divided into parts taking the form of book-entry securities with a par value which was established in the management rules and regulations of the fund. Those parts shall be called loan securitization units. The number of securitization units of each fund is determined in the management rules and regulations. The responsibility of

663. As amended (last amendment by DL 211-A/2008, of 3 November). *See* João Calvão da Silva, *Titularização de Créditos* (Coimbra: Almedina, 2003); and Diogo Leite de Campos & Manuel Monteiro, *Titularização de Créditos* (Coimbra: Almedina, 2001).

each person entitled to securitization units as regards the bonds of the fund shall be limited to the value of the securitization units subscribed.

541. Funds may have fixed or variable assets. Funds have variable assets when their management rules and regulations provide for the following, cumulatively or exclusively: (a) the acquisition of new loans, either when the fund has loans with a maturity date shorter than its duration, to substitute those loans on the date of their maturity, or in addition to the loans acquired on constitution of the fund; (b) the carrying out of new issues of securitization units. Funds have fixed assets when it is not possible to modify the respective assets or liabilities.[664]

542. Funds must apply their assets in the initial or subsequent acquisition of loans, which must not represent less than 75% of the assets of a fund. Funds may also, as an accessory activity, apply their liquidity reserves in the acquisition of securities listed in a regulated market and short-term public or private debt securities, provided that this is appropriate to the efficient management of the fund.[665] In order to provide the fund with the necessary liquidity reserves, the management companies may issue loans on behalf of the funds they administer, provided that this is permitted by the management rules and regulations.[666]

543. The issued units may be negotiated on the stock market. Portuguese law requires the existence of a depository, which is in charge of collecting payments of capital and interest in respect of the assigned receivables.

B. Constitution

544. The constitution of funds is regulated in Articles 27 to 30 of DL 453/99. The constitution of funds requires prior authorization by the CMVM. The fund shall be considered to be constituted on financial settlement of the subscription of the securitization units. The contract of purchase of the loans and the contract with the custodian shall have effect from the date on which the fund is constituted. Within three days of the constitution of the fund, the management company shall make this public by means of an advertisement in the listing bulletin of a regulated market situated in or operating within the national territory or through the information disclosure system provided for in Article 367 of the Portuguese Securities Code.

545. The State and other public legal persons, as well as credit institutions, financial companies, insurance forms, pension funds and pension fund management companies are permitted to grant loans for securitization purposes, as are other legal persons having had their accounts legally certified by an auditor registered with the

664. Article 10 of DL 453/99, of 5 November. Article 11 sets the conditions under which it may acquire new loans.
665. Article 12 of DL 453/99, of 5 November.
666. Article 13 of DL 453/99, of 5 November.

CMVM for the previous three years.[667] Only securitization funds and securities companies, however, are permitted to acquire credit for securitization.[668]

546. Loans suitable for securitization must fulfil the following pre-requisites: (a) their transmissibility is not subject to legal or conventional restrictions; (b) they are of a pecuniary nature; (c) they are not subject to any conditions; (d) they are not subject to litigation and are not given as a guarantee nor are they judicially pledged or apprehended.

Notwithstanding the special legal requirements applicable to the securitization of tax credits, the State and social security are permitted to grant loans for securitization purposes even if these loans are subject to conditions or litigation, in which case the originator shall not guarantee that these loans may exist or be an enforceable liability.

Future loans may also be granted for securitization purposes, provided that they arise from established relations and are for a known or estimable amount.

Insurance companies, pension funds and pension fund management companies shall only grant the following for securitization purposes: (a) mortgages; (b) loans on the State and other public legal persons; (c) loans from pension funds relative to the contributions of their participants, without prejudice to the benefits to be attributed to these parties.

547. The originator is obliged to reveal to the grantee any material events which could significantly affect the total value of the loan and of which the originator has knowledge on the date on which the loan takes effect. When the originator is a credit institution, a financial company, an insurance firm, a pension fund or a pension fund management company, a contract must always be drawn up at the same time as the loan is granted, whereby the originator or, in the case of pension funds, the fund management company is duty bound to carry out, in the name of and in representation of the grantee, all acts which prove to be appropriate to the proper management of the debt and, if such is the case, of the guarantees, being responsible for cover, administrative services relating to the loan, all relations with the debtors and defensive measures, modifications and terminations related to the guarantees, should any exist. Debt management may, in all other situations, be provided by the grantee, the originator or by a qualified third party. Management and cover for tax credits granted by the State and social security for securitization purposes shall be carried out, by means of compensation, by the originator or the State, through the General Directorate for Taxation.[669]

548. In case of bankruptcy of the debt manager, the sums in its possession arising from payments related to loans granted for securitization purposes shall not form part of the bankrupt estate.

667. Article 2 of DL 453/99, of 5 November.
668. Article 3 of DL 453/99, of 5 November.
669. Article 5 of DL 453/99, of 5 November.

C. Management Companies

549. Article 15 of DL 453/99 provides that the management of funds must be undertaken by a securitization fund management company. Companies managing securitization funds are financial companies which adopt the status of public company, and must have their headquarters and conduct the management of their operations in Portugal. The management company's corporate name must include the expression securitization fund management company [*Sociedade gestora de fundos de titularização de créditos*], or the abbreviation SGFTC. They must have as their sole object the management of one or more funds on behalf of the holders of securitization units in those funds.

550. Management companies must not, partially or totally, convey the powers to administer the funds which are conferred upon them by law to third parties. They may, nonetheless, have recourse to services provided by third parties, whenever this is convenient to the conduct of their activity, namely for the effects of managing the loans held by the funds and the respective guarantees, as well as the application of liquidity reserves.[670]

551. Management companies shall act on behalf of and in the interest of the holders of the securitization units of the fund,[671] and shall carry out all acts and operations necessary or appropriate to the proper management of the fund, in accordance with criteria of a high level of diligence and professional competence.

552. Article 18 of DL 453/99 sets forth, among others, the following functions of management companies: to apply of the fund's assets in the acquisition of loans, in accordance with the law and the management rules and regulations; to practice all acts and enter into any agreements necessary for the issuance of securitization units; to take out loans on behalf of the fund; to manage the sums paid by debtors related to loans comprising the fund; to calculate and have payments made corresponding to income from and redemption of the securitization units; to pay any expenses which, according to the terms of the management rules and regulations, are payable by the fund; to keep the books of the fund in order; to comply with information duties established by law or by the management rules and regulations; to provide the CMVM with information; to practice any acts necessary for proper debt management and the corresponding guarantees, if the management is not carried out by the originator or by a third party; to authorize the disposal and taxation of the fund's loans.

553. Article 21 of DL 453/99 prohibits management companies from carrying out the following operations: issuing loans on their own behalf; encumbering in any

670. Article 16(2) of DL 453/99, of 5 November.
671. Article 32(2) of DL 453/99, of 5 November, provides that notwithstanding the right to demand compliance with the law and the terms of the management rules and regulations, the holders of securitization units are not permitted to issue instructions to the management company as regards the administration of the fund.

way or disposing of the loans comprising the fund; acquiring securities of any type on their own behalf, with the exception of public, domestic or foreign funds, and of securities equivalent to these; assigning credit, including the provision of guarantees, on their own behalf or on behalf of the funds they manage; acquiring property on their own behalf, apart from that which is essential to their premises and operation.

554. Only in exceptional cases, may the CMVM, on joint request by the management company and the custodian, authorize the substitution of the management company, provided that this is in the best interests of the holders of securitization units in the fund.[672] If the authorization of the management company is revoked by *Banco de Portugal*, or if there is another reason for the winding up the company, the CMVM may decide that the management company is to be substituted.

D. Custodian

555. The securities comprising a fund must be entrusted to a single custodian. According to Article 24 of DL 453/99, the custodian shall be responsible for the following: (a) to receive deposits of the fund's securities and keep all documentary and other proof relating to the loans comprising the fund which have not been kept by the originator; to receive deposits or register securities which comprise the fund; (b) to carry out all applications of the assets of the fund which are delegated to it by the management company, in accordance with the instructions of the latter; (c) to pay interest and capital on the loans comprising the fund, when the management rules and regulations provide for this and in accordance with the instructions of the management company, and to carry out all other acts which are deemed appropriate to the proper management of debts; (d) to pay the periodic returns payable to the holders of the securitization units, pursuant to the instructions issued by the management company, and to redeem those securitization units; (e) to carry out any other instructions issued to it by the management company; (f) to propose its substitution of the management company to the CMVM; (g) to ensure, in operations relating to the securities comprising the fund, that payment or other benefits are delivered within the deadlines and in line with due market practice; (h) to ensure that the income of the fund is applied in compliance with the law and the management rules and regulations; and (i) to assume the role of overseer and to guarantee to holders of securitization units that the terms of the management rules and regulations shall be compiled with.

556. The relations between the management company and the custodian shall be governed by a written contract.[673] It is the custodian's duty to verify that all instructions issued by the management company comply with the law and the management rules and regulations, prior to such instructions being carried out. Article 25 of Decree 453/99 provides that the management company and the custodian shall

672. Article 22(1) of DL 453/99, of 5 November.
673. Article 23(4) of DL 453/99, of 5 November.

be jointly responsible for ensuring compliance with all duties set down by law and in the management rules and regulations, and shall act in the interest of holders of securitization units. The management company and custodian are also jointly responsible for ensuring the holders of the securitization units of the veracity, rigour, and sufficiency of the information contained in the management rules and regulations, and also that this information is up to date. The responsibility of the custodian shall not be affected in cases where the guardianship of the securities of the fund is entrusted by it to a third party, either partially or totally.

E. Management Rules and Regulations

557. According to Article 29 of DL 453/99, the management company shall draw up management rules and regulations for each fund it administers. The management rules and regulations must, at least, contain the following information: (a) the name and duration of the fund, as well as details of the decision which authorized the constitution of the fund; (b) details of the management company and the custodian; (c) the characteristics of the loans, or categories of identical types of loan comprising the fund and its management structure, if the management service is provided to the fund, through the management company or custodian, by the originator or a qualified third party; (d) the rights inherent to each category of securitization unit to be issued by the fund; (e) rules relating to the order of priority for payments to be made by the fund; (f) the terms and conditions for the liquidation of the fund, in particular as regards the conveyance of loans held by the fund on the date on which it is liquidated; (g) contracts to be entered into by the management company, on behalf of the fund, with a view to ensuring coverage of any foreseeable risks, in particular the risk of insufficiency of income received from the fund's debtors to comply with the duty to pay periodic returns and for the redemption of the securitization units; (h) the terms and conditions of loans which the management company is permitted to issue on behalf of the fund; (i) the remuneration for the services of the management company and the custodian, the means of calculating and making these payments, as well as any other expenses and charges which must be met by the fund; (j) the duties of the management company and the custodian; and (k) the terms and conditions under which the disposal of matured loans is permitted.

558. In the case of funds with variable assets, the management rules and regulations must also contain information relating to the loans to be acquired subsequent to the constitution of the fund, as follows: (a) the characteristics of the loans; (b) the maximum value of loans to be acquired; (c) the dates for which the acquisitions are planned and the value of each; and (d) the procedures to be adopted if, for exceptional reasons, it is not possible to implement the planned acquisitions. In the case of funds with variable assets for which the issuance of new securitization units is planned, the management rules and regulations must also contain information on the rights conferred by the securitization units to be issued, the value of such issues, the dates for which the issues are planned and any potential consequences of the new issues for the existing securitization units.

559. If the management rules and regulations permit the modification of the assets of the fund, the terms and conditions for such a modification must be established.

560. The management rules and regulations must provide for all expenses and costs to be met by the fund, in particular the remuneration for services to be provided by the management company, the custodian, or by third parties, if this is permitted by law.[674]

F. Securitization Units

561. Article 31 of DL 453/99 provides that securitization units are securities, and must be of the book-entry type. Securitization units must not be issued without the sum corresponding to the issue price effectively forming part of the assets of the fund. On the date of constitution of the fund, the subscription accounts of the securitization units shall be transformed into accounts of registration of securities, pursuant to the terms of the Portuguese Securities Code.[675] The subscription of securitization units implies acceptance of the management rules and regulations and confers upon the management company the powers necessary for acts related to the management of the fund.

562. Article 32(1) of Decree 453/99 provides that securitization units confer upon their holders the following cumulative or exclusive rights, under the terms and conditions established in the management rules and regulations: (a) the right to payment of periodic returns, (b) the right to redeem the par value of the securitization units, and (c) the right, on termination of the liquidation of the fund and apportionment of the proceeds thereof, to receive a quota of the total remaining after payment of periodic returns and all other expenses and charges met by the fund and proportionally owing to them. The risk of simple delay or failure to comply with the duties corresponding to the loans comprising the fund is incurred by the holder of securitization units.

563. If provided for in the management rules and regulations, funds may issue securitization units of different categories conferring equal rights but at variance with those conferred by the other securitization units, particularly regarding the level of preference for payment of periodic income, the redemption of the par value, or payment of the proceeds of liquidation.

674. Article 26 of DL 453/99, of 5 November.
675. Article 31 of DL 453/99, of 5 November.

G. Liquidation and Apportionment

564. According to Article 38 of Decree 453/99, funds shall be liquidated and the proceeds apportioned on expiry of the duration of the fund. Funds may only be liquidated and the proceeds apportioned prior to the end of the said term, if this is permitted by the management rules and regulations, that is, in cases where all securitization units are held by a single entity.

Funds may also be liquidated and the proceeds thereof apportioned prior to the end of the duration of the fund if the CMVM makes a decision to this effect, if the authorization of the management company is revoked or if there is another reason for winding up the company, or if the management company is not substituted.

The holders of securitization units do not have the power to demand the liquidation of funds and the apportionment of the proceeds thereof.

III. Pension Funds: Concept, Constitution and Statutory Provisions

565. DL 12/2006, de 20 de Janeiro,[676] defines pension funds as assets solely allocated to one or more pension plans or to a health care plan and their assets are allocated only to the beneficiaries through compliance with that plan. The contents of pension plans must be previously approved by the insurance control entity – the Insurance Institute of Portugal [*Instituto dos Seguros de Portugal*].

Pension funds, similar to investment funds, are autonomous patrimonies that are managed by special pension funds management companies [*Sociedades Gestoras de Fundos de Pensões*] or by Life Insurance Companies [*Companhias Seguradoras do Ramo Vida*].[677]

There is total separation of assets between the fund and its members, participants and beneficiaries.

566. In the composition of the equity of pension funds, the respective management entities should keep in mind the objectives and purposes to be met by the same, observing the principle of spreading risks, as well as the security, profitability, and liquidity of the applications made. The equity of savings funds shall be comprised of securities, units in collective investment undertakings, short-term debt instruments, bank deposits, or other assets of a monetary nature. In the case of savings funds adopting the form of a pension fund or an independent fund from one of the types of insurance in the life assurance branch, the equity can also be made up of land, buildings, and credits resulting from mortgage loans.[678]

676. As amended (last amendment by Law 35/2018, of 20 July).
677. Article 2 of Decree 158/2002, of 2 July, provides that the legally authorized management companies of securities investment funds are competent to manage savings funds constituted in the form of a securities investment fund or in the form of a pension fund. The insurance companies legally authorized to carry out life assurance activities in Portugal are competent to manage savings funds legally constituted in the form of an independent fund from the life assurance branch of the insurance sector. Each management entity is permitted to manage one or more savings funds.
678. Article 3 of DL 158/2002, of 2 July.

567. Participants may only request the reimbursement of the value of the pension saving plan in the following cases: (a) retirement due to the participant's age; (b) long-term unemployment of the participant or of any of the members of his/her household; (c) permanent incapacity of the participant or of any of the members of his/her household to work, whatever the cause; (d) serious disease of the participant or of any of the members of his/her household; (e) the participant having reached the age of sixty years; (f) attendance or enrolment of the participant or of any of the members of his/her household in a course of vocational education or higher education, whenever this generates expenses in the year in question; and (g) payments concerning mortgage credit relating to the residential immovable property of the participant.

§3. *Fideicommissum*

568. The fiduciary substitution is regulated on Articles 2286 to 2296 of the CC. It constitutes a hereditary substitution, inspired by the Roman *fideicommissum*, in virtue of which the testator entrusts a first inheritor, the fiduciary, with the mission of preserving the whole or a part of the inheritance in favour of a second inheritor, the substitute. By death of the fiduciary, goods are transferred to the substitute.[679]

569. Rather than an assignment entrusted from the testator to the fiduciary, and a subsequent conveyance in favour of the second inheritor, there is a double and successive calling to the inheritance: first in favour of the fiduciary, and second (once a term is over, or a condition has been fulfilled) in favour of the substitute. But both of them inherit from the testator.

570. An enchainment of several people between the first fiduciary and the inheritor cannot occur. Using the fiduciary substitution, the testator may make only one successive calling to the inheritance.[680]

571. Although the fiduciary acquires the property upon the rights composing the trusteeship subjected to substitution, this property is a temporary or conditional one, since it must be transferred to the substitute upon the former's death. Moreover, he/she must preserve the goods composing the trusteeship, making his/her position very similar to that typical of a usufructuary. As a result, many legal provisions on usufruct are analogically applicable to the fiduciary's status.[681]

572. The fiduciary needs authorization of the Court to alienate goods comprising the object of the trusteeship. The fiduciary is in charge of transferring the trusteeship to the substitute.

---

679. *See* Rabindranath Capelo de Sousa, *Lições de Direito das Sucessões*, vol. I, 4th edn (Coimbra: Coimbra Editora, 2000), 220–222.
680. Article 2288 CC.
681. Article 2290(2) CC.

573. If, for any reason, the substitution turns out to be invalid, or the substitute is unable to inherit from the testator, the fiduciary will be deemed a pure inheritor.[682]

§4. Foundations

574. Foundations are an adequate solution to construct and develop a charitable or protective (spendthrift) trust. Their legal regime is set in Articles 185 to 194 of the CC, and in Law 24/2012, of July 9th (as amended by Law 150/2015, of 10 September).

575. A private foundation is a legal person set up by an individual or a group of individuals, for a purpose such as philanthropy, art, education, or science. It must be created through a notarized deed or a will, and must be recognized by a supervising authority. Only after recognition of its social purpose does it acquire full legal capacity. The foundations are governed and represented by a board that is responsible for its administration.

576. Since the law does not allow foundations for private purposes, but only for relevant social interest purposes,[683] they are very limited in scope, and are not currently used as a fiduciary mechanism.

682. Articles 2289 and 2293(2) CC.
683. Article 188 CC and Article 3 of Law 24/2012.

Chapter 2. Security: *Fiducia cum Creditore*

§1. INTRODUCTION

577. Portuguese law accepts as a general principle the prohibition of the *pactum commissorium*,[684] that is, the automatic appropriation by the creditor of the thing pledged or mortgaged upon the failure of the debtor to pay the principal obligation. By virtue of this *pactum*, the creditor, if the debtor does not pay the guaranteed debt, would be allowed to appropriate the trusted goods directly, instead of requiring a mandatory sale of it. The prohibition at issue intends to prevent the creditor from getting unfairly rich at the debtor's expense, which could happen if the creditor were endowed with the power to appropriate debtor's goods directly, whose value is disproportionally higher than the credit's amount. In this sense, it is not accepted that parties may agree that in the event of non-fulfilment of the debt, the creditor-fiduciary may permanently and automatically appropriate the goods that constitute the object of the *fiducia*.[685]

§2. TITLE TRANSFER FINANCIAL COLLATERAL ARRANGEMENTS

578. DL 105/2004, of 8 May, provides the legal regime of financial collateral arrangements, on both categories: the title transfer financial collateral arrangement [*alienação fiduciária em garantia*] and the security financial collateral arrangement [*penhor financeiro*].[686]

The title transfer financial collateral arrangement is a legal device of fiduciary nature. It means an arrangement, including repurchase agreements, under which a collateral provider transfers full ownership of financial collateral to a collateral taker for the purpose of securing, or otherwise covering, the performance of relevant financial obligations. The financial collateral to be provided must consist of cash financial instruments, or credits over third parties.[687]

579. According to Article 14, the collateral taker shall, at the latest on the due date for the performance of the relevant the financial obligations covered by the title transfer financial collateral arrangement: return the original financial collateral or equivalent collateral; or return an amount of money: the value of the financial collateral on the due date for the performance of the relevant financial obligations as

684. Article 694 CC.

685. The normal proceeding of a security right is as follows: once the debt is unfulfilled, the creditor demands the mandatory sale of the goods, through a judicial process, in such a manner that the money obtained in the auction is first assigned to the payment of the credit, and only if there is a remainder will this be given to the debtor-settlor.

686. *See* Ch. 2, of part V.

687. According to Article 5 of DL 105/2004, of 8 May, cash means money credited to an account in any currency, or similar claims for the repayment of money, such as money market deposits. Financial instruments comprise shares in companies and other securities equivalent, money market instruments and claims relating to or rights in or in respect of any of the foregoing. Credits over third parties refer to loans granted by a credit institution.

agreed upon by parties according to reasonable criteria; set off the value of the collateral against the relevant financial obligations. The credit of the provider (the value of the financial collateral) shall be agreed upon by parties according to reasonable criteria.

580. If an enforcement event[688] occurs while any obligation of the collateral taker to transfer equivalent collateral under a title transfer financial collateral arrangement remains outstanding, the obligation may be the subject of a close-out netting provision.[689]

581. A close-out netting provision means a provision of a financial collateral arrangement, or of an arrangement of which a financial collateral arrangement forms part, or, in the absence of any such provision, any statutory rule by which, on the occurrence of an enforcement event, whether through the operation of netting or set-off or otherwise: (i) the obligations of the parties are accelerated so as to be immediately due and expressed as an obligation to pay an amount representing their estimated current value, or are terminated and replaced by an obligation to pay such an amount; and/or (ii) an account is taken of what is due from each party to the other in respect of such obligations, and a net sum equal to the balance of the account is payable by the party from whom the larger amount is due to the other party.

582. A close-out netting provision can take effect in accordance with its terms: (a) notwithstanding the commencement or continuation of winding-up proceedings or reorganization measures in respect of the collateral provider and/or the collateral taker; and/or (b) notwithstanding any purported assignment, judicial or other attachment or other disposition of or in respect of such rights.

§3. Sale with a Buy Back Clause (Sale with a *Pacto de Retro*)

583. The sale with a buyback clause (sale with a *pacto de retro*) is ruled by Articles 927 to 933 CC. A buyback clause is a provision in a contract that allows the seller of property the right or opportunity to repurchase the property under stated conditions.[690]

584. After a contract of sale with *pacto de retro*, where the price is usually less than in definite sale for the reason that in a sale with *pacto de retro* the vendor still expects to re-acquire the property. The essence of a *pacto de retro* sale is that the

---

688. An enforcement event means an event of default or any similar event as agreed between the parties on the occurrence of which, under the terms of a financial collateral arrangement or by operation of law, the collateral taker is entitled to realize or appropriate financial collateral or a close-out netting provision comes into effect.

689. Article 12 ex vi Article. 15.

690. *See* Decision of the Supreme Court of 16 March 2011 (Process: 279/02), at http://www.dgsi.pt/jstj.nsf/954f0ce6ad9dd8b980256b5f003fa814/418d25ba10652ad68025785c004e5eee?OpenDocument.

title and ownership of the property sold is immediately vested in the acquirer. However, within two years for movable property or five years for immovable property,[691] the sale is subject to the resolutory condition of repurchase by the vendor. Article 928(1) of the CC makes this right dependent on the return of the price paid to the seller. The fiduciary character of the vendee's title is evidenced by the stable position of the seller before the hypothetical third parties who acquire the object sold from the acquirer. According to Article 932 of the CC, when registered, the *pacto a retro* is enforceable against third parties.

585. The sale made with the clause of selling back to the seller causes an effect very similar to that of the fiduciary conveyance *cum creditore*, since it can serve a purpose of guaranteeing the payment of a debt that the vendor must assume before the vendee. The vendor could be interested in retrieving the object sold a posteriori, and the acquirer could be interested in enjoying the thing sold for a period of time (between the time of the sale and the time when the vendor exercises the right to retrieve the object sold), provided that it is guaranteed that he/she will be able to recover the price paid, together with the expenses caused by the contract.[692] Therefore, such a modality of sale adapts itself to the outline of the *fiducia cum creditore*. For example, when the contracting parties agreed that the sum that the seller owes to the acquirer is compensated with the sale's price. The seller admits that the price has been paid, and the acquirer receives the title upon the object sold, but this is not a definitive title, since the seller may exercise the right to retrieve the object sold once he/she has 'returned' the sale's price (i.e., the amount of the debt that the seller had previously contracted before the acquirer) to the acquirer. As can easily be observed, the delivery of the object sold to the acquirer fulfils a function of guarantee with regard to the return of the price (i.e., payment of the debt), since neither the seller is interested in selling nor is the acquirer interested in buying. Such function of a contract of sale *a retro* has been recently admitted as valid by the Supreme Court of Justice.[693]

691. According to Article 929 CC.
692. Article 931 CC.
693. Decision of the Supreme Court of 19 September 2006 [Process 06A2092], available at http://www.dgsi.pt/jstj.nsf/954f0ce6ad9dd8b980256b5f003fa814/b179002da602513e802571f100557bde?OpenDocument. *See* Miguel Pestana de Vasconcelos, *Direito das Garantias* 2nd ed, (Coimbra: Almedina, 2019), 465–491.

Part V. Security

Introduction

586. According to the principle of the debtor's universal patrimonial liability, foreseen in Article 601 of the CC, the debtor is responsible for the fulfilment of his/her obligations with his/her patrimony as a whole, both present and future. When the debtor does not pay a debt which is due and payable on demand, the creditor may act judicially against the debtor requesting the seizure of enough goods of his/her patrimony. When there are several creditors that may claim against the debtor for the payment of their credits, and the debtor's patrimony is not enough to satisfy all the credits, the general rule is that every creditor has the right to be paid under the same conditions as the rest of them (*par condicio creditorum*), in such a manner that every credit will be satisfied pro rata parte.[694] Debtors, however, may accord preferential treatment to certain creditors. Creditors may get a higher level of safety, characterized by the certainty that their credit will be paid before others, which might become particularly important if the debtor's patrimony is not enough to pay all the debts he/she owes. Further, securities may be *ab initio* constituted in goods belonging to a third party's patrimony, of course with his/her consent. And, finally, securities have *erga onmes* efficacy, and the creditors keep a *ius destrahendi* although the goods are not in the debtor's patrimony anymore.

587. Securities alter the functioning of the principle of debtor's universal patrimonial liability, because they imply a direct tie of guarantee between specific goods in the debtor's patrimony and a definite credit. They are a powerful support of the position of the creditor, for in the event of the debtor's non-fulfilment, they entitle the former to request the mandatory sale of the goods in which the security lies, as well as to apply the price so obtained to the satisfaction of his/her credit.

588. As a general principle, securities are accessory rights, whose legal existence depends on the existence of the debt to be secured. Portuguese law adheres to the principle of accessority and allows only a few exceptions.[695] Thus the security right is dependent upon the coming into existence and the continued existence of the claim it is intended to secure. There can, therefore, be no security right if the

694. Article 604 CC.
695. Menezes Cordeiro, Tratado de Direito Civil X (Coimbra: Almedina, 2015).

claim to which the security relates is a nullity. Moreover, the security right is extinguished when the principal claim is extinguished. It should be noted that the principle of accessority operates in one direction only: the principal operation remains operative regardless of the destruction or disappearance of the property placed under a security right or its acquisition by another.

589. Securities share the defining feature of being authentic rights in rem over property belonging to the debtor, or over property belonging to a third party. These are, therefore, collateral security over the property over which the security right is held, which may be followed by the creditor in the satisfaction of the debt even if the debtor has in the meantime transferred the property to a third party. Security rights are thus indissolubly connected to the debt which they guarantee. Once the debt is extinguished, the security is extinguished with it.

590. The immovable assets burdened by security rights must be earmarked and clearly specified in the constitutive deed – principle of specificity.[696] The principle of specificity determines that for each object of property law, a separate property right must exist. A global or general security right over all the immovable and movable assets of the security debtor is not allowed.[697]

591. On Chapter 1, I will start by the analysis of the following security rights held over immovable assets: statutory preferences, mortgage, retention right, and assignment of rents. On Chapter II, dedicated to security rights over movable assets, I will analyse the statutory preferences, the pledge, the financial collateral arrangements, and the right of retention.

---

696. Article 716(2) CC.
697. Article 716(1) CC.

Chapter 1. Securities in Immovable Property

§1. Introduction

592. The constitutive deed of a security in immovable property must specify the immovable property that is encumbered, the claim or claims that are secured and the total amount of such claims (principle of specificity). It is, however, sufficient that the secured debt can be determined and that the deed mentions the maximum amount for which the mortgage is granted. An open-ended security right that would cover all future debts of the mortgagor without limitation on the amount is invalid.

593. When the requirements of validity are fulfilled, the security holder is protected against latter dealings by the owner of the encumbered property or right. This is a result of the in rem or *erga omnes* character of real security rights, which allows the creditor to enforce his/her right against any person who has acquired the assets. The right of pursuit enables the holder to enforce his/her security right on the property even if it has passed into the hands of a third party.

594. A wide range of corporeal immovable assets may be subject to security rights provided they exist, are res *in commercio* and do not belong to the would be security creditor. An undivided share in land held in co-ownership may be the object of a security right.[698] Limited real rights in land are regarded as immovable assets and may be subject to security rights as long as they can be dealt with separately to the landed property to which they relate. Therefore, a usufruct is capable of being charged but not a right of use, because of its highly personal nature. Since the existence of the security right is dependent on the continued existence of the holder's interest in land, security rights over time-limited interests and long-term leases are not common in practice.

§2. Statutory Preferences

595. In this section, I will devote my attention to privileges with which some credits are endowed in relation to definite debtor's immovable goods. Usually, the term 'privilege' is used to refer to the preference for payment that some credits enjoy before others (the so-called privileged credits). A statutory preference is a right to preferential payment out of the proceeds of sale of an asset in execution. Preferences are given to certain classes of creditors and may be general (relating to all assets) or special (relating to a specific asset or a specific class of assets). The existence of privileged creditors implies an exception to the principle of *par condicio creditorum*. Because the remaining creditors are affected inevitably by them, preferential credits have a definite opposability before third parties (*erga omnes* efficacy).

698. Although in theory the creditor could sell one-half co-ownership share, in practice its market value would be less than one-half of the value of the whole property.

596. Unlike securities, preferences presuppose the concurrence of several creditors, all of them with the purpose of requesting payment from the same debtor, whose patrimony, however, is not enough to satisfy all of them. Statutory preferences prevail over the other real rights, mortgages included.

597. The law assigns priority to specified categories of creditors, ordering them in a detailed way. The order depends not on the time the debt came into existence but on the nature of the privilege. They can operate in respect of both movable property (general (Articles 736 and 737 of the CC) and special (Articles 738 to 742 of the CC)) and immovable property (special (Articles 743 to 744 of the CC)).

598. As regards immovable property, credits respecting taxes and court fees (in legal proceedings related to the immovable property) have statutory preference over other claims on the debtor's immovable property.[699]

599. If there was an amount remaining after satisfying the privileged credits related to a debtor's certain immovable goods, this amount should be added to the debtor's other goods for payment of the rest of the debts. If, on the contrary, some of the credits with a special immovable privilege had been not completely satisfied, they should be treated, according to their nature, as general privileged credits.[700]

§3. Mortgage

I. Concept and General Features

600. The mortgage entitles the creditor the right to be paid by the value of immovable goods belonging to the debtor or to a third party with preference over creditors who have an unsecured claim.[701] As a guarantee right, it is exercised to secure the fulfilment of a duty, and as a real right it empowers its holder to request the mandatory sale of the goods to apply the price so obtained for the satisfaction of his/her right, in case of non-fulfilment of the guaranteed obligation. The debt may be future or conditional and might include interests for a maximum period of three years.[702]

601. A mortgage is statutory, judicial, or voluntary, depending on whether it came into being by operation of law, by court order, or by a voluntary deed. There are statutory provisions creating '*legal*' mortgages for specific categories of creditors such as the tax authorities, municipalities, and the creditor of a maintenance debt. According to Article 708 of the CC, the creditor may require registration of the mortgage over any immovable property of the debtor.[703]

---

699. Articles 743 and 744 CC.
700. Article 752 CC.
701. Or a secured claim but that will not prevail (e.g., a posterior mortgage).
702. Articles 686 and 693 CC.
703. Such a mortgage, however, may be subject to reduction.

602. The judicial decision that condemns someone to pay a sum of money also allows the creditor to register a mortgage over immovable property of the debtor.[704] If the debtor is condemned to perform other obligations, mortgage is allowed only after their conversion into pecuniary obligations.

603. A voluntary mortgage can be created by a unilateral deed. It must be in a public deed and it is subject to registration. Registration of mortgages is a formality *ad substantiam*, being a requisite for their validity.[705]

604. The person who mortgages an immovable belonging to his/her patrimony does not have to be, necessarily, the debtor of the guaranteed right. The mortgage is in fact a real right, in such a way that the mortgagee has not only a preference for the satisfaction of his/her credit before other creditors, but also he/she may pursue the mortgaged estate and request the forced sale of it regardless of whom the mortgaged estate currently belongs to.

605. The security right is indivisible. The whole of the burdened property serves as security for the debt. Part payment of the principal claim does not proportionally reduce the extent to which the asset is burdened. However, parties may agree on the reduction (voluntary reduction foreseen in Article 719 of the CC) or it may be decided by the court upon request of the debtor (Article 720(2) of the CC).

II. Object

606. A mortgage can be granted both on immovable property (land, buildings) and real rights on such property. According to Article 688 of the CC, a mortgage can be vested on the following rights: ownership; usufruct, and superficies.[706]

607. A co-owner is entitled to dispose of his/her share in the property right and to burden it with real rights. This means that he/she can vest a security right on his/her undivided share without the cooperation of the other owners.[707] His/her security right is only extended to a share, and the creditor would only be able to enforce its security right after determining his/her share. If the physical division of the thing is impossible, the only solution is the sale of the immovable. In such a case, the creditor will enforce the security right on the part of the proceeding of the sale.

While the mortgage remains effective, the division of the thing requires consent of the creditor.[708] The mortgage will then be limited to the part allocated to the debtor.[709]

704. Article 710 CC.
705. Article 687 CC.
706. Servitudes are excluded because they do not exist independently of the ownership of the immovable property in which they are vested. The right of use and habitation of immovable property is excluded because it is strictly personal.
707. Article 689(1) CC.
708. Article 689(1) CC.
709. Article 689(2) CC.

608. The security rights are not confined to the land or the buildings. It extends to all the accessories that can be considered as immovable. Movables that are fixed to immovable property or that are used for the exploitation of such property are also considered as immovable property.

609. The constitutive deed is required to identify the immovable property that is subject to the security right. It is not possible to create a mortgage on all existing immovable property of the debtor without specification. The immovable property is required to be in existence at the time of the vesting of the mortgage. Future immovables are excluded.

If the rights on the immovable property are conditional or if they can be dissolved or avoidable, the security can only be vested subject to the same conditions and limitations.

It is not possible to create a mortgage over a share in an undivided heritance or a share in marital property.[710]

III. Content of the Right

610. The security debtor remains the owner of the property subject to the security and is generally in possession of, and entitled to use and enjoy, the property. His/her capacities may not be circumscribed by the provisions of the security deed, but are in any event limited by the real right of the security creditor. The owner of a mortgaged estate retains his/her ownership, and especially the powers to use and enjoy the estate, given that the mortgage does not imply transfer of possession in favour of the mortgagee. Therefore, the owner of the mortgaged estate even retains the power to sell the estate or to constitute limited real rights in it. But of course, the estate will be transferred with the burden that the mortgage signifies, in such a way that the purchaser may not prevent the estate from being mandatorily sold at the request of the mortgagee, in case of non-fulfilment of the guaranteed debt.

An agreement on the prohibition to sell or to charge the mortgaged good is not valid. However, parties can agree that the credit will become due at the moment of the transfer or charge.[711]

611. The owner must employ the care of a reasonable person in safeguarding the immovable asset burdened by the security right and is liable if, through his/her fault, the security creditor is deprived of his/her security or if the value thereof has diminished. Although he/she has the duty to maintain the property in good repair, he/she is not obliged to put the property to its most beneficial use. So long as the owner

710. Article 690.
711. Article 695 CC.

puts his/her property to a lawful purpose which is not in breach of his/her obligations contained in the security right, the security creditor can have no legitimate complaint, even if the use of property for that purpose is not the most beneficial use, or indeed, depreciates the property.[712]

612. However, the constitution of a mortgage does not eliminate the power of the mortgaged estate's owner to convey it freely. As the owner, he/she may deal with the property insofar as he/she does not infringe the security of the creditor. In particular, it is accepted that he/she may grant a lease over the property and burden it by way of a second mortgage. In the case of conveyance, the mortgage will continue to be a burden upon the estate, whoever the new owner is, and provided the right of mortgage is necessarily recorded in the Land Registry. The acquirer of a mortgaged thing, who has registered his/her acquisition and is not personally liable for the payment of the secured credit, has the right to redeem the mortgage through any of the following: full payment of the creditor; or paying to creditors an amount within the limits of the value of the good.[713]

613. When one mortgage expires, the property will fully guarantee the other credits.[714]

614. As a general principle, Portuguese law adheres to the principle of accessority.[715] The purpose of a security right is to secure an underlying obligation. Therefore, the existence of such a secured obligation is a prerequisite for the security right.[716] However, Article 727(1) of the CC allows the mortgage to be transferred without the guaranteed claim to guarantee a claim of another creditor. Consent of the creditor and the debtor is, however, required.[717] If the mortgaged thing belongs to a third party, his/her consent is required. The latter credit is secured within the limits of the amount of the former credit.[718]

615. Article 729 of the CC also allows the transmission of the priority rank to another creditor secured with a mortgage over the same property.

---

712. The owner is, however, only allowed to exercise his/her property rights in accordance with the interests of the secured creditor (Article 700 CC). As a result, he/she is not allowed to do anything which would endanger the sufficiency of the security right. A diminution of the mortgagee's rights by a diminution in the value of the mortgaged property can lead to an acceleration of the secured claim (Article 725 CC). The owner is allowed to cut trees or brushes, to collect fruits, and to sell component parts of the thing. Parties may agree that the thing must be insured (Article 702 CC).
713. Article 721 CC.
714. Article 713 CC.
715. The mortgage expires if the obligation is extinguished – whether by payment, or by prescription, or by some other means – or if the creditor renounces it. The renunciation must be express and in writing in a certified deed (Article 731(1) CC).
716. The security in respect of a prescribed debt has no effects. If the obligation is extinguished – whether by payment, or by prescription, or by some other means – the security is extinguished (Article 730 CC).
717. Article 424 CC.
718. Article 728 CC.

616. In case of damage caused to the property, a distinction is to be made between damage that is the result of an external cause and damage caused by the owner (negligent conduct). In case of damage caused by the owner, the lender has the right to claim the immediate repayment of the loan, and the owner cannot fend off this claim by offering an alternative security.[719]

617. If the property is in danger of being lost, the mortgagee may ask the court to take the necessary precautionary measures. If the property over which the mortgage subsists is lost or destroyed, the mortgagee may ask the court to establish a mortgage of equivalent value over other property or demand immediate payment of the debt.[720] If the property is insured and the insurer becomes liable to pay the debtor for its loss or destruction, the mortgagee may satisfy the debt from this sum, with the same priority rank. The same regime applies when there is an expropriation.[721]

IV. Sale of the Mortgaged Estate

618. Although security rights give their holders the power to demand the mandatory sale of the goods in which they lie, they do not grant the power to appropriate these goods directly. A *pactum commissorium* – which is a security agreement which, in its simplest form, allows the security creditor to acquire ownership of the burdened property on default of the debtor – is not valid.[722] The justification of this prohibition is the prevention of the security creditor from obtaining a windfall disproportionate to the debtor's indebtedness by exploiting the weak and desperate financial position of the debtor. The alienation of the goods burdened with mortgage must be carried out through judicial procedures, as provided by law.

619. There is no specific form of enforcement for secured creditors. As a result, the mortgagees are required to observe the general rules of enforcement proceedings as any other creditor. It should be recalled that the right to seize the encumbered property is not limited to secured creditors. A seizure by unsecured creditors, however, will only rarely occur, since secured creditors will outrank them in the distribution proceedings.

620. If the debtor defaults in his/her payments to the creditor, he/she is entitled to start enforcement proceedings. As a result, all other secured claims that attach to the property will become due. Once one creditor has started the proceedings, the other mortgage holders and unsecured creditors are required to join the proceedings.

719. Article 725 CC.
720. Article 701 CC.
721. Article 693 CC.
722. Article 694 CC. However, agreements entered into by parties after the default of the debtor in order to be enforced outside the legal framework are valid (*datio in solutum*).

621. In the event of a sale, the rights of all the mortgage holders will be transferred from the immovable property to the proceeds of the sale. This effect takes place in order to free the immovable property from all the charges and to make a transfer of the property to the buyer possible without any encumbrance. The proceeds will be distributed among the mortgage holders according to their rank.

622. At any time, the debtor has the right to pay off the debt and to redeem the mortgaged property. The cancellation of the property rights is required to be registered in the Land Registry. In such a case, this can be done on the basis of a unilateral declaration by the creditor that is stated in a notarial deed, or in a court's decision.

623. The owner of the charged thing might prevent other goods from being attached until the security is exhausted, and ensure that the charged thing is only seized to the extent necessary to pay the creditor. When the owner of the thing is not the debtor, he/she is entitled to oppose to the creditor any defence even when the debtor has renounced it.[723] The owner of the thing might oppose into the seizure as long as the original debtor is entitled to void the agreement or still might get a pay-off.[724]

§4. Retention Right

624. A right of retention is the right to retain, by operation of law, physical control over another's movable assets as security for the payment of money or labour expended on improving property or compensation for damages caused by it.[725] If the retention right impinges upon an immovable, the creditor has the right to be paid as if a mortgagee creditor.[726]

625. Article 755 of the CC provides a retention right over immovable property, for example, to the depositary for guaranteeing the payment of the amounts due because of the deposit; to the beneficiary of a *commodatum* if he/she has the right to be compensated for damages; to the mandatary in relation to the anticipated amounts because of the task developed; to the *negotiorum gestorum*; and finally to a party of a preliminary contract of sale when there was *tradition* of the thing to the future acquirer.

626. The retention right cannot be transmitted without assignment of the credit.[727] It has priority over the mortgage.[728] The retention right extinguishes by

723. Articles 697 and 698 CC.
724. Article 698(2) CC.
725. Article 754 CC.
726. Article 759(1).
727. Article 760 CC.

the restitution of the property; if the obligation is extinguished – whether by payment, or by prescription, or by some other means – the security is also extinguished. Destruction of the property and renunciation by the creditor also extinguish the security.

627. As regards retention over immovable property, the mortgage regime applies by default.

§5. Assignment of Rents

628. The assignment of rents is ruled in Articles 656 to 665 CC. By virtue of the assignment of rents, in case of default by the debtor, the creditor has the right to receive rents from immovable property or movable property subject to registration.

629. Parties are free to agree upon possession of the goods: they may remain with the owner/debtor, or be transferred to the creditor or, even, to a third party.[729] If the creditor enters into possession of the property, the management must be done according to the criterion of a *bonus paterfamilias*, and is liable for charges.[730]

728. Article 759(2) CC. The STJ issued an Uniformization Case Law, Decision 4/2014, of 19 May, interpreting the limits of this prevalence in insolvency proceedings. This case law has been developed, for example, in the Decision of 3 October 2017 [Process 212/11.1T2AVR-B.P1.S1], available at: http://www.dgsi.pt/jstj.nsf/954f0ce6ad9dd8b980256b5f003fa814/d09b09132aff809080258 1ae004ee0e2?OpenDocument.

729. Article 661 CC.

730. Article 663 CC.

Chapter 2. Securities in Movable Property

§1. Statutory Preferences

630. The law sets forth several situations where the creditor has a right to preferential payment out of the proceeds of sale of a movable asset in execution. Preferences over movable property may be general (relating to all assets) or special (relating to a specific asset or a specific class of assets). Only the former are considered rights in rem.

631. According to Articles 738 to 742, the following credits give rise to a preference: costs of legal proceedings, unpaid taxes, expenses with seeds, water or energy for rural estates; compensation for damages; and credits of the intellectual property holder. These claims enjoy a preference with regard to the debtor's definite movable goods, and exclude all others to the extent of their amount until the value of the movable at issue.

632. As already mentioned with reference to special immovable privileges, after paying privileged credits, any amount remaining will be added to the debtor's remaining goods for the payment of the non-privileged credits. On the contrary, if one of the specially privileged credits is not completely satisfied, it will be treated either as a common credit without any preference.

§2. Pledge

633. The pledge lies in movable goods and does give the creditor the right to keep possession of the goods which are the object of the guarantee until the credit is completely satisfied. If mortgage is the paradigmatic guarantee real right in the field of immovable goods, pledge occupies this role in the sphere of movable goods. Thus, the main and first differential element between these two rights is the nature of the object (immovable *versus* movable) upon which they fall. Secondly, while the mortgage does not imply the possessory transfer of the mortgaged estate into the mortgagee's hands, the pledge, at least according to the classical regulation in Civil Code and given the movable character of its object, implies the transfer of the possession in favour of the pledge creditor.

I. Concept and General Features

634. According to its classical description, the pledge could be defined as a guarantee real right that falls upon someone else's movable goods with the goal of securing a debt, and that allows the holder to retain the possession of the object given as pledge, and to request the mandatory sale of the pledged goods in case of non-fulfilment of the guaranteed debt, in order to satisfy the credit with the price so obtained. The credit may be future or upon condition.[731] The creditor whose claim is secured with pledge will be named, 'pledge creditor' and the debtor that gives one of his/her movable goods as a pledge for guaranteeing the payment of a debt 'pledge debtor'.

635. The pledge is created by the delivery of the pledged property to the creditor or through a document that confers exclusive control of the thing to the creditor or a third party.[732]

II. Object

636. A pledge may subsist not only over individual specified items of property, but over assets represented by claims that the debtor has as creditor in respect of third parties, which the pledgee may in turn claim in default of payment of the original debt, and over other rights attached to movable property.[733]

The pledge does not cause the transfer of property of the pledged goods but only the transfer of possession into the creditor's hands. This possessory conveyance fulfils a function of publicity: further creditors of the same debtor will be able to know the limits of the latter's solvency, since specific goods in his/her patrimony remain burdened in guarantee of a definite credit.[734] In addition, the transfer of possession to the pledge creditor avoids the debtor alienating the pledged good to third parties in good faith, who would deserve protection for trusting in the appearance of ownership that normally arises from the possession.

III. Content of the Right

637. The creditor is entitled to the possessory remedies to protect his/her possession even against the owner,[735] and has the right to compensation for improvements. When the thing pledged diminishes value or becomes insufficient for the payment of the debt, the creditor may claim for a reinforcement of the guarantee.[736]

638. To protect the debtor, the pledgee is under a legal obligation to keep the property in his/her custody and is liable for its loss and deterioration.[737] The pledgee is further prohibited from using it without the debtor's consent and may not dispose

731. Article 666(3) CC. *See* Decision of the Supreme Court of 30 November 2006 [Process: 5B4152], at http://www.dgsi.pt/jstj.nsf/954f0ce6ad9dd8b980256b5f003fa814/be8b0f7e5a5092f68025729500 4c352d?OpenDocument.
732. Article 669(1) CC.
733. Article 666 CC.
734. *Pignus gordianum*, where a registered security would not only cover a specific claim but every other claim that the security creditor has against the security debtor, is not valid under Portuguese law.
735. Article 670(a) CC.
736. Article 670(3) CC.
737. Article 671(a) CC. If the creditor uses the thing or does not take adequate care of it, the owner can demand an adequate security [*caução*] or its deposit with a third party (Article 673 CC).

of it, whether by way of pledge or by allowing third parties enjoyment of it.[738] The creditor is also obliged to return the property when the claim is extinguished. If the property yields fruits, the creditor may gather and consume them, setting their value against, first, expenses, then interest and then capital.[739]

639. If there is reason to believe that the thing will deteriorate or diminish value, both the creditor and the debtor, upon judicial authorization, are allowed to sell the thing. The debtor may prevent the sale, by offering an alternative *security*.[740] The amount received as price of the sale will, therefore, secure the claim of the creditor. If the property over which the pledge subsists is lost or destroyed, the pledgee or may ask the court to establish a pledge of equivalent value over other property or demand immediate payment of the debt.[741] Parties may agree that the thing must be insured.[742]

640. The security right can be separated from the secured debt. A transfer of the security right to a third party is possible without the transfer of the secured obligation. The pledge can be transferred without the guaranteed claim to guarantee a claim of another creditor[743] but consent of the creditor and the debtor is required.[744] If the pledged thing belongs to a third party his/her consent is required. The latter credit is secured within the limits of the amount of the former credit.[745] The pledger must deliver the property to the new creditor.[746]

641. It is not valid an agreement on the prohibition to sell or to charge the pledged good. However, parties can agree that the credit will become due at the moment of the transfer or burdening.[747]

642. Unless parties agree otherwise, the security right is indivisible,[748] it encumbers the whole of the movable property. It means that the creditor cannot be forced to reduce the subject matter of the pledge if a debt is partially paid off.

643. The pledge is extinguished by the restitution of the property or the document that confers exclusive control over the thing. If the obligation is extinguished – whether by payment, or by prescription, or by some other means – the security is also extinguished. Destruction of the property and renunciation by the creditor also extinguish the pledge.[749]

738. Article 671(b) CC.
739. Article 672 CC.
740. Article 674 (3) CC.
741. Article 701 CC ex vi Article 678 CC.
742. Article 702 ex vi Article 678 CC.
743. Article 727 (1)CC ex vi Article 676 CC.
744. Article 424 CC.
745. Article 728 CC ex vi Article 676 CC.
746. Article 582 (2) CC.
747. Article 695 ex vi Article 678.
748. Article 696 CC ex vi Article 678.
749. Article 677 CC.

IV. Assignment and Sale of the Pledged Goods

644. If the charge is not redeemed, the creditor acquires the right to be paid through the proceedings of the sale of the property at a public auction.[750] Parties may agree on the sale of the thing without legal intervention. They may also agree that the property will be allocated to the creditor at a value determined by the Court.[751]

645. The owner of the charged thing might prevent other goods from being attached until the security is exhausted, and can ensure that the charged thing is only seized to the extent necessary to pay the creditor.[752] When the owner of the thing is not the debtor, he/she is entitled to oppose the creditor using any defence even when the debtor has renounced it.[753] The owner might oppose the seizure as long as the original debtor is entitled to challenge the original agreement or might get a pay-off.[754]

§3. Security Financial Collateral Arrangements

646. DL 105/2004, of 8 May, provides the legal regime of financial collateral arrangements, on both categories: a title transfer financial collateral arrangement [*alienação fiduciária em garantia*] and a financial collateral arrangement [*penhor financeiro*].[755]

647. A security financial collateral arrangement means an arrangement under which a collateral provides financial collateral by way of security in favour of, or to, a collateral taker, but full ownership of the financial collateral remains with the collateral provider when the security right is created. The financial collateral to be provided must consist of cash, financial instruments, or credits against third parties. 'Cash' means money credited to an account in any currency, or similar claims for the repayment of money, such as money market deposits. 'Financial instruments' means shares in companies and other securities equivalent, money market instruments and claims relating to or rights in or in respect of any of the foregoing. Credits against thirds parties must result from a loan *granted* by a credit institution.[756]

648. According to Article 6 of DL 105/2004, the provision of financial collateral implies the financial collateral being delivered, transferred, held, registered, or otherwise designated so as to be in the possession or under the control of the collateral taker or of a person acting on the collateral taker's behalf. Parties can agree that the

750. Article 675(1) CC.
751. Article 675 (3)CC.
752. Article 697 CC ex vi Article 678 CC.
753. Article 698 CC ex vi Article 678.
754. Article 698(2) CC ex vi Article 678.
755. *See* Part IV, Ch. 2, §2.
756. Article 5 of DL 105/2004, of 8 May.

collateral taker is entitled to exercise a right of use in relation to the financial collateral provided under the security financial collateral arrangement. 'Right of use' means the right of the collateral taker to use and dispose of financial collateral provided under the security financial collateral arrangement as its owner within the limits of the security financial collateral arrangement.[757]

649. Where a collateral taker exercises a right of use, he/she thereby incurs in an obligation to transfer equivalent collateral to replace the original financial collateral on or before the due date for the performance of the relevant financial obligations covered by the security financial collateral arrangement. Alternatively, the collateral taker shall, on the due date for the performance of the relevant financial obligations, either transfer equivalent collateral, or if and to the extent that the terms of a security financial collateral arrangement so provide, set off the value of the equivalent collateral against or apply it in discharge of the relevant financial obligations.[758]

650. According to Article 13: an 'equivalent collateral' means the following: (i) in relation to cash, means a payment of the same amount and in the same currency; (ii) in relation to financial instruments, means financial instruments of the same issuer or debtor, forming part of the same issue or class and of the same nominal amount, currency and description or, where a financial collateral arrangement provides for the transfer of other assets following the occurrence of any event relating to or affecting any financial instruments provided as financial collateral, those other assets. The equivalent collateral transferred in discharge of an obligation shall be subject to the same security financial collateral agreement of the primitive collateral and shall be treated as having been provided under the security financial collateral arrangement at the same time as the original financial collateral was first provided.

651. The use of financial collateral by the collateral taker does not render invalid or unenforceable the rights of the collateral taker under the security financial collateral arrangement in relation to the financial collateral transferred by the collateral taker in discharge of an obligation.

652. Article 11 of DL 105/2004 sets forth that on the occurrence of an enforcement event, the collateral taker shall be able to realize in the following manners, any financial collateral provided under, and subject to the terms agreed in, a security financial collateral arrangement: (a) in case of financial instruments by sale or appropriation and by setting off their value against, or applying their value in discharge of, the relevant financial obligations; and (b) cash by setting off the amount against or applying it in discharge of the relevant financial obligations. An 'enforcement event' means an event of default or any similar event as agreed between the parties on the occurrence of which, under the terms of a financial collateral arrangement or by operation of law, the collateral taker is entitled to realize or appropriate

757. Article 9 of DL 105/2004, of 8 May.
758. Article 10 of DL 105/2004, of 8 May.

financial collateral or a close-out netting provision comes into effect. Article 12 recognizes the close-out netting provisions. A close-out netting provision can take effect as follows: (a) notwithstanding the commencement or continuation of winding-up proceedings or reorganization measures in respect of the collateral provider and/or the collateral taker; and/or (b) notwithstanding any purported assignment, judicial or other attachment or other disposition of or in respect of such rights. A close-out netting provision means a provision of a financial collateral arrangement, or of an arrangement of which a financial collateral arrangement forms part, or, in the absence of any such provision, any statutory rule by which, on the occurrence of an enforcement event, whether through the operation of netting or set-off or otherwise, as follows: (i) the obligations of the parties are accelerated so as to be immediately due and expressed as an obligation to pay an amount representing their estimated current value, or are terminated and replaced by an obligation to pay such an amount; and/or (ii) an account is taken of what is due from each party to the other in respect of such obligations, and a net sum equal to the balance of the account is payable by the party from whom the larger amount is due to the other party.

653. Appropriation is possible only if it has been agreed upon by parties in the security financial collateral arrangement and they have agreed in the security financial collateral arrangement on the valuation of the financial instruments.

§4. Right of Retention

654. According to Article 754 of the CC, a right of retention is the right to retain, by operation of law, physical control over another's movable assets as security for the payment of money or labour expended on improving the property or compensation for damages caused by it, for example, the person in charge of doing some works pertaining to a debtor's movables. Some creditors may retain in possession the debtor's goods until the debtor repays them the corresponding debt.[759]

Article 755 of the CC provides a retention right over movable property to the depositary for guaranteeing the payment of the amounts due because of the deposit; to the beneficiary of a *commodatum*; to the mandatary in relation to the anticipated amounts because of the task developed; to the transporter; to the lodger; to the *negotiorum gestorum*; and finally to a party of a preliminary contract of sale when there was *traditio* of the thing.

655. The retention right extinguishes: by the restitution of the property; if the obligation is extinguished – whether by payment, or by prescription, or by some

759. *See* Decision of the Supreme Court of 12 March 2013 [Process: 1664/05] at http://www.dgsi.pt/jstj.nsf/954f0ce6ad9dd8b980256b5f003fa814/5607b405b6a2a45f80257b320052d7c3?OpenDocument.

other means; by destruction of the property; and renunciation by the creditor of the security. The retention right cannot be transmitted without cession of the credit.[760]

656. Article 758 of the CC sets forth that if the retention right impinges upon movable property, the legal regime of pledge applies by default.

760. Article 760 CC.

Selected Bibliography

Books

General Works

Albuquerque, Ruy & Martim Albuquerque. *História do Direito Português*, vol I 10th ed. Lisboa: 1999.
Almeida Costa, M.J. *História do Direito Português*, 5th ed. Coimbra: Almedina, 2012.
Capelo de Sousa, Rabindranath. *Lições de Direito das Sucessões,* vol. I 4th ed. Coimbra: Coimbra Editora, 2000.
Capelo de Sousa, Rabindranath. *Lições de Direito das Sucessões,* vol. II, 3rd ed. Coimbra: Coimbra Editora, 2002.
Carvalho Fernandes, L. *Teoria Geral do Direito Civil*, vol. I. 6th ed. Lisboa: Universidade Católica, 2012.
Carvalho Fernandes, L. *Teoria Geral do Direito Civil*, vol II. 5th ed. Lisboa: Universidade Católica, 2010.
Cassiano dos Santos, F. *Direito Comercial Português I*. Coimbra: Coimbra Editora, 2007.
Castro Mendes, J. *Teoria Geral do Direito Civil.* Lisboa: Universidade Católica, 1978.
Coutinho de Abreu, Jorge. *Curso de Direito Comercial* I, 11th ed. Coimbra: Almedina, 2018.
Coutinho de Abreu, Jorge. *Curso de Direito Comercial*, II 6th ed. Coimbra: Almedina, 2019.
Coutinho de Abreu, Jorge & Coutinho de Abreu, Jorge (ed.), *Código das Sociedades Comerciais em Comentário*. Coimbra: Almedina, 2010.
Disney, A.R. History of Portugal and the Portuguese Empire. CUP, 2009.
Gomes Canotilho, J. J. *Direito Constitucional e Teoria da Constituição*, 7th ed. Coimbra: Almedina, 2003.
Gorjão-Henriques, M. *Direito da União,* 9th ed. Coimbra: Almedina, 2019.
Machado, Jónatas. *Direito da União Europeia.* Coimbra: Gestlegal, 2018.
Menezes Cordeiro, António. *Tratado De Direito Civil Português I-* Parte Geral, II-Coisas, 3rd ed. Coimbra: Almedina, 2005.
Menezes Cordeiro, António. *Tratado de Direito Civil X*. Coimbra: Almedina, 2015.
Mota Pinto, C./ Pinto Monteiro, A./Mota Pinto, P. *Teoria Geral do Direito Civil*, 4th ed. Coimbra: Coimbra Editora, 2005.

Newitt, Malyn. *Portugal in European and World History*. London: Reaktion Books, 2009.
Oliveira, F. P, et al. *Regime Jurídico da Urbanização e Edificação Comentado*, 4th ed. Coimbra: Almedina, 2017.
Oliveira Ascensão, J. *Teoria Geral*, I. Coimbra: Coimbra Editora, 2000.
Passinhas, Sandra. Propriedade e Personalidade no Direito Civil Português. Coimbra: Almedina, 2017.
Pereira Coelho, F./Oliveira, G. *Curso de Direito da Família*, 5ed. Coimbra: Imprensa da Universidade, 2016.
Sousa Antunes, H. *Direitos Reais*. Lisboa: Universidade Católica Portuguesa, 2017.
Vieira Cura, A. *Organização Judiciária Portuguesa*. Coimbra: Gestlegal, 2018.

Monographs

Albuquerque, Pedro. Direitos Reais - Relatório sobre o Programa, Conteúdo e Métodos de Ensino. Coimbra: Almedina, 2009.
Calvão da Silva, J. *Titularização de Créditos* 3rd ed. Coimbra: Almedina, 2003.
Carvalho, Orlando. *Direito das Coisas*. Coimbra: Centelha, 1977.
Carvalho Fernandes, L. *Lições de Direitos Reais*, 6th ed. Lisboa: Quid Iuris, 2009.
Garcia, M. O. Arrendamento Urbano Anotado – Regime Substantivo e Processual. Coimbra: Coimbra Editora, 2014.
Garcia, M. O. Arrendamentos para Comércio e Fins Equiparados. Coimbra: Coimbra Editora, 2006.
González, José Alberto. *Direitos Reais e Direito Registal Imobiliário*, 4th ed. Lisboa: Quid Iuris, 2009.
Henrique Mesquita, M. *Obrigações Reais e Ónus Reais*. Coimbra: Almedina, 1990.
Henrique Mesquita, M. *Direitos Reais*. Coimbra: 1967.
Jardim, Mónica. Efeitos Substantivos do Registo Predial – Terceiros para Efeitos do Registo Predial. Coimbra: Almedina, 2015.
Jardim, Mónica. Escritos de Direito Notarial e Direito Registal. Coimbra: Almedina, 2015.
Menezes Cordeiro, A. *Tratado de Direito Civil Português*, II, 3rd ed. Coimbra: Almedina, 2005.
Menezes Leitão, L. *Direitos Reais*, 8th ed. Coimbra: Almedina, 2019.
Mota Pinto, C., *Direitos Reais*. Coimbra: 1972.
Oliveira, F. P./Vassalo Abreu, A. Instalação de Empreendimentos Turísticos em Propriedade Plural: 'Quid est?'. Coimbra: Almedina, 2014.
Oliveira, F. P./Passinhas, S./Lopes, D. Alojamento Local e Uso de Fracção Autónoma. Coimbra: Almedina, 2018.
Oliveira Ascensão, J. *A Tipicidade dos Direitos Reais*. Lisboa: Petrony, 1968.
Oliveira Ascensão, J. *Direito Civil, Reais*, 5th ed. Coimbra: Coimbra Editora, 1993.
Passinhas, Sandra. A Assembleia de Condóminos e o Administrador na Propriedade Horizontal, 2nd ed. Coimbra: Almedina, 2002.
Pestana de Vasconcelos, M. *Direito das Garantias,* 3rd ed. Coimbra: Almedina, 2019.
Pinto Duarte, R. *Tipicidade e Atipicidade dos Contratos*. Coimbra: Almedina, 2000.
Pinto Duarte, R. Curso de Direitos Reais, 3rd ed. Lisboa:Principia, 2013.

Pires de Lima/Antunes Varela. *Código Civil Anotado* III, 2nd ed. Coimbra: Coimbra Editora, 1987.
Santos Justo, A. *Direitos Reais*, 5th ed. Coimbra: Coimbra Editora, 2017.
Sottomayor, Maria Clara. Invalidade e Registo – A Protecção do Terceiro Adquirente de Boa Fé. Coimbra: Almedina, 2010.
Vassalo Abreu, A. Titularidade Registral do Direito de Propriedade Imobiliária versus Usucapião (Adverse Possession). Coimbra: Coimbra Editora, 2013.
Vieira, José Alberto. Direitos Reais: Perspectiva Histórica do Seu Ensino em Portugal. Lisboa: Coimbra Editora, 2008.

Articles and Notes

Abrantes, José João. 'Law of Successions'. In *Portuguese Law – an Overview*, edited by Carlos Ferreira de Almeida, Assunção Cristas & Nuno Piçarra. Coimbra: Almedina, 2007, 239-250.
Bacelar Gouveia, J., 'Fundamental Rights'. In *Portuguese Law – an Overview*, edited by C. Ferreira de Almeida, Assunção Cristas & Nuno Piçarra. Coimbra: Almedina, 2007, 89-97.
Carvalho Fernandes, L. 'Terceiros para Efeitos de Registo Predial'. *ROA* 57 (1997): 1283-1320.
Carvalho, Orlando de. 'Terceiros para Efeitos de Registo' *BFD* 70 (1994): 97-106.
Caupers, João & Duarte, Tiago. 'Legal Studies'. In *Portuguese Law – an Overview*, edited by C. Ferreira de Almeida, Assunção Cristas & Nuno Piçarra. Coimbra: Almedina, 2007, 53-60.
Freitas do Amaral, D./Caupers, João. 'Administrative Law'. *Portuguese Law – an Overview*, edited by C. Ferreira de Almeida, Assunção Cristas & Nuno Piçarra. Coimbra: Almedina, 2007, 99-112.
Henrique Mesquita, M. 'A Propriedade Horizontal no Código Civil Português'. *RDES*23 (1976): 79-152.
Lima Rego, M./Ferreira de Almeida, C. 'Contract Law'. In *Portuguese Law – an Overview*, edited by C. Ferreira de Almeida, Assunção Cristas & Nuno Piçarra. Coimbra: Almedina, 2007, 183-196.
Nogueira da Silva, C. 'Legal History'. In *Portuguese Law – an Overview*, edited by C. Ferreira de Almeida, Assunção Cristas & Nuno Piçarra. Coimbra: Almedina, 2007, 15-28.
Passinhas, Sandra. 'Empreendimentos Turísticos em Propriedade Plural'. In Alves Correia (ed.), *Empreendimentos Turísticos*. Coimbra: CEDOUA, 2010.
Passinhas, Sandra. 'Fundamental Rights in Actions to Protect Immovables'. In Sonia Martín Santisteban e Peter Sparkes (ed.), *Protection of Immovables in European Legal Systems*, Cambridge University Press, 2015, 31-63.
Passinhas, Sandra. 'Proporcionalidade e Adaptabilidade: a Jurisprudência do TEDH'. In Nuno Pinto de Oliveira and Benedita McCrorie (ed.), *Pessoa, Direito e Direitos*, edited by. Braga: Universidade do Minho, 2016, 201-236.
Passinhas, Sandra. 'Desafios Jurídicos à Eficiência Energética em Propriedade Comum e/ou de Terceiros: da Geração Térmica ou Elétrica ao Carregamento de Veículos Elétricos'. In *Direito da Eficiência Energética,* edited by Suzana Tavares da Silva. Coimbra: Instituto Jurídico, 2017, 257-288.

Selected Bibliography

Pereira Nunes, V./Ferreira de Almeida, C. 'Portuguese Law System as Civil Law'. In *Portuguese Law – an Overview*, edited by C. Ferreira de Almeida, Assunção Cristas & Nuno Piçarra. Coimbra: Almedina, 2007, 29-42.
Poiares Maduro, M./Pereira Coutinho, F. 'EU Law and Portuguese Law'. *Portuguese Law – an Overview*, edited by C. Ferreira de Almeida, Assunção Cristas & Nuno Piçarra. Coimbra: Almedina, 2007, 51-71.
Trabuco, Cláudia. 'Intellectual Property Law'. In *Portuguese Law – an Overview*, ed. C. Ferreira de Almeida, Assunção Cristas & Nuno Piçarra. Coimbra: Almedina, 2007, 215-227.
Henriques, Paulo. 'Terceiros para Efeitos do Artigo 5.º do Código do Registo Predial' 79 *BFD* 70 (2003), 389-452.

General Case Law and Surveys

Portuguese case law is available online on: www.dgsi.pt. On this free-access website, managed by the ICT Services of the Ministry of Justice, case law of the Courts of Appeal (Lisboa, Porto, Coimbra, Guimarães, Évora) and of the Supreme Court of Justice are available.
The Portuguese Official Journal is freely accessed in www.dre.pt
Several legislative acts can also be found on www.pgdlisboa.pt

Index

The numbers here refer to paragraph numbers